MUMFORD ON MODERN ART IN THE 1930s

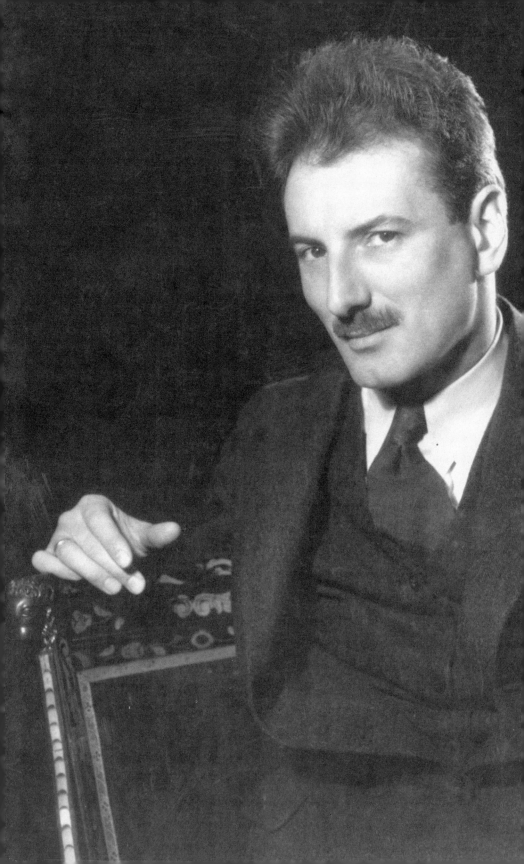

MUMFORD ON MODERN ART IN THE 1930s

EDITED AND WITH AN INTRODUCTION BY
ROBERT WOJTOWICZ

University of California Press   Berkeley   Los Angeles   London

University of California Press, one of the most distinguished university presses in the United States, enriches lives around the world by advancing scholarship in the humanities, social sciences, and natural sciences. Its activities are supported by the UC Press Foundation and by philanthropic contributions from individuals and institutions. For more information, visit www.ucpress.edu.

University of California Press
Berkeley and Los Angeles, California

University of California Press, Ltd.
London, England

Library of Congress Cataloging-in-Publication Data

Mumford, Lewis, 1895–1990.
   Mumford on modern art in the 1930s / edited and introduced by Robert Wojtowicz.
      p.   cm.
Selection of articles originally published in the New Yorker, 1932–1937.
   Includes bibliographical references and index.
   ISBN-13, 978-0-520-24858-8 (cloth : alk. paper), ISBN-10, 0-520-24858-9 (cloth : alk. paper)
      1. Art, Modern—20th century.   2. Art criticism—New York (State) — New York—History—20th century.   3. New Yorker (New York, N.Y. : 1925).   I. Wojtowicz, Robert.   II. Title.

N6490.M832   2007
709'.04—dc22   2006009142

Manufactured in the United States of America

16   15   14   13   12   11   10   09   08   07
10   9   8   7   6   5   4   3   2   1

This book is printed on Natures Book, which contains 50% post-consumer waste and meets the minimum requirements of ANSI/NISO Z39.48-1992 (R 1997) (Permanence of Paper).

To R.E.S.

CONTENTS

THE ART GALLERIES, 1936–1937

ACKNOWLEDGMENTS

In summer 1990, Sophia Wittenberg Mumford invited me to lunch at a restaurant near her farmhouse in upstate New York and asked if I would consider becoming her late husband's literary executor. Lewis Mumford, her husband of sixty-seven years and one of America's preeminent cultural critics, had died the previous January, and Sophia Mumford was adamant that someone carry his considerable intellectual legacy into the next century. I accepted, knowing, of course, that his legacy was already in good order. Before retiring from writing, Lewis Mumford had deposited the bulk of his papers at the University of Pennsylvania, and he had placed his drawings, selected photographs, and personal library at Monmouth University. Moreover, he had assiduously collected and published many of his miscellaneous writings, including letters, articles, and reviews as well as his "random notes" and "personalia," in two anthologies—*Findings and Keepings* (1975) and *My Works and Days* (1979)—that preceded his 1982 autobiography, *Sketches from Life*.

Over the next several years, Sophia Mumford and I met regularly for lunch, discussing the current academic and popular reception of her husband's ideas, but also growing deeper together in friendship. Before her death in 1997, she gave her approval to several potential projects composed of material that I believed Lewis Mumford had modestly overlooked when reviewing his life's work. One of these was a collection of his "Art Galleries" columns for the *New Yorker,* which is the subject of this book.

Without the assistance of several colleagues and friends, *Mumford on Modern Art in the 1930s* would have never been completed. Foremost is Stuart L. Frazer, Interlibrary Loan librarian at Old Dominion University's Perry Library. For many years, the *New Yorker* published two editions, metropolitan and national, and although the "Art Galleries" column was always included in the former, it was sometimes omitted from the latter, which is the one most often represented in research libraries and in microfilm collections. Frazer assiduously contacted libraries across the United States until all of the columns were found. Clay L. Vaughan of Old Dominion University's Hofheimer Art Library helped to locate numerous secondary sources, and he and Linda F. McGreevy of the Department of Art graciously provided me with helpful feedback after reading a draft of the introduction. Kurt Rehkopf generously shared his insights into the relationship between Mumford and Alfred Stieglitz. Sarah S. McCaskill patiently assisted with proofreading. I am extraordinarily grateful as well to Robert E. Shepard, my good friend and literary agent, for placing this book with the University of California Press. Stephanie Fay has been a thorough editor, guiding this project through its various stages with great skill and tact. Her assistant, Sigi Nacson, has been helpful and efficient at every turn.

Permission to reprint material from the *New Yorker* was obtained through the kind asistance of Leigh Montville of Condé Nast Publications. Funding for several of the illustrations used in this book was generously provided by the Dean's Faculty Publication Fund of the College of Arts and Letters at Old Dominion University.

Robert Wojtowicz
Norfolk, Virginia

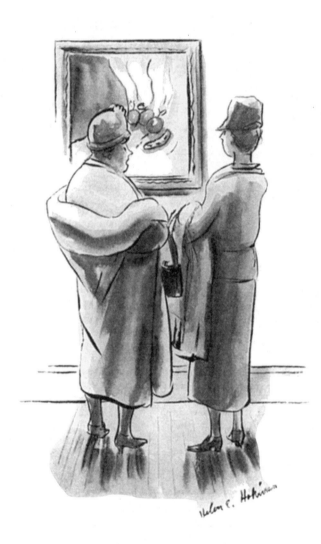

"Mr. Cortissoz said one thing and Mr. McBride another.
I'm going to ignore it entirely."

INTRODUCTION

For me art in all its forms awakened or intensified my own experiences of actual life. The years I spent writing weekly art reviews for the *New Yorker Magazine* from 1932 to 1937 played an essential part in my emotional education which complemented my experience in love. What is more, I learned to read the hidden meaning of the artist's unconscious symbols—so often a prophecy of events that the artist is quite unaware of.

—Lewis Mumford, *My Works and Days* (1979)

Lewis Mumford (1895–1990) is widely celebrated as a seminal critic of architecture, urbanism, technology, and American culture, but he is less recognized for his important work in art criticism. Mumford, in fact, regarded the study of art as essential to understanding the human condition, and this thread is woven into his writings across seemingly disparate fields. He began writing art criticism in the early 1920s, and his influence peaked in the mid-1930s when he became a regular columnist for the *New Yorker*. Appearing under the heading "The Art Galleries," his columns provide an unusual window into the rapidly evolving American art scene during the Great Depression. Mumford, although open to new movements emanating from Europe, advocated a progressive American modernism that was both socially aware and formally inventive. On a deeper level, his columns uncovered a creative alienation among modern artists that he believed to be symptomatic of a larger cultural disintegration, one in which the emergent evils of Nazism and fascism were only the most obvious manifestations.

Mumford on Modern Art in the 1930s assembles for the first time Mumford's work as an art critic—long buried in back issues of the *New Yorker*—into a single accessible volume that complements several collections of his architectural criticism already in print.[1] Many of the themes he addresses in "The Art Galleries" overlap with his more familiar architectural criticism: the guiding role of the past in stimulating creativity in the present, the increasing congestion of the modern metropolis, the alarming lack of human control over modern technology, and the pressing need to restore organic balance to everyday living. Other themes, such as the driving role of abstraction in modern expression, are wholly specific to the visual arts. Read together, the pieces form a prelude to Mumford's subsequent studies of human forms and values on which his larger critical reputation now rests.

The path that led Mumford to art criticism was both inadvertent and circuitous. Born in 1895 to a single mother, he was raised in modest circumstances on New York's Upper West Side.[2] Some of his fondest early memories involved trips with his stepgrandfather around the city and, in particular, to the Metropolitan Museum of Art and the American Museum of Natural History. Among the many books he recalled reading during his youth were Giorgio Vasari's *Lives of the Most Eminent Painters, Sculptors and Architects* and John Ruskin's *Modern Painters*.[3] A gifted but indifferent student, Mumford graduated from the prestigious Stuyvesant High School in 1912 with only average grades. He attended both the day and evening sessions of the City College of New York but left higher education before earning his baccalaureate degree.

Despite his lackluster academic performance, Mumford flourished intellectually outside the classroom. He was determined to become an independent writer and philosopher, finding an unusual role model in the Scottish polymath Patrick Geddes. Geddes, whose writings Mumford first encountered in a college biology class, preached an interdisciplinary, evolutionary, and organic approach to understanding modern society in which art would become a major component in fostering postindustrial human renewal.[4] Geddes's impact on Mumford was total, and it is significant to note here that among Geddes's early publications are guidebooks to major art exhibitions in Manchester and Glasgow, both published under the disarmingly simple title of *Every Man His Own Art Critic*.[5] The guidebooks were basic primers in art appreciation, but imbued with the Scotsman's peculiar outlook on social evolution. In many of his later writings, Geddes urged the gathering of factual information about cities and their regions via a firsthand observation process that he termed "regional survey." Consequently, Mumford walked the streets of New York, notepad in hand, scribbling notes and drawing scenery. He eventually began experimenting with watercolors as well, and although he never pursued his artistic efforts very far, they brought him a great deal of personal pleasure.[6]

By the early 1920s, Mumford had established himself as a freelance writer and journalist on a variety of topics—sociology, politics, urban planning, and the arts—for a variety of journals, including the *Dial*, the *Sociological Review*, the *Freeman*, the *American Mercury*, the *New Republic*, and the *Journal of the American Institute of Architects*. He completed his first book, *The Story of Utopias*, in 1922 while still under the influence of Geddes, and it established "eutopia"—the "good place" achievable through rational, organic planning—as the dominant theme of his entire writing career.[7] Near the book's conclusion, Mumford argued that a major step toward reaching this goal would be the reintegration of artists into the social mainstream: "In the good life, the purely esthetic element has a prominent place; but unless the artist is capable of moving men to the good life, the esthetic element is bound to be driven farther and farther away from the common realities, until the world of the artist will scarcely be distinguishable from the phantasia of dementia præcox. . . . If the arts are not to disintegrate utterly, must they not focus more and more upon eutopia?"[8] *The Story of Utopias* garnered positive notices, and it helped launch Mumford's career in cultural criticism.

During the 1920s, Mumford traveled in two distinct social and intellectual circles largely based in New York City: the first revolved around architecture and urban and regional planning and the second around literature and the fine arts. His writings both reflected these dual contacts and transcended them via the all-embracing theme of organic, cultural renewal. Through his work for the *Journal of the American Institute of Architects*, Mumford was introduced to the first group, an informal think tank known as the Regional Planning Association of America, which included architects, planners, conservationists, economists, writers, and philanthropists.[9] The association advocated the decongestion of the modern metropolis and the creation of affordable housing in accordance with the regionalism of Geddes and the garden city model of Ebenezer Howard, the English reformer. The architect Clarence Stein led the group, and Mumford served as its secretary and publicist. The association is best known for its promotion of the Appalachian Trail—the brainchild of member Benton MacKaye—and for its development of two planned communities in the New York metropolitan region inspired by the garden city: Sunnyside Gardens, Queens, and Radburn, New Jersey. Combining the theoretical background derived from Geddes and the practical experience drawn from the association, Mumford emerged as the enfant terrible of architectural critics in numerous essays and reviews of the 1920s.[10] His 1924 book *Sticks and Stones* was a radical retelling of American architectural history from a social perspective, and it branded him an iconoclast opposed to romantic revivalism and supportive of emerging European modernist ideals.[11]

Mumford's second circle was composed of established writers, critics, and artists who worked for the myriad literary and political journals that flourished in New York during this period. The scholar Casey Nelson Blake identified its core members—Randolph Bourne, Van Wyck Brooks, Waldo Frank, and Mumford—as the "Young Americans," radical critics who profoundly reshaped the postwar intellectual climate of the United States.[12] Others in this circle included Harold Stearns, Hendrik van Loon, Joel Elias Spingarn, John Dewey, Paul Rosenfeld, Walter Pach, and Alfred Stieglitz. Unlike the Regional Planning Association of America, this group was never organized, although several of its members initially gathered around Stearns, who edited an ambitious cultural omnibus published in 1922 as *Civilization in the United States*.[13] Mumford's piece concerned the imperiled state of American cities, and, as a measure of the young writer's growing reputation, Stearns positioned it first in the volume.[14] Once associated with this group, Mumford was quickly drawn into its lively debates concerning modernism in the arts and America's place vis-à-vis new developments in Europe. Greenwich Village, then in its heyday as a crucible of creative and social experimentation, was the locus of many of the group's activities. Mumford and his wife, Sophia (1899–1997), a former *Dial* colleague whom he married in 1921, actually resided in the Village briefly before decamping to Brooklyn Heights and, subsequently, to Sunnyside Gardens. Their son, Geddes, named for Mumford's early mentor, was born in 1925.

Within the group, Mumford drew closest in friendship to Van Wyck Brooks, a colleague at the short-lived *Freeman* and an accomplished literary critic. Brooks surveyed the state of American literature in his essay for *Civilization in the United States*, but it was his earlier piece "On Creating a Usable Past" that first caught Mumford's attention.[15] Believing that America had dwelt too long in the cultural shadow of Europe, Brooks urged his younger colleagues to join him in unearthing America's "usable past," its writers and artists from earlier generations who had made original, creative contributions to a nascent national culture but who had not been given their proper due by contemporary critics.[16] In response to Brooks's challenge, Mumford's next book, *The Golden Day*, identified a literary pantheon of five nineteenth-century writers: Ralph Waldo Emerson, Henry David Thoreau, Walt Whitman, Nathaniel Hawthorne, and Herman Melville.[17] Mumford's fourth book, a biography of Melville, deepened his investigative journey into the "usable past." [18] Both Mumford and Brooks believed that contemporary writers and artists would be spurred to new creative heights once these connections to their forebears had been reestablished.

If Brooks was Mumford's strongest literary influence, then Joel Spingarn similarly affected Mumford's ideas concerning art criticism and aesthetics.[19] An eminent critic and former Columbia University professor, Spingarn wrote on the state of American criticism for Stearns's volume.[20] He believed that criticism was itself a creative act, and, recognizing Mumford's potential in this area, he urged his younger colleague to undertake a closer study of aesthetics, including the works of Edmund Burke, Samuel Taylor Coleridge, Friedrich von Schiller, George Santayana, and especially Benedetto Croce. Even though, as Mumford later recalled, he "was put off by the aesthetically irrelevant nature of most of this literature," he found much to ponder, specifically in Croce's ideas concerning the roles of intuition and expression in criticizing works of art.[21]

In 1924, Mumford published a fictionalized dialogue about Croce's ideas in the American Mercury, which he titled "Æsthetics: A Palaver."[22] The dialogue was based upon a conversation that Mumford had had with Spingarn, Brooks, and two other friends at Troutbeck, Spingarn's Dutchess County, New York, country house three years earlier.[23] What disturbed Mumford about Croce's aesthetics was the philosopher's separation of an object's practical qualities from its aesthetic and his insistence on criticism for the sake of criticism. Mumford, who, like Geddes, sought to break down such intellectual barriers, could not accept this kind of categorization. Not surprisingly, Charles Adams, the character who expressed Mumford's viewpoint in the dialogue, used an organic metaphor in the manner of Geddes to state his position:

> To begin with, I can't accept the Crocean divorce between the practical and the æsthetic or ideal: it is a dialectical subterfuge, and its sole effect is to embarrass criticism with tautologies. Soil, seed, plant, and flower are one in life, and I would take the metaphor over bodily and say that they are one in literature: cut the flower away from the plant and it soon ceases to be a flower. Art can grow and reproduce and scatter its seeds in the hearts of men only when the conditions . . . are favorable. The good critic is therefore a gardener who pays attention to all the conditions that environ the production of a work of art. It is only when he has secured the best possible conditions in his own community that he is free to taste and enjoy, and to lead others to this pleasure.[24]

Despite Mumford's criticism of Croce, Spingarn liked "Æsthetics" so much that he had it privately printed as a pamphlet.[25] Their deepening friendship, moreover, soon prompted Mumford and his wife to begin spending their summers in the village of Leedsville adjacent to Trout-beck, where Spingarn hoped to nurture an artists' and writers' colony. Although Spingarn's vision never fully materialized, the Mumfords found themselves drawn to country living, purchasing a small farmhouse in Leedsville in 1929.[26] For the next seven years they divided their time between the city and the country.

Through Stearns's project Mumford also met the artist and critic Wal-ter Pach, who developed extensive connections to European modern artists during his many years of living abroad.[27] Pach earlier had assisted Arthur B. Davies and Walt Kuhn in organizing the 1913 International Exhibition of Modern Art, a controversial traveling survey of European and American modern art that became known popularly as the Armory Show after its New York venue, the Lexington Avenue Armory.[28] Pach included three of his own works in the American section, and he wrote some of the supporting material for the exhibition. At each of its stops—New York, Chicago, and Boston—the Armory Show scandalized both critics and the public, who were unaccustomed to the radical experi-ments of the fauves, cubists, expressionists, and other European mod-ernists. Viewers especially savaged Marcel Duchamp's infamous 1912 painting *Nude Descending a Staircase (No. 2)* because of its abstracted and fragmentary treatment of the human nude. Yet despite widespread resistance modern art had gained a foothold in the United States. Along with Duchamp and the collector Walter Arensberg, Pach subsequently formed the Society of Independent Artists to provide American mod-ernists with a sympathetic forum for their works via annual exhibitions. Mumford did not attend the Armory Show, since he would have been only seventeen years old during its New York run. "I was then too young and callow even to visit that exhibition, let alone respond to it," he wrote in his autobiography.[29] Nevertheless, he was well aware of the Armory Show's significance by the time he met Pach.

Pach contributed an essay simply titled "Art" to *Civilization in the United States,* and it opened Mumford's eyes to several key artists of the late nineteenth and early twentieth centuries, including Winslow Homer, Albert Pinkham Ryder, John La Farge, and Maurice Prendergast.[30] Fur-thermore, Pach argued for the development of modern art along dis-tinctly American lines: "There is no question to-day but that America must evolve along the lines of contemporary thought throughout the civ-ilized world. There will be a local tang to our art. Certain enthusiasms and characteristics, as we develop them, may give emphasis to special

phases of our production, but there is no longer the possibility of an isolated, autochthonic growth, such as seemed to be forecast up to about
the time of the [American] Revolution."[31]

No account of Mumford's formation as an art critic is complete without mention of his relationship with the photographer, art critic, and
gallery owner Alfred Stieglitz.[32] More than thirty years Mumford's senior,
Stieglitz discovered photography while living and studying in Berlin during the 1880s. Stieglitz resettled in New York in 1890 and became involved
in writing and editing for the *American Amateur Photographer* and for
Camera Notes, all the while continuing his pursuit of truthful subjects
drawn from everyday life on the city's streets. Eager to promote photography as an emerging fine art medium, he founded the Photo-Secession, an
avant-garde group that embraced a pictorialist aesthetic, in 1902. Stieglitz
edited and published the group's lavishly produced journal *Camera Work,*
which contained critical and technical essays as well as photographic illustrations. He solidified his position as a leading advocate for photography by opening the Little Galleries of the Photo-Secession in 1905. In a typ-
ically modern twist, the exhibition space soon became known as 291, its
address on Fifth Avenue, after Stieglitz expanded the scope of its exhibitions to include works in all media by leading European and American
modernists, including Auguste Rodin, Pablo Picasso, Arthur Dove, Marsden Hartley, and Georgia O'Keeffe, whom Stieglitz married in 1924. 291
closed its doors in 1917, but Stieglitz continued to mount exhibitions occasionally at the Anderson Gallery until he opened the Intimate Gallery in
1925. Four years later, he launched his last gallery, An American Place,
which focused more narrowly on American art.

Stieglitz was not part of Stearns's project, and his introduction to
Mumford occurred around 1924 through Paul Rosenfeld, a mutual
friend and critic whose convivial weekly salons brought together New
York's literary and artistic elite.[33] Stieglitz and Mumford began ex-
changing letters the following spring, and, despite the differences in their
ages, they forged a deep friendship over the next several years.[34] Mumford was keenly aware of the expectations that often develop in men-
toring relationships, since he had already rejected Patrick Geddes's offer
of a position as his amanuensis. Stieglitz and Mumford, however, seemed
almost perfectly attuned in their mutual quest to uncover a genuinely
American artistic expression, with the former encouraging the latter to
expand his outlook on modernism and the role that American artists
were to play in its evolution.

Mumford and Stieglitz exchanged more than letters and ideas. At a time when journalistic ethics had not yet solidified, Stieglitz felt free to bestow gifts on his younger "protégé." In evident gratitude for an O'Keeffe review in the *New Republic,* for example, Stieglitz gave works by O'Keeffe and Marin to the Mumfords to hang in their home.[35] In 1929, there was a gift of *Equivalents,* photographs of clouds that number among Stieglitz's most important landscape studies.[36] Several years later, Stieglitz set aside back issues of *Camera Work* for Mumford's library.[37] Still struggling as a writer, despite some measurable successes, Mumford reciprocated in less material ways. When in 1927 he joined with Brooks, Rosenfeld, and Alfred Kreymborg to launch the *American Caravan,* a literary yearbook, they dedicated the first volume to Stieglitz, "a teacher," or, more correctly, their teacher.[38] Seven years later, Mumford, Rosenfeld, and several other literary colleagues produced a Festschrift entitled *America and Alfred Stieglitz: A Collective Portrait.*[39] Reproduced in the present volume, Mumford's essay, "The Metropolitan Milieu," deftly situates Stieglitz within the context of a growing and changing New York in the decades bracketing the turn of the twentieth century.[40]

Mumford began writing art criticism during a period of great flux in the American art scene.[41] Having been exposed to European avant-garde movements at the Armory Show, artists and critics became sharply divided between conservatives who wished to preserve the academic tradition and radicals who embraced modernism in its innumerable forms. Realism, formerly the dominant American art movement, had already been transformed in the first decade of the twentieth century by the socially aware content of New York's "Ash Can" artists and by the formal experiments of numerous returning expatriates who had drunk deeply of fauvism, cubism, expressionism, and other European styles. As early as 1910, Arthur Dove abandoned subject matter altogether in his nonrepresentational paintings, the first American artist to do so.

The pace of change accelerated greatly after the Armory Show. Photography, long an influence on modern painting, was freely acknowledged in the work of the precisionist group that gathered around Stieglitz, while Marcel Duchamp nurtured a New York branch of Dada, the fleeting, absurdist movement of the immediate postwar period. Imported from Europe in the 1920s, surrealism further upset the status quo with its disturbing subject matter. On an institutional level, upstarts such as the Museum of Modern Art (founded 1929) and the Whitney Museum of American Art (founded 1931) would soon challenge the cultural hegemony of establishments such as the Metropolitan Museum of Art and the Brooklyn Museum, while private galleries, including Stieglitz's, captured the attention of a growing cognoscenti.

Although Mumford matured as a writer and critic in this charged environment, even in his earliest pieces he sought a middle ground for American modernism, one that would be based in society's organic reintegration and renewal. With no particular credentials in art criticism, Mumford began writing book reviews and essays for the *Freeman* in 1920, and this led to more prominent exposure in the pages of the *American Mercury,* the *New Republic,* and *Harper's Monthly.* Once established, Mumford joined a select company of American critics that included Walter Pach, Royal Cortissoz, Frank Jewett Mather, Henry McBride, Katherine Dreier, Thomas Craven, and George L. K. Morris. Toward the end of the decade, Mumford began writing exhibition reviews for the *New Republic* as well, reviews that eventually brought him to the attention of the *New Yorker*'s editors.

Mumford's art criticism, like his architectural criticism, was highly individualistic and synthesized from a variety of academic sources and personal contacts. He remained firmly independent in his views, displaying an unusually catholic appreciation for various styles and movements. In making judgments, he rejected formalism, the dominant critical mode then championed by the English critics Clive Bell and Roger Fry, as too narrowly focused on the object itself. Instead, Mumford, along with Paul Rosenfeld and other critics in Stieglitz's orbit, favored what scholar Susan Noyes Platt identified as a "generic expressionism," a transcendental and environmental approach that emphasized the viewer's emotional response to the work of art.[42] This approach, as adapted by Mumford, considered the social, moral, political, and economic issues of contemporary life to be essential to the study of art, and it strongly paralleled both the ideas of Geddes and the educational philosophy of the American scholar John Dewey.[43] Toward the end of the decade, Mumford ruminated on what he viewed as the critic's elusive qualifications:

What, then, does substantiate the judgment of a work of art? The answer is a slightly disheartening one to those who would rely upon books and rules and applicable formulas; for the ultimate instrument for measuring a work of art is a man and his whole experience. If a critic has seen thousands of pictures and studied them over and over again; if he has experienced the esthetic moment directly, as it occurs in life, when a man's hand or a group of buildings or a cliff or a woman's body isolates itself from its practical associations and establishes some more immediate and direct relationship with one's inner experience; if the critic has observed and pondered and made love and experienced joy and sorrow, there will come a time when he will be able to declare, with a certain exactitude and confidence: This is good and that is bad: this is mediocre or the other is astounding. He cannot prove that his verdict is correct; there is, indeed, no final proof for any other observer except that induced by his sympathy and his confidence in the man. Lacking that, a mountain of formal demonstration would not convince a mouse.[44]

Mumford's emphasis on "inner experience" as an essential part of a critic's apparatus increased over the next several years as he immersed himself in the study of Freudian and Jungian psychology. This interest was sparked largely by his friendship with Henry A. Murray, a Harvard psychologist who shared Mumford's scholarly fascination with Herman Melville.[45] Thereafter, the role of signs and symbols in art, as well as the myths behind its creation, assumed a greater prominence in Mumford's writings.

Like many budding writers, Mumford initially used reviews as a way to bolster his meager income; more important, they were a means for him to immerse himself in the literature of a given field and to build his expertise. The 1920s saw the publication of several landmark studies in the general history of art as well as more specialized tomes on particular periods or cultures. Of particular importance was the American publication of Elie Faure's magisterial four-volume *History of Art*—translated by Walter Pach—which Mumford praised for its contextual approach in two separate reviews.[46] "What M. Faure has done is re-read the history of the world," Mumford wrote in a 1922 review of the first two volumes. "His point of departure, indeed his originality, consists in taking man's images for his documents. In short, he has written a history of men's minds, as revealed in the image."[47] Of Helen Gardner's more compact *Art through the Ages,* soon to become a standard college text, Mumford wrote: "For all that a descriptive guide book can properly do, Miss Gardner's survey is excellent; and he who asks more from it, does not know the essential limitations of books."[48] He reviewed more scholarly studies as well, even treading in unfamiliar historical territory. For example, he deemed Agnes E. Meyer's *Chinese Painting as Reflected in the Thought and Art of Li Lung-Mien* "a vigorous contribution to our knowledge and intuition of Chinese culture."[49]

Mumford took special interest in the history of American art, and this, of course, coincided with his studies of American architecture and literature. Few books in this subject area, however, appeared until the 1920s, since the field was still largely obscured by a broader scholarly interest in European art. When Suzanne La Follette's comprehensive survey *Art in America* appeared in 1929, Mumford was genuinely ecstatic that the first step had been taken to rectify this historical deficiency.[50] La Follette privately admitted her indebtedness to Mumford's *Sticks and Stones* in researching her own book, which examined architecture as well as painting and sculpture.[51] In the quest to recover America's usable past, moreover, Mumford believed that La Follette had justly elevated American art in the face of its European detractors. He wrote:

> Miss La Follette has good sense and a nicely balanced mind; and what she proves is what history proves: namely, that art has had its good and its bad moments in America, and that it is today in probably as healthy a state as literature or science, to say nothing of industrialism. And just as we have in the past had our Joseph Henrys and Willard Gibbses to put alongside the Clerk Maxwells and Kelvins, so we have had a Ryder or an Eakins to put alongside a Redon or a Courbet, a Richardson to place beside a Bentley, or a Roebling to measure up with a Paxton or an Eiffel.[52]

By this time Mumford was in the process of gathering information for his own general study of the arts in late-nineteenth-century America, and he found La Follette's book to be invaluable to his own research, even if he did not agree with all of her judgments about individual artists.

Mumford's more general essays on art ranged over a wide territory. His intellectual indebtedness to Geddes, as well as to his childhood excursions, is evident in such early pieces as "The Marriage of Museums" (1918), which advocated building a physical and intellectual path across Central Park between the Metropolitan Museum of Art and the American Museum of Natural History.[53] By combining museological approaches, he argued, visitors would have a greater sense of an artifact's cultural and historical context. His outlook quickly broadened. Three years later, he penned "Beauty and the Picturesque," in which he defined "Beauty" in relation to objects that fulfill their function and purpose, while relegating "the Picturesque" to objects that exist solely on an aesthetic plane.[54] Mumford's definitions thus subverted the standard aesthetic categories established by eighteenth-century British writers in favor of ones measured by their relationship to twentieth-century functionalism. He wrote: "Beauty is inseparable from use; it is the outward token of an inward grace; its appearance is the manifestation of a humanized life; and its existence and development constitute, in fact, a sort of index to a community's vitality."[55] He returned to this theme in a 1927 essay for *Harper's Monthly* on the related aspects of taste: "Taste, regarded in the large, is not something that can be cultivated in an old curiosity shop or a museum: it is a much more robust and fundamental matter than this, and it has its roots not in historic treatises and guide-books, but in the myths of religion, the needs of social life, the technic of industry, and the daily habits of a people. All the fine historic models of the past, just because they were historic, had no base in contemporary civilization: so far from springing out of modern necessities, they shrank from them."[56]

Primarily under Stieglitz's and Rosenfeld's influence, Mumford began to indicate a preference in his criticism for art with organic content, es-pecially the human figure. Nevertheless, Mumford saw positive value in abstraction, which was gaining ground among American modernists and their supporters. He explored this theme in a 1927 essay for the *New Republic:*

> Abstract art—that is, art in which the meaning does not depend upon the accurate representation of objects—is now firmly established; but abstrac-tion itself is only a method: a picture is not a neutral arrangement of lines and spaces, like a Greek fret: it is such an arrangement as will produce a definite spiritual effect, and it is successful only when it stimulates in the be-holder an immediate feeling of the painter's own capacities and reactions. If the effect is void, no mastery of technique will justify it; if the effect is gen-uine and the synthesis an exhilarating one, almost any means, from a palette knife to a camera, can be justified.[57]

Mumford reacted most positively toward abstract art when it was placed within the context of modern architecture. "In architecture and the ac-cessory arts, pure pattern is a highly desirable quality," he wrote in an exhibition review that same year, "and in our own day we are perhaps more likely to find such patterns in terms of mechanical forms than we are, like the older craftsmen, in flowers, animals and growing things."[58] To Mumford abstract art generally reflected modern society's empty pre-occupation with technology; conversely, he believed that organic com-positions by artists such as Georgia O'Keeffe existed on a higher emo-tional plane, effectively filling this modern void.[59]

By the mid-1920s Mumford was writing occasional exhibition re-views for the *New Republic,* some of which focused approvingly on Stieglitz's protégés. On Marin, for example, Mumford wrote in Decem-ber 1926: "The fusion of the inner and the outer eye, focused uncon-sciously in the living gesture of the brush, not brought together by any set formula of design, puts Marin at the very summit of his art; and this means, at the present moment, of American art."[60] Mumford concluded the review by suggesting that a permanent Marin collection be estab-lished. "Today we can find our Marins with Stieglitz," he continued.

"But where shall we find them tomorrow? What answer have our museums to make to this question?"[61] Privately he confided to Stieglitz: "Yours is the intimate gallery in a deep sense: what goes on there cannot be lightly drawn to the surface, and exhibited to others. In that sense, the Marins will wait long for another home."[62]

The following March, Mumford wrote one of his most controversial pieces: a review of O'Keeffe's paintings, to which he ascribed an overt eroticism: "[O'Keeffe] has beautified the sense of what it is to be a woman; she has revealed the intimacies of love's juncture with the purity and the absence of shame that lovers feel in their meeting; she has brought what was inarticulate and troubled and confused into the realm of conscious beauty, where it may be recalled and enjoyed with a new intensity; she has, in sum, found a language for experiences that are otherwise too intimate to be shared."[63] As scholar Barbara Buhler Lynes noted, this was a view that Stieglitz and his associates had long espoused—despite O'Keeffe's objections—and that Mumford helped to fix in the public's imagination.[64] Marin, O'Keeffe, and others in Stieglitz's circle continued to hold prominent places in Mumford's art criticism well into the next decade.

Meanwhile, Mumford was diligently at work on the "usable past" project first inspired by Van Wyck Brooks earlier in the decade. Between 1924 and 1929, Mumford had produced one book on American architecture and two books on American literature, and for his next effort he decided simultaneously to narrow his time frame to late-nineteenth-century America and to broaden his subject matter to include the full spectrum of the arts. The result was *The Brown Decades* (1931), Mumford's cultural analysis of the arts in America between the end of the Civil War and the turn of the twentieth century.[65] The book brought to the surface the buried achievements of Emily Dickinson in literature; H. H. Richardson and Louis Sullivan in architecture; John and Washington Roebling in engineering; Frederick Law Olmsted in landscape architecture; and Thomas Eakins and Albert Pinkham Ryder in painting. Mumford's book was groundbreaking in drawing attention to Richardson and Sullivan, who have been viewed ever since as the period's chief progressive architects, but it also cast new light on Eakins and Ryder, who were then somewhat underappreciated painters.

In researching the section on painting for the book, Mumford devoured the literature then emerging on American art.[66] He also had access to the numerous exhibitions of American art mounted in New York's museums and galleries during this period. In 1930, for example, the Museum of Modern Art held a major retrospective of the careers of Ryder, Eakins, and Winslow Homer, effectively codifying the scholarly reevaluation that had been going on since those artists' deaths.[67] That Mumford would have missed this pertinent exhibition is highly unlikely. He published an advance draft of his chapter on American art in the October 1931 issue of *Scribner's Magazine,* just ahead of *The Brown Decades'* fall release.[68]

The chapter "Images—Sacred and Profane" is Mumford's most lasting contribution to the historiography of American art. As with his related analyses of literature and architecture, he hoped that by writing a historical survey of the visual arts he would inspire his contemporaries to build upon the achievements of their predecessors. Since the chapter appeared last in the book's sequence, he also used it to summarize his views on contemporary American culture. Mumford devoted most of his attention to Eakins, the era's grittiest realist, and Ryder, the era's most idiosyncratic romantic. In Mumford's view, Eakins made his art "face the rough and brutal and ugly facts of our civilization, determined that its values should grow out of these things, and should not look for its themes to the historic symbols of Europe."[69] The reclusive Ryder was clearly Mumford's favorite American artist, occupying a position similar to that of Melville in his literary criticism. "No one except Melville . . . had such a deep sense of the beauty and treachery of the sea as Ryder did," Mumford wrote, "and no one, not even Melville, expressed this more completely and poignantly, suggesting in the fathomless ocean the fathomless mystery of life itself."[70] Winslow Homer, George Fuller, John La Farge, and Mary Cassatt also figured prominently in Mumford's analysis, while John Singer Sargent and James Abbott McNeill Whistler were handily dismissed.

Before concluding his chapter, Mumford briefly discussed the contributions of photography to the art of the "Brown Decades." He was firmly committed to the still-unorthodox view that photography should be classified with the fine arts. According to Mumford, the first artist to master this medium fully was Stieglitz: "Stieglitz's mission in photography was like [Frank Lloyd] Wright's in architecture: he was to demonstrate its manifold potentialities. He had faith in the photograph as a means of education; he foresaw the increasing importance of the photographically illustrated paper; he preached the lesson of the concrete symbol, the symbol beyond words, so necessary in an age that had closed half the world to itself by the great educational device of literacy."[71] Far from being a passive observer, Stieglitz, in Mumford's view, had an exceptional ability to record and to interpret modern life. "For Stieglitz photography was not merely a matter of making pictures," Mumford wrote: "it was an attitude toward life as a whole, an acknowledgment of the personalities and forces around him, an attempt to embrace them, hold them, comment upon them, interpret them, continue along the lines of their development."[72] Most important, Mumford regarded Stieglitz as both a vital link to the Brown Decades—Stieglitz in fact provided Mumford with a firsthand account of his experiences for the book—and an inspiring presence in the first half of the twentieth century.[73]

Mumford identified a general decline in creativity among American artists in the early years of the twentieth century that in many ways paralleled the situation with American architects. Nevertheless, he recognized as significant the contributions of the Ash Can artists and the work of Charles Burchfield and Edward Hopper. Among contemporary artists, Mumford cited Boardman Robinson, Benton, Marin, and O'Keeffe as continuing this creative impulse. Lest the reader miss Mumford's didactic objective, he restated it clearly near the book's conclusion: "The influence of the Brown Decades upon our own, or the parallel developments of their original artists and ours, can of course be exaggerated: but it is important, since the relationship is a reciprocal one, that we should recognize the solid foundation on which, consciously or unconsciously, we build."[74]

Critics, while generally enthusiastic about *The Brown Decades'* contributions to American architecture, tended to gloss over Mumford's analysis of the painting of the period. "Although Mr. Mumford does justice to literature and painting, the most convincing pages in his book are those devoted to architecture, including, very properly, landscaping, city planning and engineering," Albert Guerard wrote in the *New York Herald Tribune*.[75] William Murrell, writing in *Creative Art*, praised the discussion of art in *The Brown Decades* as "an excellent and sympathetic study of conditions and temperaments" but took issue with Mumford's biases concerning contemporary artists.[76] "The tribute to the work and influence of Alfred Stieglitz in photography is both timely and just," Murrell wrote; "but the gratuitous presentation of Marin and O'Keeffe as lineal descendants of the 'Brown Decades' will be felt by many to be but the ill-advised stretching of an honest loyalty to Stieglitz himself."[77] Nevertheless, the book's most important achievement lay in its insightful cultural analysis of the period rather than its treatment of specific artists. Pach recognized this and expressed his satisfaction with the book to Mumford privately:

I have just finished *The Brown Decades,* and it's a fine book. . . . [T]he estimates of Homer, Eakins, and Ryder are weighty and just—and again with an element of beauty that does away with any prosaic tinge that might attach [itself] to those other words. But it is not the individual portraits and interpretations that leave the main impression on my mind: it really is the period that is portrayed—I might almost say created, for no one I know has isolated those decades before, and I am sure that the future will more than confirm your seeing of them.[78]

By the early 1930s, art history was more firmly established as an academic discipline in the United States than architectural history, so Mumford's chapter on the visual arts had far less of an impact than the book's other chapters. This is reflected in the standing accorded *The Brown Decades* in subsequent scholarship. Although Elizabeth Johns called it the "classic study of the role of the arts in America in the late nineteenth century," most scholars of American art have tended to overlook Mumford's contribution.[79]

One might characterize Mumford in the 1920s as someone who wrote art criticism on an occasional basis rather than as a critic with a regular following. That situation changed dramatically when, in 1931, he joined the staff of the *New Yorker.* He was employed initially as the magazine's architecture critic, and he assumed the additional duties of art critic the following year. The story of his association with the magazine has been told elsewhere in detail, but it is useful here to recount the circumstances of his hiring.[80] Harold Ross, the *New Yorker*'s cantankerous editor, was searching for a new critic to head up "The Sky Line," a regular department that covered architecture. Having admired Mumford's writing for the *New Republic,* Ross coaxed a trial piece from Mumford in June 1931 on the recently unveiled plans for Rockefeller Center.[81] Ross was delighted with the resulting review, and he offered the architecture position to Mumford. As a contented freelance writer, however, Mumford initially resisted being tied to a regular engagement, leading to a cat-and-mouse pursuit that lasted for several months. Undoubtedly, the deepening Depression factored into his decision to accept Ross's offer—and the regular paycheck that accompanied it—that fall. With a small family to support and two mortgages to pay, Mumford could not have maintained his pre-Depression lifestyle without the income from the *New Yorker.*

Mumford's first fall-to-spring cultural "season" at the *New Yorker* netted nine "Sky Line" columns on topics ranging from the new George Washington Bridge to the Museum of Modern Art's milestone Modern

Architecture: International Exhibition. Ross was pleased with his new columnist, but at the same time concerned that a slowing real estate market would limit potential new material. Sometime in the early spring of 1932, he inquired if Mumford would consider writing "The Art Galleries," another of the *New Yorker*'s regular departments, as well.[82] Mumford would replace Murdock Pemberton, the magazine's first art critic and an original member of the renowned "Round Table" of *New Yorker* writers that had gathered at the nearby Algonquin Hotel during the previous decade.[83] This shuffling of personnel was typical of what the longtime *New Yorker* contributor Brendan Gill called "the hysteria of Ross's reckless hiring, firing, and switching about of jobs in the early days of the magazine."[84] Ross's terms were extremely generous: $75 per department, with three columns for every four issues of the magazine during a standard ten-month fall-to-spring season.[85] The offer, slightly modified due to the magazine's slumping revenues, remained on the table through the summer. "We still want you to do the art department but possibly not as often as was proposed," Ross wrote Mumford in mid-August. "It is the depression, you know."[86]

Mumford agreed to Ross's terms in time for the start of the 1932–33 cultural season. Yet when the critic submitted three columns—two "Art Galleries" and a "Sky Line"—all at once in mid-September, Ross was caught, uncharacteristically, off guard. "My God," he wrote Mumford, "don't ever do that again."[87] Mumford responded the next day with a careful mix of modesty and irony. "I knew I was crazy to write those three pieces all in one day, after a hasty day in the city: but when I sent them in, I didn't think you'd be crazy enough to print them," he explained. "It shall not happen again: I am a methodical man and don't usually have brainstorms."[88] A few days later, Ross, with his usual dryness, provided the last word. "Your first Art Gallery piece got in the issue of October 1st," he wrote. "Reading it over in proof I liked it better than ever. I had no idea you did all three of the pieces in one day. It must have been a long day."[89]

If Ross was worried about the magazine's financial health, he was nonetheless generous in allocating space for Mumford's columns, which began running with nearly the frequency Ross first envisioned and which settled into a monthly schedule of roughly three "Art Galleries" published for every "Sky Line." Ross also asked Mumford to write the brief copy for the art section of the magazine's "Goings On about Town" department.[90] Outside the major daily newspapers, few critics at the time had such regular exposure, especially to a national audience. Moreover, no critic since has wielded such double-barreled influence in art and architecture simultaneously. In his first year at the magazine, Mumford had already shaken the city's architect, planners, and real estate moguls. Now it was time for the city's artists, museum directors, and gallery owners to be similarly challenged.

Fortunately, the number of exhibitions mounted in the city's museums and galleries had not decreased significantly, and Mumford kept pace with the quickly evolving scene. By the 1930s, the city's leading art and cultural institutions were just beginning to cluster along Fifth Avenue on Manhattan's Upper East Side, an area initially settled by the Metropolitan Museum in the late nineteenth century and subsequently dubbed "Museum Mile" in the late twentieth century. To the north, the Museum of the City of New York opened its new building at 104th Street in January 1932, and to the south, the Frick Collection completed a major expansion on its grounds at the corner of Seventieth Street several years later.[91] There were notable exceptions to this evolving geographic concentration. The Brooklyn Museum stood in another borough entirely, while the Whitney Museum operated from a group of renovated townhouses on West Eighth Street in the Village.[92] In Midtown, the Museum of Modern Art occupied a single townhouse at 11 West Fifty-third Street, having moved in 1932 from rented space in the Hecksher Building at Fifth Avenue and Fifty-seventh Street; a truly modern building expressive of the museum's mission was still several years in the offing.[93] Except for a small cluster in the Village, most of the private art galleries were located in Midtown in the Fifties between Fifth and Lexington Avenues, including Stieglitz's An American Place at Madison Avenue and Fifty-third Street.

The compactness of the "Art Galleries" turf suited Mumford, an inveterate walker who never learned to drive. Since his small, Sunnyside Gardens townhouse was located across the East River in Long Island City, he ordinarily commuted to Midtown by subway and made his rounds on foot, whether he was reviewing buildings or exhibitions. Only occasionally would he review venues outside New York City. Mumford worked quickly, writing his manuscripts at home and delivering them quietly to the magazine's editorial offices on West Forty-fifth Street. By temperament something of a loner, Mumford remained detached from the *New Yorker*'s other celebrated contributors as well as its industrious staff. Approaching forty and determined to establish himself as an author of weightier books, Mumford did not have the time to socialize as in his younger days. Moreover, two intense extramarital affairs—one with the architecture critic and housing reformer Catherine Bauer and the other with the sculptor Alice Decker—upended his personal life and were the chief source of the "emotional education" to which he refers obliquely in the passage used as this introduction's epigraph.[94] Despite these outside concerns, surviving correspondence indicates that Mumford and Ross quickly developed an easy rapport born of mutual respect, despite—much to Ross's regret—their infrequent face-to face contact. As Mumford's first season as art critic drew to a close, Ross wrote: "Make your plans for next winter to include doing our work, for God's sake. I think you are a big success and I had intended to tell you so personally for weeks but have failed to meet you in the office. I am in the office less than I used to be as I find it more and more impossible to do any work here. Nevertheless, I thought I would run into you sometime."[95] Eight months later, with Christmas approaching, Ross wryly informed Mumford that, around the office, the elusive critic was "suspected of being an elf."[96]

Mumford quickly mastered the literary tightrope that was required of all writers who worked for the *New Yorker*: thorough research balanced by sprightly and sophisticated prose reflective of the collective energies of the metropolis. In a humorous foreword penned in 1935 for an album of *New Yorker* cartoons, Mumford focused his critical lens inwardly on the magazine's cosmopolitan tone: "The *New Yorker* is preëminently a regional magazine. Its very special flavor springs out of this self-imposed set of limitations. . . . [O]ne is conscious always of the background of the big city. One hears the hum and putter and screech of traffic, the cackle of conversation in restaurants, the far-off hoots and whistles on the river; one's eye has glimpses of streets, alleys, corners, nooks; the smells and flavors of the city come through by a hundred subtle suggestions; even the perfume of the boudoir creeps—or should I say gallops?—through the advertisements."[97] From the very beginning, Mumford wrote the column in the first person, dropping the chatty second-person plural used by Pemberton and some of the magazine's other contributors. This helped to establish a more serious—but not too serious—tone for the column, while making the columnist more accountable for his pronouncements.

To art criticism, which is often a stodgy field freighted with lugubrious writing, Mumford brought accessible cultural observation tinged with witty irreverence. Ross encouraged this. "I was going to tell you we are all very happy about the Art column," Ross wrote to Mumford in April 1934. "Moreover, you seem to be able to meet the humorous boys on their own grounds. At any rate, I have got quite a few chuckles out of some of your recent pieces."[98] Mumford's prose was descriptive as well as analytical, since the magazine's columns were not illustrated, save for amusing pictorial vignettes near their headlines. To at least one artist-critic, Mumford too often overlooked the subtleties of pictorial form, a mainstay of conventional art criticism, but to the educated lay public, still unsure of what to think—let alone say—about modern art, "The Art Galleries" must have provided a kind of reassuring road map.[99] It is no coincidence that the magazine's celebrated cartoonists occasionally used the art museum or the contemporary art gallery as a setting for wry jokes on the confusing nature of pictorial modernism.

Mumford deliberately kept the coverage of "The Art Galleries" broad, reviewing exhibitions of old and modern European masters, living Americans, photography, decorative arts, and industrial design. He covered the earliest Whitney biennials, soon to become a regular barometer of the contemporary American art scene. Public artwork, whether sponsored privately or through government initiatives such as the Public Works of Art Project (PWAP) and the Works Progress Administration (WPA), received his attention as well. Several exhibitions during this period resurrected the artists of the Brown Decades, which permitted Mumford to reinforce or even revise some of his earlier views regarding the late nineteenth century. On the contemporary front, the struggle between conservatives and progressives continued into the 1930s, with advocates of an American regionalism, as represented in the figurative work of Thomas Hart Benton and Grant Wood, rising to meet the challenge of surrealism, which was by then the dominant European modern movement. While supportive of regionalism in architecture and planning, Mumford recognized an inherently nativist streak in this group of painters that he found objectionable. Instead, he favored the "social realism" of artists such as Reginald Marsh and William Gropper for its skewering of contemporary public and political mores.

The proclivity of modern artists to embrace abstraction or even nonobjectivity continued to perplex Mumford—as it most certainly continued to perplex his readership—but largely for different reasons. He did not oppose modern artists' innumerable formal experiments, which were so vexing to the uninitiated; for example, he repeatedly praised the biomorphic inventions of Joan Miró. Rather, Mumford balked at what he perceived to be modern artists' nihilistic content, which, in his somewhat Freudian view, revealed a world increasingly threatened by emptiness at best or totalitarianism at worst. Thus he discerned a latent pathology in the abstracted and distorted imagery of surrealism and other movements and a dehumanizing mechanization in the geometries of nonobjectivity.

Given Mumford's friendship with Alfred Stieglitz, it comes as no surprise that the critic regularly—and favorably—reviewed exhibitions at An American Place and that he continued to champion the artists in Stieglitz's circle, especially O'Keeffe and Marin. It should also be noted that Mumford was a key supporter of the Museum of Modern Art, whose promotion of European and American modernism paralleled Stieglitz's efforts on an institutional scale. Before assuming responsibility for "The Sky Line," Mumford had agreed to write a catalog essay for the museum's landmark 1932 Modern Architecture: International Exhibition.[100] That he subsequently reviewed the exhibition for "The Sky Line" created an unusual and self-confessed conflict of interest that he did not repeat in either column.[101] In fact, he declined an invitation by the museum in 1936 to write a catalog essay for a John Marin exhibition, presumably to avoid an awkward repetition of the previous situation.[102] Still, Mumford was not above criticizing the museum when he felt it was warranted. Two years earlier, he voiced his concern that the museum's Department of Painting had failed to embrace more fully the work of less-established contemporary artists and that the institution as a whole had failed to mount a major photography exhibition ("The Art Galleries: Tips for Travellers—The Modern Museum," June 9, 1934).[103]

On several occasions, Alfred H. Barr Jr., the director of the Museum of Modern Art, wrote Mumford to express his appreciation after receiving positive notices in "The Sky Line" or "The Art Galleries." In the case of the museum's survey of abstraction in modern art, Mumford's review was somewhat qualified, but Barr was grateful nonetheless ("The Art Galleries: The Course of Abstraction," March 21, 1936). "I think I never thanked you for your generous words about the Abstract show," Barr wrote to Mumford in May 1936. "I appreciate it partly because it was not a show of great general interest to the public, and I think your article in the New Yorker may easily have encouraged many people to come."[104] When Mumford reviewed the museum's major surrealism exhibition later that year, Barr was again moved to thank the critic ("The Art Galleries: Surrealism and Civilization," December 19, 1936):

> I almost never write to reviewers of our exhibitions, either in praise or complaint, but I want to break this convention to say how much I appreciate your review of the Fantastic-Surrealist show at the Museum.

> I was very much disheartened by the reviews of the art critics in the daily papers, not because they were ag[a]inst the show but because they seemed so badly informed and so irresponsible in their criticisms.
>
> Your review has done much to restore the balance, since it has been read probably by more intelligent people than any of the others.[105]

No critic ever pleases his targeted audience, but Mumford generally softened his barbs with gentle humor, and if surviving correspondence is any indication, his columns rarely elicited outright commendations or protests. One major exception was his uncharacteristically blistering review of a memorial exhibition of paintings by Bryson Burroughs ("The Art Galleries: Mirrors and the Metropolitan," April 6, 1935). The exhibition was held at the Metropolitan Museum of Art, where Burroughs had been chief curator of painting, and Mumford faulted the institution for honoring an individual whom he believed to be of questionable artistic talent and professional judgment. Burroughs embraced a conservative, neoclassical mode in his own work that was heavily influenced by the French fin-de-siècle muralist Pierre Puvis de Chavannes. For Mumford, a vociferous opponent of academicism in contemporary architecture, Burroughs's images struck a similarly clichéd and outdated chord that also seemingly impaired his curatorial faculties.

Influential friends and colleagues of Burroughs immediately bombarded the *New Yorker* with letters of protest. Lloyd Goodrich, the prominent scholar of American art, who was at the time a research curator at the Whitney Museum, claimed that Mumford's piece was "disqualified by its silly violence."[106] The Whitney's director, Juliana Force, echoed Goodrich's protests. "Bryson Burroughs' sensitiveness as an artist combined with his rare scholarship, made him of inestimable value to the Art of our day, and to the Museum which had the good fortune to 'HARBOR' him," she wrote.[107] Artist C. M. Penfield argued that Mumford's "personal" attack on Burroughs undermined the magazine's high journalistic standards: "So, Mr. Editor, please take a reef in this situation or give Mr. Mumford a vacation and see if he cannot attain a more cheerful and therefore more helpful point of view and more in line with your standard; help him to acquire a basis of criticism less destructive and less colored with a personal bias. It is not worthy of you to publish or of him to write an attack upon the memory of a man who has passed on."[108] Since the *New Yorker* did not ordinarily publish readers' letters, these missives were transcribed and sent to Mumford, and the matter was dropped.

Although writing for the *New Yorker* consumed much of Mumford's time, he was extraordinarily active on numerous fronts. He still wrote occasionally for the *New Republic* and other journals. In 1934, he accepted a prestigious appointment to the New York City Board of Higher Education, and he joined the executive committee of the leftist American Artists' Congress, delivering the opening address at its inaugural session in 1936.[109] Most significant, he was deeply involved in the researching and writing of the Renewal of Life, an ambitious book series that examined Western civilization from the perspectives of technology, urbanism, and intellectualism.[110] The initial idea for the series took root around 1929–30, and Mumford spent the next several years cultivating the work into its ultimate, multivolume format. *Technics and Civilization* (1934), the series' first volume, examined the history of technology from the Middle Ages to the twentieth century, concluding with a call for greater human control over a world increasingly driven by technological advances. Art emerged as a minor but important subtext in the book, essentially as a path through which humanity could better understand its own motives. Mumford was emboldened by *Technics and Civilization*'s critical success to undertake the series' next volume, a parallel study of cities, but he became increasingly frustrated that his journalistic duties were interfering with his more serious writing.

As early as spring 1933, Mumford began to grow restive with his dual responsibilities at the *New Yorker*. "Do you want to chuck your present art critic?" Mumford asked Ross in April. "By now you probably realize, as you didn't last spring, that *all* art critics are unsatisfactory, and only by changing them regularly can you even get the sensation momentarily that one is a little better than another."[111] Ross, pleased with the status quo, demurred.[112] Like clockwork, Mumford again offered to resign the "Art Galleries" post as the next season drew to a close. "I am still having fun with the department:" he wrote to Ross in April 1934, "but I can easily conceive that no one else is."[113] Ross responded quickly and firmly. "We want you to go ahead and are somewhat surprised at your having any doubt whatever," he wrote. "You wouldn't have if I had ever had a chance to see you in the office."[114] Ross forestalled Mumford's annual resignation plea in April 1935 by offering to double Mumford's salary to $150 per column with the promise of additional space.[115] Mumford evidently found the terms irresistible, and he continued to write both columns into the next season. Yet at the beginning of March 1936 he again raised the familiar plea. "What about next year?" Mumford asked Ross. "Has the present arrangement worked out from your standpoint, or do you want to fire me?"[116] Ross once again demurred, and the arrangement continued uninterrupted into the 1936–37 season.[117] This would be Mumford's last under the "Art Galleries" banner.

Even as Mumford stole time away from the *New Yorker* to work on his cities manuscript, other, more personal matters commanded his attention. After many years' difficulty, Mumford and his wife welcomed the birth of their second child, their daughter, Alison, in April 1935, just as their marriage threatened to unravel because of the affair with Alice Decker. Crowding in their Sunnyside Gardens townhouse finally prompted the family in summer 1936 to move to their farmhouse in Leedsville year-round. This relocation to the Dutchess County countryside required that, during the *New Yorker*'s fall-to-spring season, Mumford travel ninety miles by train to New York City nearly every week. He would spend several days researching and writing whichever column was due, staying nights in a hotel.[118] The rigor of this schedule soon exhausted him, and in February 1937 he indicated that he would quit writing "The Art Galleries," although he would continue to pen architecture criticism for the magazine—except for a wartime hiatus—until 1963.[119] Even a luncheon with associate editor Katharine S. White—perhaps an even more persuasive personality than Ross—failed to convince Mumford to reconsider his decision to retire from "The Art Galleries."[120] Disheartened, Ross wrote Mumford to express his appreciation nonetheless:

> All of us here are grateful to you for having done the art column at all, let alone as conscientiously as you have done it. We know we're not going to get anyone to follow you who will be as good and are reconciled to that. You will be greatly missed. I'll take the occasion of saying this now,—and finally, unless you want a more formal and fitting expression of appreciation, in which case I'll supply an elegant and eloquent one, by God.
> We'll try to make up a little of the deficiency you are creating by getting more pieces out of you on other subjects.[121]

Paul Rosenfeld, whom Mumford had earlier recommended to Ross as a potential replacement, debuted as the new "Art Galleries" columnist the following October but abruptly withdrew from the position before the month was over.[122] Longtime *New Yorker* contributor Robert M. Coates took the column's reins permanently in November.[123]

Once Mumford left the *New Yorker*, he quickly fell out of touch with new developments in contemporary art. This was a conscious intellectual choice as well as a career decision. He had very little to say about abstract expressionism, the movement that dominated American painting in the 1940s and 1950s. His belief in the essentially expressive nature of art did not predispose him toward the new and largely nonobjective mode of painting, and he was increasingly disturbed by what he perceived as its solipsistic tenor. Consequently, Mumford's influence in the art world was soon eclipsed by more avant-garde critics such as Meyer Schapiro, Clement Greenberg, and Harold Rosenberg.[124] Stieglitz's death in 1946, moreover, must have only furthered Mumford's estrangement from the contemporary art scene.

The timing of Mumford's departure from "The Art Galleries" nevertheless proved fortuitous, as his life simultaneously expanded in several directions. He ended his troubled affair with Decker in December 1937 and rededicated himself to marriage and his family.[125] At about the same time he completed work on his cities manuscript, which was published in 1938 to widespread critical acclaim as *The Culture of Cities*, the second volume of the Renewal of Life series.[126] The book established Mumford as a leading international expert on urbanism, and invitations to consult on city and regional plans in Hawaii, the Pacific Northwest, and the United Kingdom ensued. One measure of his newfound fame was his selection for a lead story in *Time* with accompanying cover photograph.[127]

This was also a period when Mumford, alarmed by the rise of totalitarianism in Europe, became a leading and outspoken advocate of American intervention on behalf of the Allied powers. He joined the upstart Committee to Defend America by Aiding the Allies, and he wrote two books on the eve of World War II that argued this interventionist viewpoint forcefully: *Men Must Act* (1939) and *Faith for Living* (1940).[128] Last, he accepted a teaching position at Stanford University in 1942, which required that he relocate his family to California and that he suspend most writing for the *New Yorker* and other periodicals.[129] Dissatisfied by the institutional bureaucracy, Mumford left Stanford in 1944, returning with his family to Leedsville, but his son, Geddes, who had enlisted in the U.S. Army, perished in combat on an Italian battlefield that same year.[130] Disconsolate, Mumford poured his energy into his writing, including a poignant memoir of his son's brief life.[131]

Still, Mumford did not entirely abandon his interest in art. Already in *Technics and Civilization* (1934) he had begun to explore the role of artists like Rembrandt in humanizing an increasingly technological society. As he developed the Renewal of Life further, the arts moved to a central position in his organic philosophy. In the series' third volume,

The Condition of Man (1944), Mumford included images from various epochs in the history of art, complementing the religious, philosophical, and psychological history of man that he discussed in the text.[132] Significantly, Mumford chose one of Stieglitz's views of Lake George, New York, for the book's final image.[133] The events leading up to World War II had convinced him that, more than ever, the arts must be an integral part of man's self-renewal. Sensing that postwar artists had become increasingly self-absorbed in the face of the atomic age's manifold scientific and political problems, Mumford called upon them to become more active leaders in this transformative process.

In 1951, Mumford lectured on these potent themes to rapt audiences at Columbia University. His lectures were subsequently published as *Art and Technics* (1952), and they contain his most searching analysis of the visual arts and visual culture.[134] His objective was not to define a theory of aesthetics but rather to restore art to a place of primacy in postwar society. To support his argument, Mumford drew upon such diverse sources as cultural anthropology, classical mythology, Freudian and Jungian psychology, and technological history. In six lectures, he built a seamless case for the arts' necessity, function, and purpose in postwar society, and he argued that the reconciliation of art and technics would provide for a better and more stable future. He concluded the lecture series with a plea for cultural integration in which technics would serve human needs and art would express human values. Once again, he singled out the abstract and surrealist movements as emblematic of modern man's demoralization: "Our technics has become compulsive and tyrannical, since it is not treated as a subordinate instrument of life; while, at the same time, our art has become either increasingly empty of content or downright irrational, in an effort to claim a sanctuary for the spirit free from the oppressive claims of our daily life. The images of the abstract painters do justice to the blankness and disorganization of our lives; the images of the surrealists reflect the actual nightmare of human existence in an age of mass exterminations and atomic catastrophes."[135] Rather than laying the blame on artists, however, Mumford believed that society itself must undergo a fundamental change: "What I am saying here, in effect, is that the problems we have inquired into within the special realms of art and technics are illustrative of much larger situations within modern society; and that, therefore, we cannot solve these problems until we have achieved a philosophy that will be capable of reorienting this society, displacing the machine and restoring man to the very center of the universe, as the interpreter and transformer of nature, as the creator of a significant and valuable life, which transcends both raw nature and his own original biological self."[136] The greatest obstacle to renewal in the Cold War period, according to Mumford, was the American government. "The present curtailment of political and intellectual freedom in the United States, as the result of insidious changes that have taken place within the last decade, is only a symptom of a larger loss: the abdication of the human personality," he wrote, generally alluding to the contemporary political climate of McCarthyism and the Cold War. "Our acceptance of this curtailment with so little effective protest gives the measure of our moral collapse."[137] Such acquiescence, he believed, only underscored his argument for radical change in modern society.

Critics, while generally receptive to *Art and Technics,* were quick to point out the weakness of its conclusion. "The renewal of life is admittedly 'the great theme of our age,' and the individual effort 'to recover our capacity for living' is important, but exhortation is not enough, and 'purposeful action' remains undefined," Herbert Read wrote in the *New Republic.* "Such definition, on the very practical level of education and social organization, is now the supreme need."[138] A reviewer for the *Times Literary Supplement* agreed: "Mr. Mumford's masterly analysis of the causes of our cultural decadence is incontrovertible; but his remedies are necessarily vague and, one fears, only practicable as the aftermath of a cataclysm we must all hope to avert."[139] More recently, however, the scholar Casey Nelson Blake called *Art and Technics* "an accessible and penetrating exploration of the moral predicament of art in a technological society."[140]

After the publication of *Art and Technics,* Mumford made only occasional excursions into art theory and criticism, principally in "The Sky Line," where, over the course of several columns, he addressed the changing role of public art vis-à-vis modern architecture and urban renewal projects in Europe and the United States. In his subsequent books—*In the Name of Sanity* (1954), *The Transformations of Man* (1956), *The City in History* (1961), and *The Myth of the Machine* (1967, 1970)—he brought his observations about art, technology, and politics to even more pessimistic conclusions.[141] Together with *Art and Technics,* they explore similar themes of moral devaluation, personal renewal, and cultural reintegration, but his prescription for change in each is undeniably vague. Although regionalism in architecture and planning was Mumford's general solution for the physical reorganization of society, the restructuring of its moral fiber was another matter. His personal philosophy, a generalized humanist compendium—rooted in the Judeo-Christian tradition, but with passing references to the shared values of Islam and several Eastern religions—was not easily grasped by the general reader. Mumford intended that the individual should discover these truths for himself, but he did not disclose how the "renewed" individual would work with others in the rebuilding of society.

In the specific case of modern art, Mumford's aesthetic and formal directives tended to exclude works that did not deal with organic subject matter, thus curtailing the very freedom of creative expression that he so avidly defended. Having essentially retreated from the New York art world in the late 1930s, Mumford no longer maintained the direct contact with modern art and modern artists that had so vividly informed the writing of "The Art Galleries." Younger artists did not capture his attention the way that O'Keeffe and Marin had a generation earlier, and emerging content-based movements such as pop art only earned his derision. A crucial balance was thus lost in his criticism during the postwar period, when he began to view art less as a field of individual creative development and more as a symptom of collective cultural decline.

Toward the end of his career, Mumford drew a bitter parallel between himself and Thomas Eakins, who in old age had likewise found himself in a nearly solitary position, increasingly undervalued by the public. In a 1972 review of Gordon Hendricks's *The Photographs of Thomas Eakins,* Mumford—with only the thinnest of veils separating his own life and work from the artist's—wrote: "Eakins had no need for publicity or the adulatory patter and chatter that now erect an elaborate verbal screen to conceal the artist's autistic withdrawal from reality. Whatever the restrictions of the scientific and aesthetic conventions that dominated Eakins's art, his life and work have now a special contribution to make to a generation that, morally speaking, has reached the end of its rope."[142]

Mumford on Modern Art in the 1930s seeks to draw attention once again to Mumford's important legacy as an art critic, which has been all but eclipsed by his writings in other fields. From the very beginning of his career, he followed an interdisciplinary process of critical inquiry in which the literary and visual arts, the liberal arts, urbanism, and technology were treated as part of the same cultural continuum. In the "Art Galleries" columns, which are collected in this volume for the first time, he touches on all of these subject areas, even as he focuses more narrowly on the vibrant New York museum and gallery scene of the mid-1930s.

These columns also contain some of Mumford's liveliest and most in-spired prose, written at a time when he still retained his optimism about the future of twentieth-century civilization. His success as an art critic was due in no small part to the unstinting support of Harold Ross, his sympathetic editor at the *New Yorker,* a magazine that valued both thor-oughness and wit. As these columns attest, Mumford supplied both in abundance.

NOTES

The epigraph is taken from Lewis Mumford's *My Works and Days: A Personal Chronicle* (New York: Harcourt Brace Jovanovich, 1979), 211.

1. Mumford's columns are especially difficult to locate because two editions of the *New Yorker* were published early in his tenure. For the benefit of advertisers, the publisher launched a national edition in 1929, which appeared simultaneously with the standard metropolitan edition. "The Art Galleries" appeared in most na-tional editions except in the years 1933 and 1934. "The Sky Line" appeared less frequently in the national edition during the mid-1930s. See Thomas Kunkel, *Ge-nius in Disguise: Harold Ross of the New Yorker* (New York: Random House, 1995), 168. Mumford's architectural criticism is collected in the following vol-umes: Lewis Mumford, *From the Ground Up: Observations on Contemporary Ar-chitecture, Housing, Highway Building, and Civic Design* (New York: Harcourt, Brace, 1956), *The Highway and the City* (New York: Harcourt, Brace and World, 1963), *The Urban Prospect* (New York: Harcourt, Brace and World, 1968), *Ar-chitecture as a Home for Man: Essays for Architectural Record,* ed. Jeanne M. Davern (New York: Architectural Record Books, 1975), and *Sidewalk Critic: Lewis Mumford's Writings on New York,* ed. Robert Wojtowicz (New York: Princeton Architectural Press, 1998). Mumford's *Sidewalk Critic* includes three "Art Galleries" columns, covering material related to architecture and design.

2. Mumford wrote an autobiography covering the first half of his life, and he also published two anthologies that contain autobiographical passages. See Lewis Mumford, *Sketches from Life: The Autobiography of Lewis Mumford, The Early Years* (New York: Dial Press, 1982), *Findings and Keepings: Analects for an Au-tobiography* (New York: Harcourt Brace Jovanovich, 1975), and *My Works and Days.* For a detailed, biographical account of Mumford's life, see also Donald L. Miller, *Lewis Mumford: A Life* (New York: Weidenfeld and Nicolson, 1989).

3. Mumford, *Sketches from Life,* 449, 88.

4. On Geddes's life and work, see Helen Meller, *Patrick Geddes: Social Evo-lutionist and City Planner* (New York: Routledge, 1990); see also Volker M. Wel-ter, *Biopolis: Patrick Geddes and the City of Life* (Cambridge, MA: MIT Press, 2002). On the complex relationship between Mumford and Geddes, see Frank G. Novak Jr., "Introduction: Master and Disciple," in *Lewis Mumford and Patrick Geddes: The Correspondence,* ed. Frank G. Novak Jr. (New York: Routledge, 1995), 1–39.

5. Patrick Geddes, *Every Man His Own Art Critic at the Manchester Exhi-*

bition, 1887 (London: John Heywood, 1887); and Geddes, *Every Man His Own Art Critic (Glasgow Exhibition, 1888): An Introduction to the Study of Pictures* (Edinburgh: William Brown; Glasgow: John Menzies, 1888).

6. More than three hundred of Mumford's sketches, which include portraits and both urban and rural landscapes, are deposited at Monmouth University in West Long Branch, New Jersey. See Vincent DiMattio and Kenneth R. Stunkel, *The Drawings and Watercolors of Lewis Mumford,* Studies in Art History 8 (Lewiston, NY: Edwin Mellen Press, 2004).

7. Lewis Mumford, *The Story of Utopias* (New York: Boni and Liveright, 1922). *Eutopia* is the ancient Greek term from which Sir Thomas More derived the more familiar *utopia*.

8. Ibid., 296–97.

9. On the history and membership of the Regional Planning Association of America, see Edward K. Spann, *Designing Modern America: The Regional Planning Association of America and Its Members* (Columbus: Ohio State University Press, 1996).

10. For a general overview of Mumford as a critic of architecture and urbanism, see Robert Wojtowicz, *Lewis Mumford and American Modernism: Eutopian Theories for Architecture and Urban Planning* (New York: Cambridge University Press, 1996).

11. Lewis Mumford, *Sticks and Stones: A Study of American Architecture and Civilization* (New York: Boni and Liveright, 1924).

12. See Casey Nelson Blake, *Beloved Community: The Cultural Criticism of Randolph Bourne, Van Wyck Brooks, Waldo Frank, and Lewis Mumford* (Chapel Hill: University of North Carolina Press, 1990).

13. Harold Stearns, ed., *Civilization in the United States: An Inquiry by Thirty Americans* (New York: Harcourt, Brace, 1922).

14. Lewis Mumford, "The City," in Stearns, *Civilization,* 3–20.

15. Van Wyck Brooks, "The Literary Life," in Stearns, *Civilization,* 179–97, and "On Creating a Usable Past," *Dial* 64 (April 11, 1918): 337–41.

16. On Brooks's call for a "usable past," see Alan Trachtenberg, "Mumford in the Twenties: The Historian as Artist," *Salmagundi* 49 (Summer 1980): 29–42.

17. Lewis Mumford, *The Golden Day: A Study in American Experience and Culture* (New York: Boni and Liveright, 1926).

18. Lewis Mumford, *Herman Melville* (New York: Harcourt, Brace, 1929).

19. On Spingarn's influence on Mumford, see Lewis Mumford, "J. E. Spingarn: The Scholar as Activist," review of *J. E. Spingarn,* by Marshall Van Deusen, *New York Review of Books* 18 (March 23, 1972): 13–17.

20. Joel Elias Spingarn, "Scholarship and Criticism," in Stearns, *Civilization,* 93–108.

21. Mumford, "J. E. Spingarn," 13.

22. Lewis Mumford, "Æsthetics: A Palaver," *American Mercury* 3 (November 1924): 360–65.

23. Mumford, *Sketches from Life,* 481–82.

24. Mumford, "Æsthetics," 365.

25. Lewis Mumford, *Æsthetics: A Dialogue,* Troutbeck Leaflets 3 (Amenia, NY: Troutbeck Press, 1925).

26. Mumford, *Sketches from Life*, 485.

27. For a discussion of Pach's life and work, see Laurette E. McCarthy, "Walter Pach: Artist, Critic, Historian, and Agent of Modernism" (PhD diss., University of Delaware, 1996).

28. On the history of the Armory Show, see Walt Kuhn, *The Story of the Armory Show* (New York: private publication, 1938). On the show's subsequent influence, see Milton W. Brown, *American Painting: From the Armory Show to the Depression* (Princeton: Princeton University Press, 1955).

29. Mumford, *Sketches from Life*, 444.

30. Walter Pach, "Art," in Stearns, *Civilization*, 227–41.

31. Ibid., 231.

32. For an account of Alfred Stieglitz's life and work, see Richard Whelan, *Alfred Stieglitz: A Biography* (Boston: Little, Brown, 1995). For a more specialized study, see Barbara Buhler Lynes, *O'Keeffe, Stieglitz and the Critics: 1916–1929* (Ann Arbor: UMI Research Press, 1989). On Stieglitz's importance in the dissemination of modernism in the United States, see Sarah Greenough et al., *Modern Art and America: Alfred Stieglitz and His New York Galleries* (Washington, DC: National Gallery of Art; Boston: Little, Brown, 2000).

33. Whelan, *Alfred Stieglitz*, 474–75.

34. Mumford's letters to Stieglitz and some carbon copies of Stieglitz's letters to Mumford are deposited in the Alfred Stieglitz Correspondence Files, Alfred Stieglitz/Georgia O'Keeffe Archive, Yale Collection of American Literature, Beinecke Rare Book and Manuscript Library, Yale University, New Haven (hereafter referred to as AS/GOA). The first letter from Mumford is dated April 30, 1925, and apparently responds to a letter from Stieglitz now unlocated (AS/GOA). A handful of Stieglitz's letters to Mumford are deposited at the Lewis and Sophia Mumford Papers, Annenberg Rare Book and Manuscript Library, University of Pennsylvania, Philadelphia (hereafter referred to as LMP). Stieglitz's first letter to Mumford is dated July 6, 1925 (LMP, folder 4703).

35. Lewis Mumford, "O'Keefe [*sic*] and Matisse," *New Republic* 50 (March 2, 1927): 41–42; Mumford to Stieglitz, March 17, 1927, AS/GOA.

36. Mumford to Stieglitz, October 23, 1929, AS/GOA.

37. Mumford to Stieglitz, May 15, 1934, AS/GOA.

38. Van Wyck Brooks et al., eds., *The American Caravan: A Yearbook of American Literature* (New York: Literary Guild, 1927), dedication page.

39. Waldo Frank et al., eds., *America and Alfred Stieglitz: A Collective Portrait* (Garden City, NY: Doubleday, Doran, 1934).

40. Lewis Mumford, "The Metropolitan Milieu," in ibid., 33–58.

41. On early-twentieth-century American art criticism, see Susan Noyes Platt, *Modernism in the 1920s: Interpretations of Modern Art in New York from Expressionism to Constructivism* (Ann Arbor: UMI Research Press, 1985); and Peninah R. Y. Petruck, *American Art Criticism: 1910–1939* (New York: Garland, 1981).

42. Platt, *Modernism in the 1920s*, 45.

43. Recognizing this intellectual kinship, Mumford tried unsuccessfully to interest Geddes in Dewey's work as it was applied practically at an experimental day school in Manhattan. See Mumford, *Sketches from Life*, 325.

44. Lewis Mumford, "On Judging Art," review of *Ananias, Or the False Artist,* by Walter Pach, *New Republic* 58 (March 20, 1929): 130.

45. An edition of the Mumford-Murray letters, to be edited by Frank G. Novak Jr., is in preparation by Syracuse University Press.

46. See Lewis Mumford, "Man the Artist," review of *History of Art,* vols. 1 and 2, by Elie Faure, trans. Walter Pach, *New Republic* 33, sec. 2 (November 29, 1922): 1–2, and "The First History," review of *History of Art,* vols. 3 and 4, by Elie Faure, trans. Walter Pach, *New Republic* 39 (August 13, 1924): 335.

47. Mumford, "Man the Artist," 1.

48. Lewis Mumford, "Art Studies," reviews of *Art Studies: Mediaeval, Renaissance and Modern,* ed. members of the Departments of Fine Arts at Harvard and Princeton Universities, and *Art through the Ages: An Introduction to Its History and Significance,* by Helen Gardner, *New Republic* 47 (July 14, 1926): 236.

49. Lewis Mumford, "Chinese Culture and Art," review of *Chinese Painting as Reflected in the Thought and Art of Li Lung-Mien: 1070–1106,* by Agnes E. Meyer, *New Republic* 40, sec. 2 (October 1, 1924): 10.

50. Suzanne La Follette, *Art in America* (New York: Harper and Brothers, 1929).

51. Suzanne La Follette to Mumford, January 21 [1930?], LMP, folder 2731.

52. Lewis Mumford, "Art in America," review of *Art in America,* by Suzanne La Follette, *New Republic* 62 (March 5, 1930): 77.

53. Lewis Mumford, "The Marriage of Museums," *Scientific Monthly* 7 (September 1918): 252–60.

54. Lewis Mumford, "Beauty and the Picturesque," *Freeman* 3 (July 13, 1921): 419–20.

55. Ibid., 420.

56. Lewis Mumford, "American Taste," *Harper's Monthly Magazine* 155 (October 1927): 570–71.

57. Lewis Mumford, "The Heritage of Impressionism," *New Republic* 50 (May 18, 1927): 356.

58. Lewis Mumford, "The Moderns," *New Republic* 49 (January 12, 1927): 222.

59. Ibid.

60. Lewis Mumford, "Brancusi and Marin," *New Republic* 49 (December 15, 1926): 112.

61. Ibid.

62. Mumford to Stieglitz, December 6, 1926, AS/GOA.

63. Mumford, "O'Keefe [sic] and Matisse," 42.

64. Lynes, *O'Keeffe, Stieglitz,* 121–22.

65. Lewis Mumford, *The Brown Decades: A Study of the Arts in America, 1865–1895* (New York: Harcourt, Brace, 1931).

66. See Mumford, *Brown Decades,* 256–58, for a review of the literature Mumford consulted in writing this section of the book.

67. See *The Museum of Modern Art: Sixth Loan Exhibition. Winslow Homer, Albert P. Ryder, Thomas Eakins* (New York: Museum of Modern Art, 1930).

68. Lewis Mumford, "The Brown Decades: Art," *Scribner's Magazine* 90 (October 1931): 361–72.

69. Mumford, *Brown Decades,* 215.

70. Ibid., 221.

71. Ibid., 234.

72. Ibid., 233.

73. Ibid., 249.

74. Ibid., 245.

75. Albert Guerard, "Mr. Mumford on the Arts," review of *The Brown Decades*, by Lewis Mumford, *New York Herald Tribune Books*, sec. 11 (October 11, 1931): 3.

76. William Murrell, review of *The Brown Decades*, by Lewis Mumford, *Creative Art* 10 (January 1932): 73.

77. Ibid.

78. Walter Pach to Mumford, February 7, 1932, LMP, folder 3764.

79. Elizabeth Johns, *Thomas Eakins: The Heroism of Modern Life* (Princeton: Princeton University Press, 1983), 175.

80. See Robert Wojtowicz, introduction to Mumford, *Sidewalk Critic*, 11–29. On Ross and the history of the magazine, see Kunkel, *Genius in Disguise*, and Brendan Gill, *Here at the New Yorker* (New York: Random House, 1975).

81. Lewis Mumford, "Frozen Music or Solidified Static? Reflections on Radio City," *New Yorker* 7 (June 20, 1931): 28–36.

82. Mumford to Harold Ross, April 2, 1932, *New Yorker* Records, Manuscripts and Archives Division, New York Public Library, Astor, Lenox and Tilden Foundations, New York, box 187 (hereafter NYR).

83. Kunkel, *Genius in Disguise*, 75–76, 77.

84. Gill, *Here at the New Yorker*, 181.

85. Ross to Mumford, April 4, 1932, LMP, folder 3580.

86. Ross to Mumford, August 13, 1932, carbon copy, NYR, box 187.

87. Ross to Mumford, September 21, 1932, LMP, folder 3580.

88. Mumford to Ross, September 22, 1932, NYR, box 12.

89. Ross to Mumford, September 26, 1932, carbon copy, NYR, box 12.

90. Ross to Mumford, September 21, 1932, LMP, folder 3580.

91. For Mumford's review of the expanded Frick Collection, see Lewis Mumford, "The Art Galleries: Fifth Avenue's New Museum," *New Yorker* 11 (December 28, 1935): 41–42, reprinted in Mumford, *Sidewalk Critic*, 146–49.

92. For Mumford's review of the Whitney Museum, see Lewis Mumford, "The Sky Line: On Making a Museum—Post-Boom Tower—The Modern Restaurant," *New Yorker* 8 (June 25, 1932): 50–52, reprinted in Mumford, *Sidewalk Critic*, 80–82.

93. For Mumford's review of the Museum of Modern Art's new building, see Lewis Mumford, "The Sky Line: Growing Pains—The New Museum," *New Yorker* 15 (June 3, 1939): 40–42, reprinted in Mumford, *Sidewalk Critic*, 230–34.

94. See Miller, *Lewis Mumford*, chs. 17, 18.

95. Ross to Mumford, April 20, 1933, LMP, folder 3580.

96. Ross to Mumford, December 7, 1933, carbon copy, NYR, box 15.

97. Lewis Mumford, "The Undertaker's Garland," foreword to *The Seventh New Yorker Album* (New York: Random House, 1935), n.p.

98. Ross to Mumford, April 16, 1934, LMP, folder 3580.

99. See Ralph M. Pearson, "The Failure of the Art Critics—II," *Forum and Century* 94 (December 1935): 376–78.

100. See Lewis Mumford, "Housing," in *Modern Architecture: International Exhibition* (New York: Museum of Modern Art, 1932), 179–92. On the history of the exhibition, including Mumford's participation, see Terence Riley, *The International Style: Exhibition 15 and the Museum of Modern Art* (New York: Rizzoli, 1992).

101. Lewis Mumford, "The Sky Line: Organic Architecture," *New Yorker* 8 (February 27, 1932): 45–46, reprinted in Mumford, *Sidewalk Critic,* 71–73. Mumford wrote: "A faintly official connection with the Exhibition prevents me from saying in any but very chaste terms how good I think the show is" (*Sidewalk Critic,* 71).

102. Alfred H. Barr Jr. to Mumford, May 11, 1936, with pencil inscription by Mumford, May 28, 1936, LMP, folder 3461.

103. The museum finally mounted a sweeping photography retrospective exhibition in spring 1937, but without Stieglitz's cooperation; see Whelan, *Alfred Stieglitz,* 565; and Lewis Mumford, "The Art Galleries: Prints and Paints," *New Yorker* 13 (April 3, 1937): 67–69 (reprinted in this volume). When preparing a revised edition of the exhibition catalog, the curator, Beaumont Newhall, asked Mumford to intervene on the museum's behalf with Stieglitz to secure one of his prints for the frontispiece, which Mumford did successfully. See Beaumont Newhall to Mumford, May 18, 1938, LMP, folder 3461; Mumford to Stieglitz, May 20, 1938, AS/GOA; and Newhall to Mumford, May 22 [1938], LMP, folder 3461. The revised catalog was published as Beaumont Newhall, *Photography: A Short Critical History,* 2nd rev. edition (New York: Museum of Modern Art, 1938).

104. Barr to Mumford, May 11, 1936, LMP, folder 3461.

105. Barr to Mumford, December 23, 1936, LMP, folder 3461.

106. Lloyd Goodrich to the editor of the *New Yorker,* April 6, 1935, transcribed copy, LMP, folder 3580.

107. Juliana Force to the editor of the *New Yorker,* April 8, 1935, transcribed copy, LMP, folder 3580.

108. C. M. Penfield to the editor of the *New Yorker,* April 9, 1935, transcribed copy, LMP, folder 3580.

109. Lewis Mumford, "Opening Address," in *First American Artists' Congress* (New York: American Artists' Congress, 1936), 1–2.

110. The four volumes of Mumford's Renewal of Life series are *Technics and Civilization* (New York: Harcourt, Brace, 1934), *The Culture of Cities* (New York: Harcourt, Brace, 1938), *The Condition of Man* (New York: Harcourt, Brace, 1944), and *The Conduct of Life* (New York: Harcourt, Brace, 1951).

111. Mumford to Ross, April 18, 1933, NYR, box 15.

112. Ross to Mumford, April 20, 1933, LMP, folder 3580.

113. Mumford to Ross, April 15, 1934, NYR, box 17.

114. Ross to Mumford, April 16, 1934, LMP, folder 3580.

115. Ross to Mumford, April 11, 1935, LMP, folder 3580.

116. Mumford to Ross, March 4, 1936, transcript of note, NYR, box 20.

117. Ross to Mumford, March 16, 1936, carbon copy, NYR, box 20.

118. Miller, *Lewis Mumford,* 375–76.

119. Mumford to Ross, February 6, 1937, NYR, box 281. Mumford stopped writing "The Sky Line" at the end of spring 1942 and did not resume until fall 1947.

120. Ross to Mumford, March 5, 1937, LMP, folder 3581.

121. Ibid.

122. Mumford to Ross, February 28, 1937, NYR, box 281; Mumford to Ross, October 19, 1937, transcript of letter, NYR, box 21. See Paul Rosenfeld, "The Art Galleries: Pictures of War and Peace," *New Yorker* 13 (October 9, 1937): 62–63.

123. See Robert M. Coates, "The Art Galleries: Ceramics and a Modern Primitive—Joe Jones," *New Yorker* 13 (November 6, 1937): 43–45.

124. On the next generation of American art critics, see Stephen C. Foster, *The Critics of Abstract Expressionism* (Ann Arbor: UMI Research Press, 1980).

125. Miller, *Lewis Mumford,* 352.

126. Mumford, *Culture of Cities.*

127. "Form of Forms," *Time* 31 (April 18, 1938): 40–43.

128. Miller, *Lewis Mumford,* 402; Lewis Mumford, *Men Must Act* (New York: Harcourt, Brace, 1939), and *Faith for Living* (New York: Harcourt, Brace, 1940).

129. Miller, *Lewis Mumford,* 407–8.

130. Ibid., 424–25.

131. Lewis Mumford, *Green Memories: The Story of Geddes Mumford* (New York: Harcourt, Brace, 1947).

132. Mumford, *Condition of Man.*

133. Ibid., plate XVI.

134. Lewis Mumford, *Art and Technics* (New York: Columbia University Press, 1952).

135. Ibid., 137.

136. Ibid., 159.

137. Ibid., 162.

138. Herbert Read, "The Burden of Renewal," review of *Art and Technics,* by Lewis Mumford, *New Republic* 126 (May 12, 1952): 31.

139. "In a Machine Age," unsigned review of *Art and Technics,* by Lewis Mumford, *Times Literary Supplement* (November 14, 1952): 736.

140. Casey Nelson Blake, "Lewis Mumford, Insurgent: Introduction to *Art and Technics,*" in Lewis Mumford, *Art and Technics* (New York: Columbia University Press, 2000), xxviii.

141. Lewis Mumford, *In the Name of Sanity* (New York: Harcourt, Brace, 1954), *The Transformations of Man* (New York: Harper and Brothers, 1956), *The City in History: Its Origins, Its Transformations, and Its Prospects* (New York: Harcourt, Brace and World, 1961), and *The Myth of the Machine,* vol. 1, *Technics and Human Development* (New York: Harcourt, Brace and World, 1967), and vol. 2, *The Pentagon of Power* (New York: Harcourt Brace Jovanovich, 1970).

142. Lewis Mumford, "Thomas Eakins, Painter and Moralist," review of *The Photographs of Thomas Eakins,* by Gordon Hendricks, *New York Review of Books* 19 (September 21, 1972): 6.

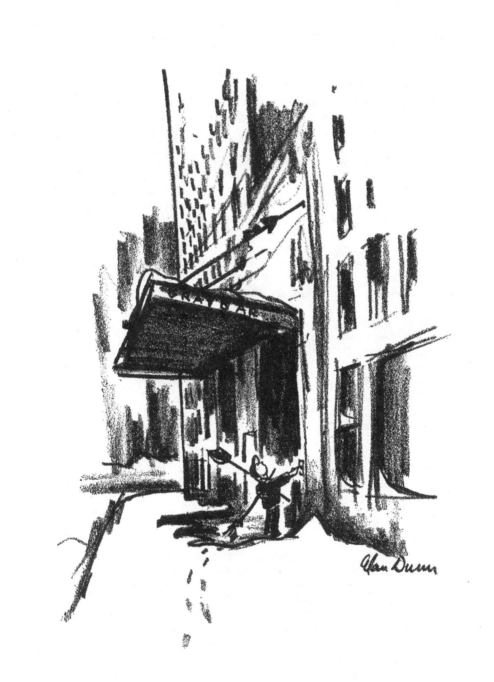

In 1934, the year Alfred Stieglitz turned seventy, Lewis Mumford and his colleagues Waldo Frank, Dorothy Norman, Paul Rosenfeld, and Harold Rugg edited an illustrated Festschrift titled *America and Alfred Stieglitz: A Collective Portrait*.[1] This volume included essays by the editors along with contributions by John Marin, Arthur Dove, Marsden Hartley, Gertrude Stein, and Sherwood Anderson, among others. Although all of the volume's essays generally project a hagiographic tone, Mumford's essay, entitled "The Metropolitan Milieu," bears special scrutiny for what it says about Stieglitz, Mumford, and the city that sustained them both.[2]

Motifs familiar to Mumford's readers abound in the essay: the overcrowding of the early-twentieth-century metropolis, the paving of the landscape, and the desiccation of daily life. Yet Mumford also introduces a fresh, overarching theme: the insurgent city waiting to be captured as an aesthetic experience. Informed by the study of such Brown Decades luminaries as Walt Whitman, John Roebling, Albert Pinkham Ryder, and, above all, Stieglitz, the theme also drew upon Mumford's emerging nostalgia for a city that was fast disappearing in the throes of redevelopment. Stieglitz, of course, recorded many of these changes with his camera from the windows of 291, An American Place, and his apartment at the Shelton Hotel. Tracing the trajectory of Stieglitz's life through his photography, Mumford discovers an organic balance restored in these intimate black-and-white images. Likewise, his prose is life affirming and, in its exploration of the photographer's human subjects, sensual.

Mumford enjoyed writing the historical background for the Stieglitz essay so much that he developed another "overflow" piece, a humorous examination of his own early life, which the *New Yorker* published in December 1934 as "A New York Childhood: Ta-Ra-Ra-Boom-De-Ay" and which generated a sequel three years later.[3] Hearing earlier of the Stieglitz essay, the *New Yorker* associate editor Katharine S. White suggested to the editor, Harold Ross, that it might be "swell" for the magazine.[4] By this time, however, the Festschrift had been accepted for publication, and Mumford declined.[5] "The Metropolitan Milieu" was subsequently reprinted in two collections of his writings: *City Development* (1945), which presented an alternative ending, and *The Human Prospect* (1955), which retained the original ending.[6] An enlightening introduction to the essay, which Mumford first penned for *City Development,* is included in the present volume. Furthermore, the spelling, punctuation, word variances, and subtitles from the 1945 version of the essay have been maintained, although the original ending has been restored.

NOTES

1. Waldo Frank et al., eds., *America and Alfred Stieglitz: A Collective Portrait* (Garden City, NY: Doubleday, Doran, 1934); also published in 1934 under Doubleday's Literary Guild imprint (New York).

2. Lewis Mumford, "The Metropolitan Milieu," in Frank et al., *America and Alfred Stieglitz,* 33–58. On the creation and critical reception of the Festschrift, see Richard Whelan, *Alfred Stieglitz: A Biography* (Boston: Little, Brown, 1995), 551–55.

3. Lewis Mumford to Don Wharton, July 19, 1934, *New Yorker* Records, Manuscripts and Archives Division, New York Public Library, Astor, Lenox and Tilden Foundations, New York, box 210 (hereafter NYR). See Lewis Mumford, "A New York Childhood: Ta-Ra-Ra-Boom-De-Ay," *New Yorker* 10 (December 22, 1934): 18–23; see also Lewis Mumford, "A New York Adolescence: Tennis, Quadratic Equations, and Love," *New Yorker* 13 (December 4, 1937): 86–94. Both essays are reprinted in Lewis Mumford, *Sidewalk Critic: Lewis Mumford's Writings on New York,* ed. Robert Wojtowicz (New York: Princeton Architectural Press, 1998), 32–51.

4. Undated memorandum (c. summer–fall 1934) from Katharine S. White to Harold Ross, Lewis and Sophia Mumford Papers, Annenberg Rare Book and Manuscript Library, University of Pennsylvania, Philadelphia, folder 3580.

5. Mumford to Katharine S. White, October 13, 1934, NYR, box 210.

6. Lewis Mumford, "The Metropolitan Milieu," with a new introduction by the author, in *City Development: Studies in Disintegration and Renewal* (New York: Harcourt, Brace, 1945), 26–60; Lewis Mumford, *The Human Prospect,* ed. Harry T. Moore and Karl W. Deutsch (Boston: Beacon Press, 1955), 146–77.

Ever since I began walking about the streets of New York, noting its people, its buildings, its industries, its activities, I have planned to write an extensive interpretation of my native city's development. The time to have done this was in 1939, when I returned for a winter's residence, after three years spent mainly in my Dutchess County home; but the mounting menace of fascism drove all such thoughts from my mind. If I never live to write that book, the following essay must serve as a substitute.

The Metropolitan Milieu is a subjective interpretation of the city: subjective in the sense that it is focused in a succession of human personalities, Whitman, Ryder, and above all Alfred Stieglitz; it is an attempt to show how a particular environment not merely molds the human personality but often reactivates it, developing compensatory interests that offset its evils and make possible a fuller human growth.

Much of the material in this essay derives directly from my own experiences and impressions. Through my grandfather, Charles Graessel, with whom I used to stroll about the city up to the age of ten, I had a direct connection with a remoter past, with sweet old Bastian, the German bookbinder on University Place, who loved Leatherstocking, or with the custom bootmaker on Canal Street who still made my grandfather's boots. I saw the sordid seventies through the eyes of my mother, who grew up in a gloomy house that still stands in the shadow of St. Marks-in-the-Bouwerie. I saw the immigrant's city through the eyes of our faithful maid, Nellie Ahearn, who gave me entry to the struggling but generously hospitable Irish Catholics of the middle West Side; as a boy in the public schools, above all during my high school period at Stuyvesant, I became intimately acquainted with a later wave of immigrants, the Polish and Russian Jewish migration; in short, long before I began deliberately to think about the city, I had absorbed much of it through my pores.

Only a born New Yorker, perhaps, could do justice to the work of such a genuine New Yorker as Stieglitz: we had a common bond even in our remembered fondness for the horse races at Belmont Park, Sheepshead, and Brighton. Indeed, it is out of our love for what the city has given us that we have attempted to stand fast against its slippery ways, to break with its more inhuman routines and its money-bound activities, and to rally together the forces of spirit for an attack upon its sleek materialism.

Stieglitz's integrity, and his concentration upon essentials, his implacable refusal to be diverted by the trivial or the loudly advertised or the pseudo-good, give his personality a unique place in the development of the city. When all its showy splendors have been reduced to their proper significance, when its inflated values have fallen, when the city itself finally saves itself by re-grouping in units that have some relation to the human scale, there will still be this to be said for the expansive New York of Stieglitz's generation: it produced an Alfred Stieglitz.

1. THE COLOR OF THE CITY

Before the Civil War, New York shared its intellectual distinction with Boston, its industrial place with Philadelphia, and its commercial supremacy with Baltimore and New Orleans. Though it had become the mouth of the continent, thanks to the Erie Canal, it was not yet the maw. After the Civil War, despite the energetic rise of Chicago, New York City became an imperial metropolis, sucking into its own whirlpool the wealth and the wreckage of the rest of the country and of the lands beyond the sea.

When Dickens first visited America, voracious pigs rooted in the streets of Manhattan. Less than a generation later, through the holy transmutation of war, most of them were turned into financiers and industrial enterprisers, and they confined their operations to Wall Street, where the troughs were deep and the wallow good. Poets became stockbrokers; Pan took a flier in railroad securities; satirical humorists hobnobbed with millionaires and turned the lance of their satire against purely legendary kings, instead of driving their steel through the middle of the real kings, the Cooks, the Vanderbilts, the Rogerses, the Rockefellers. New York had become the center of a furious decay, which was masked as growth and enterprise and greatness. The decay caused foul gases to form; the gases caused the physical body of the city to be distended; the distention was called Progress.

So the city grew. Brownstone mansions, often grotesquely scratched with Eastlake ornament, wheeled into position along Fifth Avenue; and brownstone houses, in solid speculative rows, lined the side streets as the city stumbled rapidly northward. On either side of them, in the cheaper quarters, were the new tenements, with common toilets in the halls, and dusty vestibules where, in the seventies, a row of pitchers would be exposed through the night, to be filled with milk in the morning. The crosstown traffic became less important, as the rivers ceased to provide the main entrances to the city; but the tangle of wheels on the avenues thickened: shafts interlocked, hubs scraped, horses reared; presently a bridge was built over Broadway for the pedestrian. The vivacious dangers of congestion had all appeared: exasperated drivers exchanged oaths as deadly as bullets, and gangsters, lining up for fights on the dingier side streets, exchanged bullets as lightly as oaths. Respectable folk hunched their shoulders, lowered their heads, and hypnotized themselves into somnolence by counting sheep: at all events the population was increasing.

Beer saloons, four to as many corners in most parts of the city, brought together in their more squalid forms the ancient forces of hunger and love and politics: "free lunch," "ladies' entrance," and the political boss and his underlings. The main duty of the latter was to protect vice and crime and to levy a constant tax upon virtue in whatever offensive form it might take—as justice, as public spirit, as intelligence. Whisky and beer ruled the wits and the emotional life of the city: whisky for aggressiveness and beer for good-natured befuddlement. Barber shops specialized, until the present century, in painting out black eyes that did not yield to the cold iron of the lamp-post. The swells of course drank their wine convivially at Martin's or Delmonico's; but that was as far from the beer saloon as Newport or Narragansett was from Coney Island. In the nineties Messrs. McKim, Mead, and White began to make over the city for the more polished classes: they designed the Century Club, Gorham's, Tiffany's, and many sumptuous mansions in the city for the new Borgias and Sforzas. But these cultured architects of course remained aloof from the principal buildings of the populace, the tenement and the saloon. The dingy brown front of the saloon, with the swinging doors and the sawdust floors and the slate carrying the day's menu and the soap-decorated mirrors, remained unchanged by fashion for two generations or more, obeying the biological law that the lowest organisms tend to remain stable.

In the seventies, elevated railroads were built; and for miles and miles, on each side of these ill-designed iron ways, which contrasted so unfavorably with those Berlin built only slightly later, tenement houses were planted. Thousands of people lived under the shadow of the elevated, with the smoke of the old-fashioned locomotives puffing into their windows, with the clank and rattle causing them to shout in daily conversation to overcome the roar outside. The obliviousness to low sounds, the indifference to cacophony which makes the ideal radio listener of present-day America, was part of the original acquisition of Manhattan in the Brown Decades. This torment of noise-troubled sleep lowered waking efficiency, depleted vitality; but it was endured as if it were an irremediable fact of nature. In the lull of the elevated's thunder, the occasional tinkle of the cowbells of the ragman on a side street, or the solemn I—I—I—I cas' clo's of the second-hand clothing buyer, would have an almost pastoral touch; while Carmen, on an Italian's clanking hand organ, could splash the sky with color.

Within the span of a generation, the open spaces and the natural vistas began to disappear. The older beer gardens, like Niblo's Garden, gardens that had frequently preserved the trees and open space of a whole block, were wiped out: only in the further reaches of the city did they remain, like Unter den Linden on upper Broadway, and like the roadhouses which dotted the more or less open country that remained on the West Side above 125th Street until the end of the century. The rocky base of Manhattan, always unkind to life, steadily lost its filament of soil. The trees in the streets became more infrequent as the city grew; and their leaves grew sear before autumn came. Even the great Boulevard above Sixty-fifth Street, which the ignoble Tweed had planted along Broadway for his own pecuniary benefit, sacrificed its magnificent trees to the first subway; while only the ailanthus tree, quick growing and lean living, kept the back yards occasionally green, to gladden the lonely young men and women from the country, who faced their first year in the city from hall bedrooms on the top-floor rear of unamiable boarding houses. And as the city grew, it grew away from its old markets: one of the last of these, to prove more reminiscent of the old than anticipatory of the new, was the Jefferson Market, with its medieval German tower, at Eighth Street. Vanishing from the consciousness of most Manhattanites were the open markets that had once brought the touch of the sea and the country to its streets, connecting farmstead and city home by means of little boats that plied the Hudson and Long Island Sound.

The waterfront kept a hold on the city, modifying its character, longer than the countryside did. The oyster stands remained on South and West streets; and "mast-hemmed Mannahatta" was still an accurate description up to the end of the nineties: Alfred Stieglitz has indeed recorded for us the bowsprit of an old sailing vessel, thrust like a proud harpoon into the side of our Leviathan. But most of the things that had made life pleasant and sane in the city, the old houses, red brick, with their white doorways and delicate Georgian fanlights, the friendly tree-lined streets, the salty lick and lap of the sea at the end of every crosstown street, as Melville described it in the opening pages of Moby Dick—all these things were disappearing from the eye, from the nose and touch, and so from the mind.

The water and the soil, as the prime environment of life, were becoming "immaterial," that is to say, they were of no use to the canny minds that were promoting the metropolis, unless they could be described in a legal document, appraised quantitatively, and converted ultimately into cash. A farm became for the speculator a place that might be converted into building lots: in that process, indeed, lay the meaning of this feverish growth, this anxious speculation, this reckless transformation of the quick into the dead. People staked out claims on the farther parts of the city in the way that prospectors stake out claims in a gold rush. There was always the chance that some negligible patch of earth might become, in the course of the city's growth, a gold mine. That was magic. In the atmosphere of magic, the desire to get something for nothing, a whole population hoped and breathed and lived. That in reality the environment was becoming unfit for human habitation in the process did not concern the midas-fingered gentlemen who ruled the city, nor did it affect the dull-fingered million who lacked that golden touch: their dreams were framed within the same heaven. Lacking the reality, they fed on the gilded lubricities of Mr. Bennett's, Mr. Pulitzer's, and Mr. Hearst's newspapers.

2. THE CULT OF PAPER

The ledger and the prospectus, the advertisement and the yellow journal, the world of paper, paper profits, paper achievements, paper hopes, and paper lusts, the world of sudden fortunes on paper and equally grimy paper tragedies; in short, the world of Jay Cook and Boss Tweed and James Gordon Bennett, had unfolded itself everywhere, obliterating under its flimsy tissues all the realities of life that were not exploitable, as either profits or news, on paper. Events happened to fill the paper that described them and to provide the daily titillation that relieved a commercialized routine. When they came reluctantly, they were manufactured, like the Spanish-American War, an event to which Newspaper Row contributed rather more than statesmanship did.

Behold this paper city, buried in its newspapers in the morning, intent through the day on its journals and ledgers and briefs and Dear-sir-in-reply-to-yours-of-even-date, picking at its newly invented typewriters and mimeographs and adding machines, manifolding and filing, watching the ticker tape flow from the glib automatons in Broad Street, piling its soiled paper into deep baskets, burying its dead paper in dusty alphabetical cemeteries, binding fat little dockets with red tape, counting the crisp rolls and bank notes, cutting the coupons of the gilt-edged bonds, redeemable twenty years hence, forty years hence, in paper that might be even more dubious than the original loan issue. At night, when the paper day is over, the city buries itself in paper once more: the Wall Street closing prices, the Five Star Sporting Extra, with the ninth inning scores, the Special Extra, All-about-the-big-fight, all about the anarchist assassination in St. Petersburg—or Pittsburgh.

The cult of paper brings with it indifference to sight and sound: print and arithmetic are the Bible and the incense of this religious ritual. Realities of the world not included in this religion become dim and unreal to both the priests and the worshipers: these pious New Yorkers live in a world of Nature and human tradition, as indifferent to the round of the seasons and to the delights of the awakened senses and the deeper stores of social memory as an early Christian ascetic, occupied with his devotions amid the splendid temples of a Greek Acropolis. They collect pictures as they collect securities; their patronage of learning is merely a premature engraving of their own tombstones. It is not the images or the thoughts, but the reports of their munificence in the newspaper, that justifies their gifts. The whole social fabric is built on a foundation of printed paper; it is cemented together by paper; it is crowned with paper. No wonder the anarchists, with more generous modes of life in mind, have invented the ominous phrase: "Incinerate the documents!" That would wreck this world worse than an earthquake.

Beneath this arid ritual, life itself, attenuated but real, starved but still hungry, goes on. Lovers still become radiant and breathless; honest workers shave wood, rivet steel beams, dig in the earth, or set type with sure hands and quiet satisfaction; scholars incubate ideas, and now and again a poet or an artist broods by himself in some half-shaded city square. In rebellion against this arid and ugly new environment, some country-bred person, a William Cullen Bryant or a Frederick Law Olmsted, would attempt to preserve faltering rural delights: a picnic grove here, a park there. Just before the Civil War the building of Central Park began; and despite the raids of political gangsters, despite the brazen indecent robbery of the Tweed gang—so malodorously like the political gangs of our own day—a stretch of green was carved out, not merely carved out, but actually improved, from barren goat pasture and shantydom into a comely park.

Meanwhile, the city as a whole became progressively more foul. In the late seventies the new model tenement design, that for the so-called dumbbell apartment, standardized the habitations of the workers on the lowest possible level, encouraging for twenty years the erection of tenements in which only two rooms in six or seven got direct sunlight or a modicum of air. Even the best residences were grim, dreary, genteelly fusty. If something better was at last achieved for the rich in the 1890's, on Riverside Drive and West End Avenue, it remained in existence scarcely twenty years and was replaced by mass congestion.

During the period we are looking at, the period of Alfred Stieglitz's birth and education and achievement, we are confronted with a city bent on its own annihilation. For New York used its intense energy and its taut, over-quickened life to produce meaner habitations, a more constricted environment, a duller daily routine, in short, smaller joys, than it had produced during the modest provincial period. By denying itself the essentials of a fine human existence, the city was able to concentrate more intently upon its paper figments. It threw open its doors to the Irish of the forties, to the Germans of the fifties and sixties, later to the Italians, and to the Russians and Jews of eastern Europe: the outside world, contemptuous but hopeful, sneering but credulous, sent many of its finest children to New York. Some of them pushed on, to the cornlands, the wheatlands, the woodlands, the vinelands, to the iron mines, the coal mines, the copper mines; while those that remained were forced to huddle in utmost squalor. But the congested East Side, for all its poverty and dirt, was not the poorest part of the city: it still had its open markets with their color, its narrow streets with their sociability and their vivid common life and neighborly help, its synagogues with at least the dried remnants of a common vision.

This New York produced the elevator apartment house at the end of the sixties, and the tall building, called the skyscraper after the topmost sail of its old clipper ships, a little later; and it used these new utilities as a means of defrauding its people of space and light and sun, turning the streets into deep chasms, and obliterating the back yards and gardens that had preserved a humaner environment even when people drank their water, not from the remote Croton River, but from the Tea-water Pump.

The spirit of pecuniary pride was reckless and indiscriminate; it anni-hilated whatever stood in the path of profit. It ruined the ruling classes as well as their victims. As time went on it became ever more positive in its denial of life; so that in more elegant parts of the East Side today there are splendid "modern" mansions that are practically built back to back, even worse in some respects than the vilest slums on Cherry Street. This negative energy, this suicidal vitality, was the very essence of the new city that raised itself after the Civil War, and came to fullest bloom in the decade after the World War. Beholding it in its final manifestations, a German friend of mine wrote: *Dies ist die Hölle, und der Teufel war der Baumeister.* Men and women, if they survived in this environment, did so at the price of some sort of psychal dismemberment or paralysis. They sought to compensate themselves for their withered members by dwelling on the material satisfactions of this metropolitan life: how fresh fruits and vegetables came from California and Africa, thanks to refrigeration, how bathtubs and sanitary plumbing offset the undiminished dirt and the growing tendency toward constipation, how finally the sun lamps that were bought by the well-to-do overcame the lack of real sunlight in these misplanned domestic quarters. Mechanical apparatus, the refinements of scientific knowledge and of inventive ingenuity, would stay the process of deterioration for a time: when they failed, the jails, the asylums, the hospitals, the clinics, would be multiplied. Were not these thriving insti-tutions, too, signs of progress, tokens of metropolitan intelligence and philanthropy?

But in the end the *expectation* of health and wholeness, like the ex-pectation of honesty and justice, tended within the great metropolis to disappear. In the course of its imperialistic expansion the metropolis, as Patrick Geddes put it, becomes a megalopolis, concentrating upon big-ness and abstract magnitude and the numerical fictions of finance; mega-lopolis becomes parasitopolis, dominated by those secondary pecuniary processes that live on the living; and parasitopolis gives way to patholo-polis, the city that ceases effectively to function and so becomes the prey of all manner of diseases, physical, social, moral. Within such a town, graft and corruption are normal processes; the greater part of the popu-lation shares the animus of the criminal, applauds him when he "gets away with it," and condones his crime when he is caught red-handed. The city that has good words for its Commodore Vanderbilts and Tweeds and Crokers, to say nothing of contemporary gamblers and shysters who have practiced on an even larger scale, which multiplied these antisocial types a thousand times, is a city in which a deteriorated social life, without elementary probity or public spirit, has become normalized into the accepted routine.

So every profession has its racket; every man his price. The tonsil snatcher and the ambulance chaser and the insurance fixer and the testimonial writer have their counterparts in the higher reaches of the professions. The more universal forms of dishonor become honorable, and graft and shakedowns, like the private toll exacted for automobile and marriage licenses, become so common that they even escape notice. Those who actively oppose these customary injustices and these systematic perversions of law and decency are looked upon as disappointed men who have set their own price too high. Force, fraud, lying, chicane, become commonplaces; the law is enforced by illegal methods, the constitution protected by unconstitutional practices; vast businesses are conducted in "peace" by judicious connivance with armed thugs—now passive blackmailers, now active strikebreakers—whose work proceeds under the amiable eyes of the very agents supposed to combat it. No one believes that the alternative to living with honor is to die with honor: it is easier, it is more comfortable, to live sordidly, accepting dishonor.

In such a city, an honest man looms high. He is a lighthouse on a low and treacherous coast. To attain even a human level becomes, in this megalopolitan environment, an arduous, almost a superhuman, task.

3. EARTH, WATER, SKY, MEN

Any fair picture of New York must confess the underlying sordidness of a large part of its preoccupations and activities. It is not that manufacture and shipping and the exchange of goods are necessarily antivital or antisocial processes: quite the contrary. But when these activities become central to life, when they are themselves perverted to serve chiefly as instruments in an abstract accountancy of profit and power, the human hierarchy of values is displaced; and, as in some perversion of the physiological functions, the head becomes cretinous, and the subordinate members become gigantic *and useless*. What I have elsewhere called a purposeless materialism became the essential principle of the city's life.

One must not flinch, then, from recognizing the dark elements of the picture. But one would have no true image, in fact, no image at all, if one forgot to add the light and colors that define the blackest shape; and even at its worst, these elements were always present. There is, to begin with, the physical magnificence of the scene: the sweep and curve of the bay, the grand spaciousness of the river, the rhythm of the tides that encircle it, the strike of its mica-gleaming schists as they crop out in the park or the temporary excavation, and finally, the proud upthrust of the Palisades themselves. In the very shape of the island is something tight, lean, athletic: a contrast to the glacial till of Long Island, with its fat Dutch landscape, its duckponds, its feathery asparagus beds. The skyscrapers, despite their disorder, have not diminished those positive lines in their stalagmitic up-thrust: they are almost as geometric as gypsum crystals. And before the skyscrapers were built, from Brooklyn Heights, from the Palisades, from the Belvedere in Central Park, from Morningside Heights, one could see and feel the hard flanks of Manhattan.

Above all, there is the sky; pervading all these activities is the weather. The sharp crystalline days of early autumn, with intense blue sky and a few curls of cloud, drifting through space like the little jets of steam that were once such characteristic outlets of the older skyscrapers: the splendors of sunset on the waters, over the Palisades, crossing the Brooklyn Ferry, looking toward the Jersey shore from the Brooklyn Bridge; the swift, whiplike changes from heat to cold, from fog to clarity, from the sharp jeweled contours of John Bellini to the soft tones of Whistler and Fuller. Occasionally, too, the sulphurous hell of the dog days, to whip up appetite for the dank clouds in the west and the brave crackle of lightning and the drenching showers. At the other extreme the benignity and quiet of a city quenched by snow: the jingle of sleighbells in the 1890's, the cold flash of electricity on the elevated tracks twenty years later.

The niggling interests of the day might lead to a neglect of these fundamental beauties; but they could not obliterate them. Nature remained, ready to nourish the first person who opened his eyes and breathed in the air—the clear, slightly salt-laden air, gray wings swooping and circling through it. This clear air and this intense sunlight are no small encouragements to the photographer. And the landscape as a whole has definition, a disciplined line: the rocks run as due north and south as the points of the compass, and the very sides of the island, once scraggly, have been shaped by the hands of man into sharp lines, like the margin of a Dutch canal. No matter how great the confusion on the surface, beneath it all, in the rocks themselves is order: no matter how shifty man's top layer, the foundations are solid. If the streets are dingy, there is the dazzle of the sky itself: if the alleys and yards are foul, heavy with ancient dirt, with the effluvia of the sewers or the factories, there is the sanative taste of salt in the first wind that blows from the Atlantic. The cold sea fog in spring, sweeping inland in the mid-afternoon, calls one to the ocean as imperatively as the proud, deep-throated roar of the steamer, claiming the channel as she passes out to sea. So the ocean and the sky and the rivers hold the city in their grip, even while the people, like busy ants in the cracks and crevices, are unconscious of these more primal presences, save when they read a report in the morning paper, and reach for an umbrella, an overcoat, a fan.

Along with its great landscape, New York has had its men. Even in the worst periods of the city's deterioration, there has always been a saving remnant, that handful of honest souls whose presence might have saved the Biblical cities of the plain.

There was, for one, Walt Whitman himself, "of Mannahatta a son," whose visits to the city, with even occasional public appearances, continued after the Civil War, and whose brief pictures of the city are precious records of its life. Whitman, who had rambled about every part of the city, who knew it coming inward from his native Huntington, from Coney Island when that spot was just a fishing hamlet, from the rocky wilds of the upper part of the island, where he would go walking with Bryant—Whitman knew the city at its best. While he realized the evil significance of so much of its vitality, and the impoverishment of its wealth—see his description of the fashionable parade in Central Park in '79—he was nourished by it and fed steadily on it, opera, theater, bookstalls, libraries, lecture halls; above all, the million-headed throng on the streets.

Drinking at Pfaff's, loafing on the Fifth Avenue stages with the coach drivers, crossing the Brooklyn Ferry, Whitman had caught something in the common life that was dear and permanent. He who really touches the soil of Manhattan and the pavement of New York touches, whether he knows it or not, Walt Whitman. Beneath the snobbery of the commercial élite there was in New York a genuinely cosmopolitan spirit. In those who like Whitman and Melville were well rooted in the provincial soil, this spirit was capable of reaching out for elements that were still foreign to the new country—the philosophy of Hegel and Schopenhauer, the criticism of Carlyle and Ruskin, the vision of Michelet and Hugo—and transporting them to our unfinished landscape. Melville, who had been a common sailor, and Whitman, a common printer and carpenter, were not caught by the bourgeoisie and debased into accepting their prudent paper routine. Both of them were capable of a passionate aristocracy that reserved for the spirit its primacy in the affairs of men. Whitman's democracy was the prelude to a broader-rooted aristocracy, and none knew that fact better than he.

The Roeblings were in New York, too, during the sixties, and Wash-

ington remained on, though an invalid, until the Brooklyn Bridge was finally completed in 1883. Not alone did they compose the poem of granite and steel that is the Brooklyn Bridge, one of the first of those grand
native works of art that Whitman had demanded of the sawyers and
delvers, but they brought that arduous habit of intellectual exertion, that
capability for heroic sacrifice on behalf of immaterial things, that strict
obligation to self-discipline, which came directly from the great Germany
of Kant and Goethe and Hegel, a Germany the elder Roebling—who was
a pupil of Hegel's—so well knew. It was right for a New Yorker who was
interested in science or engineering to seek Berlin during this period; so
that even though Stieglitz was unaware of the fact that he was following
in the footsteps of the great engineer who built the bridge, it was as natural for him to go to Berlin as it was for Louis Sullivan, a little earlier, to
follow the footsteps of Richardson to the Ecole des Beaux Arts in Paris.

Though none of the new buildings in New York could compare in
beauty with the High Bridge, in its original stone form, or with the
Brooklyn Bridge, there was a stir in architecture in the eighties and
nineties, due chiefly to the work of Richardson, whose influence remained even though he changed his residence from Staten Island to
Boston. Beginning with the De Vinne Building on Lafayette Street, an excellent structure created for a scrupulous and craftsmanlike master of
printing, the finest works of New York architecture were the series of loft
and factory and storage buildings that arose in the eighties: buildings
whose round arches, solid stone courses, and subtle brickwork set a
mark that few later buildings have surpassed. These buildings, moreover,
were better than the very best Europe could show in this department at
the same period; and contemporary European travelers of discernment
noted and admitted this.

Finally, there was Albert Pinkham Ryder, the most sensitive, the most
noble mind that appeared in New York after the war, a worthy companion in the spirit to that other post-war recluse, the author of Moby
Dick. If the bold sunlight of Broadway made its sheet-iron buildings look
flimsy and unreal, the moonlight of Ryder's inner landscape gave body
to reality: Ryder with his intuitions of human destiny, Death Riding
around a Racetrack, with his wistful melodies of love, the vision of
Perette, Siegfried and the Rhine Maidens, with his presentation of fate
in the little boats with a tiny sheet of sail on a broad moonlit sea, to
which he so often returned, this mystic had a strength and a purpose that
the ephemeral activities of the outer world did not possess. A benign figure, ranging up and down the streets after dark, penetrating life in its

stillness and peace more bravely than those who flung themselves into the noisiest corners of the battlefield, Ryder also became part of the soil of Manhattan. No one can be aware of the rich vitality of the city who does not know its Ryder as well as its Whitman. He needed little from the city; he gave back much.

4. THE LIVING ENVIRONMENT

The problem for the creative mind in the nineties, whether he was a young writer like Stephen Crane or a young man with a passion for photography like Alfred Stieglitz, was to face this New York of boundless misdirected energy and to capture a portion of that wasteful flow for his own purposes, using its force without accepting its habitual channels and its habitual destinations. But there was still another problem: and that was to conquer, with equal resolution, the gentility, the tepid overrefinement, the academic inertness and lack of passionate faith, masquerading as sound judgment, which were characteristic of the stale, fugitive culture of the bourgeoisie. The genteel standards that prevailed were worse than no standards at all: dead objects, dead techniques, dead forms of worship, cast a morbid shadow on every enterprise of the mind, making mind itself a sham, causing vitality to seem somehow shameful. To put the choice with the crudest possible emphasis, the problem for the creative mind was how to avoid the gangster without turning into the spinster.

Now, during the nineteenth century, great forces were at work in the world. People who prefer the tight securities of the eighteenth century or the adolescent turbulence of the seventeenth century only prove their own timidity and ineptness when they belittle these forces merely because they destroyed old patterns and worked creatively on unfamiliar lines. But if the artist was to become a force in his own right once more, as confident of his mission as the scientist or the engineer, it was important that he should not identify himself with the senseless acts of imperialist conquest, or with the senseless mechanical negation of life. When I use the word senseless I use it in both its usual meanings—first, foolish and stupid, and on the other hand, without benefit of the senses, shut off from the experiences that come through the eye, the hand, the ear, the nose, the touch of the body. For the weakness of the mechanical ideology that had put itself at the service of capitalism—and that colored even the minds that rejected it—was that it had limited the provinces of the senses, and confined its operations to a blind world of matter and motion.

Following partly from this mechanical philosophy, partly from the new routine of industry, the senses were in fact denied and defeated in all the new industrial centers; not least, certainly, in New York, which concentrated the industry and the finance of the Western continent. To become a force in this society, this city, it was necessary to open up once more all the avenues of human experience: to sharpen the eye, quicken the touch, refine the senses of smell and taste, as a preliminary to restoring to wholeness the dwarfed and amputated personalities that had been produced—the Gradgrinds, the M'Choakumchilds, the Bounderbys. In a world where practical success canceled every other aspiration, this meant a redoubled interest in the goods and methods that challenged the canons of pecuniary success—contemplation and idle reverie, high craftsmanship and patient manipulation, a willing acceptance of the emotions and an enlargement of the erotic ritual, a shift from the specialized masculine interests leading to an exploitation of power to the more generalized, more centrally biological interests expressed in love: an emphasis on the ecstasy of being rather than a concentration on the pragmatic strain of "getting there."

In the Bhagavad-Gita, Krishna says that the way to contemplation may be found through action as well as through exercises that are directly meant to intensify and illuminate the spiritual life. And it was by action, by utilizing one of the fine mechanical instruments that had been produced by the scientist and the inventor, that Stieglitz, on returning to New York in the 1890's, approached the world around him and helped restore those values that had been left out of the narrow *Weltbild* of his contemporaries. While Stieglitz, through his very use of the camera, allied himself with the new forces at work in the world, he did not, like those who have denied their own humanity, become smaller through his use of the machine. For mark this: only those who live first and who keep alive have earned the right to use the machine. Those who use machinery because they are incapable of facing the stream of life and directing it, those who seek order in automatons because they lack the discipline and courage to achieve order in themselves, become the victims of their instruments and end by becoming mere attachments to a mechanical contrivance. Not so with Stieglitz: from the beginning the machine was as subordinate to his human direction, through his understanding of its potentialities and capacities, as is the breathing of a Hindu guru. When used thus, as part of man's organic equipment rather than as a substitute for a deficient organ, the machine becomes as integral as the original eyes or legs. Assimilating the machine in this fashion, Stieglitz was armed to reconquer the lost human provinces that had been forfeited by the one-sided triumph of the machine.

In the surviving photographs of Stieglitz's early discovery of New York with the camera, one is conscious at first chiefly of his sure and resolute approach to the outward aspects of the city that had been regarded as "unpaintable," and therefore, in a fashion, as unusable. He watches the changing of the horses on a horse car in a snowstorm; he looks at a row of ugly brownstones or hovers above a maze of railroad tracks in a railroad yard, with the locomotives puffing magnificently at the sky. In his interest in these things, he is on a par with another realist, who used paint as his major medium, rather than photography, Thomas Eakins: but his scope is broader, his interests less traditional. Stieglitz does not, like his Parisian contemporary, Atget, range the city from morning to night, deliberately composing a documentary history of its life, after the fashion of Zola. He not merely observes: he waits; he eliminates; he selects. Certain aspects of the city he touches only by implication. Instead of merely mining the pitchblende, he extracts the minute particle of radium, which accounts for the strange behavior of the entire mass.

There are many parts of New York that Stieglitz ignores or leaves no record of, parts of it that have not entered his life or nourished him; there are other parts of his experience, like the grand spectacle of the horse races, which mean much to him and still are preserved only in a print or two. It is not for lack of love or interest that the epic of New York is not caught by his camera, chapter by chapter, as it unfolds from the nineties onward; to seize this was indeed part of his conscious intention. But the point is that it is not the document but the life that made it possible that he searches for and holds to: and as Emerson says, the essential fact is unaltered by many or few examples. If one doubts Stieglitz's awareness of the deeper transformations of feeling and thinking and acting that took place in his metropolis one need only examine his photographs more carefully. The external change in the city itself was profound. Within the darkened alleyways of the financial district, people lost their sense of day and night; just as they lost the occasional glimpse of the sky which makes the worst routine bearable. In the new subways they lost even the sight of the sun over the roof tops of Manhattan, which had once been theirs from the ramshackle elevated roads. Nature in its most simple form, the wonder of the morning and the night, was missing from the metropolitan routine; and *therefore*—I say "therefore" because such reactions are rarely accidents—these elements establish themselves in Stieglitz's photographs with a new force.

The chief instrument of photography is light; and the fact that Stieglitz always worked by natural light, never by artificial light, with its studied arrangements and its temptations to trickery, is an important one. But all the hours of the day become important to him: so he takes the first night pictures that have esthetic significance. The weather, likewise, is an important element for his vision: hence, too, he takes the first photographs in snow and in rain. He does not have to escape to the country to find nature, any more than he has to escape to antiquity to find beauty, in the way that the purse-proud art collectors of the period, the Mrs. Jack Gardners and the Pierpont Morgans, were doing. All these necessary elements in life were still present in the city, though they had been excluded from the routine of getting and spending. Just as Ryder continued to be in touch with nature when he had his ailanthus tree and his patch of sky, so Stieglitz found the necessary germs of a living environment even in a metropolis that had lost the most rudimentary sense of the soil, and was turning itself, step by step, block by block, into a stony waste.

During the 1900's, too, the city was losing its sense of the rivers, despite the extension of Riverside Park. For sewage pollution had driven the North River shad away and made all other kinds of fish that might be caught noxious; so that the old gaffers with their set-lines and bells had disappeared from the Hudson, along with the groups of happy naked swimmers, and another link with nature was broken, even as later, because of pollution from the oil-burning steamers, the waters of the Lower Bay lost the bluefish and weakfish that had once been so plentiful there. But Stieglitz, not less than Whitman, preserved the sense of the waters surrounding Manhattan. He photographed the ferry boats coming into their slips, the boatload of immigrants, the skyline of Manhattan from the Jersey shore, with the water establishing a base in the foreground. Water and sky come into his pictures, again and again: the river, the ocean, the bathing beach, the rain, the snow, and finally, dominating the whole landscape in every sense, the clouds. Shut out by the tall buildings, shut out by the dark courts of the new apartment houses, the very stars at night put at a distance by the myriad lights of the city, flaring, as Tennyson said, like a dreary dawn—the sky remains under all conditions the essential reminder of nature and the cosmos. In the course of Stieglitz's own development, the sky becomes a more and more essential part of his pictures; and finally, it becomes the symbol whereby Stieglitz unites his sense of the universal order with the sense of the personality, as developed in the relations of men and women.

In the stoniest pavement of the city there are cracks. And out of the bleakest soil, between these cracks, a few blades of grass will sooner or later show, whose seeds are borne by the birds; here, even, the germ of a tree will take root and spring up, if no foot disturbs it. It is in the cracks between the new buildings that Stieglitz finds the sky; it is in the surviving cracks in the pavement that Stieglitz finds his trees; and in his most characteristic pictures of the city, so far from emphasizing the massiveness and the obduracy of its stones, he emphasizes the presence of life. One of the most moving and impressive pictures he ever made was that of a little tree in Madison Square Park, young and vernal in the rain, with a street sweeper in the foreground and the dim shape of a building in the background: the promise of life, its perpetual reawakening and renewal, are in that print.

Wherever Stieglitz turns his head in this city, he looks for the touch of life, seizes it, emphasizes it; and by this means he sets himself in opposition to those who would glorify the negation of life and sanction its subordination to metropolitan business, material concentration. Meanwhile, all the forces of urban aggrandizement are on the make: advertising, insurance, and high finance, the divine trinity that rules the world of industry and perverts its honest labors for its own ends, gather together in the city and out of its egotism and self-inflation rose higher and higher skyscrapers, first in the southern end of the island, then, forming a sort of double vertebral column, from Thirty-fourth Street upward, in the new central district. The new office buildings and lofts are flanked by apartment houses as stupidly planned, as extravagantly designed, as crazily and as dishonestly financed as the business buildings themselves. The megalopolitan architects who designed these puerile structures gloated over the prospect of a whole city composed of skyscrapers, with aerial drives for the rich, and in the murky canyons below the working and living quarters for the poor—artificially lighted! artificially ventilated!—a city in which sunlight would be supplied by sunlamps, grass by green tiles, and babies, presumably, by mechanical incubation. (No extravagance of Aldous Huxley's satire was beyond the serious commonplace luncheon conversation of the self-infatuated schoolboys who were financing and planning and building the "city of the future," on paper.)

A generation after his first pictures of New York, Stieglitz surveys the city once more, now from the seventeenth story of an office building at Fifty-third Street, surrounded by the architectural bluff and fraud of the boom period. He ironically portrays these structures with no further hint of nature than the indication of the hour of the day, through the degree of light and shadow that falls on their trivial façades. He shows the skyscraper—the mock city of the future—in the last state of mechanical perfection and human insignificance, devoid at last of even the possibility of earning money: financial liabilities, as well as the social liabilities their reckless misuse had already made them. There, in effect, is the ultimate result of putting nature at a distance and subordinating all the values of living to the paper routine of pseudo-work and profit-pyramiding. These skyscrapers of Stieglitz's last photographs might be the cold exhalations of a depopulated world.

And at the end, with a sardonic gleam in his eyes, he photographs the turning point: the tearing down of a seven-story building at Sixtieth Street and Madison Avenue in order to make way for a new two-story building. The nightmare was over. The human scale had begun to return. Finally, the sterile dream of imperialist conquest externalized itself in that last gesture of the impotent: Rockefeller Center. But this was already an aftermath, which, like an auto rolling backward downhill, continued on its course because the driver preferred the sensation of motion, even if it were motion backwards, to the recognition of his inability to reverse the direction and go forward.

5. SYMBOLS OF VITALITY

While the tree and the sky are dominating symbols in Stieglitz's work, brought to sharper focus by their steady exclusion from the urban landscape, there are two others that were important, both in his personal life and in his vision: the race horse and the woman. The thoroughbred horse, quivering in every muscle, nostril open, eyes glaring, hooves delicately stamping, ready for the race or the rut: symbol of sheer animal vitality, bred and nurtured with a single eye to that final outburst of speed which carries horse and rider down the home stretch to victory. From the black heavy-flanked Waterboy or the low-slung, short-legged chestnut Sysonby, to the great Man o' War and his present-day successors, these horses represented the pinnacle of animal achievement: proofs of man's skill and intelligence in alliance with the world of life, symbolic of those new strains of wheat, those new hybrids or sports in flowers and fruits, whose conquest was ultimately more important to man than were half the mechanical contrivances on which the metropolitan mind doted.

And if the horse was animal vitality, woman was—if one may combine the words—animal spirituality, that form of spirit which, unlike the lonely ascetic endeavors of man, fulfills itself in the very organs of the body, in the warmth of the arms, in the tenderness that emanates from the breast, in the receptivity of the lap, in the utilization of every physical fiber for the higher ends of life, making the body not the enemy of the mind but the friendly guide and initiator; favoring the warm intellect, touched by the earth, the intellect of Goethe, as contrasted with the cold intellect, the intellect divorced from the earth, the intellect of womanless men like Leonardo. Man tends to overvalue his eyes and his muscles: the organs of definition and of physical conquest. Woman teaches him to use his lips, his sense of touch, and to diffuse some of the fierce tactile sensitiveness that is at first concentrated so exclusively in his generative organ. Here is a vitality even deeper-fibered than that of the thoroughbred horse; for it reaches, through the very structure of woman's body, toward a completer biological fulfillment, never being fully organized or alive except when the relationships lead, through the lover or the baby, to the ultimate breast and womb.

The masculine world, with its strife of markets, with its stultifying ambitions to corner wheat or to cheapen steel, to invent this or that substitute for organic life, to conquer by an equation or a formula this or that territory of the intellect, this masculine world, particularly in our own cultural epoch, has tended toward an asceticism that has left little energy or time for the fundamental biological occupations. The seed was sound and fruitful: the great outburst of vitality marked by the rising birth rate of the nineteenth century proved it: but the soil was too dry and sour and lacking in humus to give the plant itself full growth. So that it was the classes at the periphery of our mechanical civilization, more often the not-serious people, the unbusinesslike, the wastrels and gamblers and sports, the "low" and the "vicious," among the males, who still preserved an alert eye appreciative of the flanks and fetlocks and neck of a horse, or the flanks and belly and buttocks of a woman.

Compare the stock exchange and the race track. Economically, both are mainly gambling devices; and humanly speaking they are both low forms of activity. But one is indoors; it is conducted in a clamorous jumble of noises by means of a series of telegraphic symbols; the realities with which the gamble deals, the automobile factories and packing plants and mail-order houses and banana plantations, are present only as verbal abstractions. The other activity is held outdoors under the sky; the track, heavy or fast, is affected by accidents of the weather; the gamble has to do with visible horseflesh and visible human skill and courage; and in the procession to the post, the suspense of the start, the stretching out of the field, and the final climax of the home stretch, there is a superb esthetic spectacle. The drama itself does not terminate abruptly with the end of the race: the tension is prolonged by the return of the jockey to the judge's stand, where he awaits for an instant, with upraised arm and whip, the nod that gives him the victory in a fairly won race.

Dégas came closer than anyone else among the painters to representing this drama; but there is something, in the four-dimensional continuity of it, that evades even the most skilled of painters; indeed, the impulse to grasp this continuity was responsible for the critical steps in the invention of the motion-picture camera. At the bottom of this interest is the horse himself; and until the automobile usurped this interest, the horse and the gambling connected with the races were ways in which the American, caught in his artful commercial merry-go-round, kept a little of his residual sense of the primitive and the organic. Right down to the end of the first decade of the present century, the Speedway at 155th Street was maintained as a common race track for trotters; and the designer of Central Park, a generation earlier, was forced, in the interests of more general recreation, to plan his horse drives so as to curb racing.

If Stieglitz did not photographically utilize this deep interest of his in the horse races—there is, however, the fine print of Going to the Post— it was only perhaps because its intensity was incompatible with that patient suspended animation which makes photography possible. Stieglitz was too near the race horse, as one is too near the lover in an embrace, to be able to photograph him. And yet the horse symbolized to him, as it did to the author of *St. Mawr* and to the author of *Roan Stallion* in a later generation, something essential in the life of man: that deep animal vitality he had too lightly turned his back on and renounced in his new mechanical preoccupations. So Stieglitz conceived, though he never carried out, a series of photographs of the heads of stallions and mares, of bulls and cows, in the act of mating, hoping to catch in the brute an essential quality that would symbolize the probably unattainable photograph of a passionate human mating.

6. SEX AND LOVE

Just as the old rural interest in animals could enter the city only deviously by way of the race track, so sex itself, despite its endless manifestations, had no central part in the routine of the civilization that had reached a mechanical apex in New York. Where sex was most obvious, in the burlesque houses and musical comedies and in the murky red-light district, it was also most furtive and shamefaced: a grudging admission, not a passionate conviction; an itch, not an intensity; a raw piece of flesh flung to a caged animal, who responded in his reflexes, like a Pavlovian dog, without benefit of mind. Foreign observers noted that women tended to dominate the pioneer society of America, and to hold its males in nominal subservience to ideals of courtesy and chivalry toward womanhood. But although the traditional scarcity of women in a new country gave woman a privileged position and permitted her a freedom of travel and a freedom of choice in mating unknown among similar classes in Europe, the result was to widen the political scope of woman at the expense of her sex life. Instead of ruling with and through her sex, the American woman, despite her studious attention to her own beauty, her figure and her dress, learned to preserve her freedom and power by keeping sex at a distance. It was on the assumption that "nothing could happen" that the sexes came together so easily, and that women in America, up to the second decade of the present century, were given their "freedom."

And in any fundamental sense nothing did happen, even after the American girl extended her flirtations to the length of concluding them in bed. The whole business of sex remained peripheral: sexual expression symbolized freedom or sophistication; indeed, it often sank so low as to justify itself as hygiene. People married and became the parents of children and were driven to seek divorce before they had even scraped the surface of intimacy. This negation of sex was helped, perhaps, rather than hindered by the devices of birth control. Contraceptive devices put between passion and its fulfillment a series of mechanical or chemical obstacles which, though small in themselves, could never be completely routinized into oblivion: the least objectionable device from the standpoint of intercourse was also the most dangerous in the possibilities of serious lesion. If this is still largely true today, a hundred years after the initial movement toward birth control in America, it was even more true a generation ago, when the crudeness and uncertainty of the various devices used added to the clumsiness and anxiety that attended their employment. With sex, the dish often became lukewarm before it could be served; and with the loss of warmth and flavor went a loss of appetite; for why, if the final result were favored by lukewarmness, should people ever bother to reach in the first place a hotter temperature?

Lusty men and passionate women of course remained in this society; but the whole tone of sex remained practically as low as it had been in Victorian days. Although talk about sex, and even possibly physical indulgence, became more common, the actual manifestations often remained placidly anemic: a girl might have a dozen lovers without having known an orgasm, or have a dozen orgasms without having achieved any fundamental intimacy with her lover. On the surface, decorum or the defiance of decorum; beneath it, irritation, frustration, resentment—resentment on the part of the male for the unarousableness of the female, about whom the faint aroma of anxious antisepsis clung like an invisible petticoat; resentment on the part of the female against the male both for his bothersome insistence and his lack of really persuasive aggression. In the course of business, the work in the office and the factory, the activities of the home, the club, the social gathering, men and women saw each other too little on their more primitive levels to overcome all these obstacles and find each other. They sought by the chemical means of drink to reach these levels more quickly—only to lose the sting and sharpness of sex, when what they needed was patience and leisure and sympathy and above all free energy and vitality, for all of which a tumescent animal befuddlement was in no sense a substitute. For what was left for sex but the dreary crowded moments before sleep, when all energy had been spent upon every aspect of living except sex?

One emphasizes the state of sex in American society because here again Stieglitz was to preoccupy himself with symbolic representations of the elements that were lacking in the scene around him. As a young student in Europe, he had found his own sense of manliness and sexual confidence reinforced and cultivated by the great traditions of the arts, above all by Rubens, whose portrait of Hélène de Fourment, an exuberant naked girl wrapped in fur, he had seen on his first visit to Vienna, at a critical moment when it had re-echoed and eloquently justified the impulses he found within himself. The health, the animal vitality, the unashamed lushness of sex in Rubens's paintings, are all as conspicuous as the absence of these qualities in the unhealthy sentimentality that has hung around sex in the Western world, since Christianity attempted to transfer to heterosexual relations the sick moonlight glamour of unfulfilled yearning that derived ultimately, perhaps, from the romantic homosexual love of the Greeks. Rubens was a long step back to reality from the misty mid-regions inhabited by Poe's pallid maidens, girls who were reproduced in paint in the adolescent sweetness of George Fuller's paintings in the seventies, and still further attenuated in the popular Dewing ladies who ruled the nineties. The ideal maiden of adolescent America was a sort of inverted pariah: untouchable by reason of her elevation. In defiance of Nature, her womanliness and her untouchability were supposed to be one. But what was sex, how could it exist, how could it nourish the personality, if it were not in fact the most essential demonstration of touchability—if the intercourse of lovers, at all its levels, from the intuitions at a distance to the final stages of union, were not accompanied at every moment by that direct sense of touch, that tact, which removes the need for words and signs and breaks down the formidable distance between object and subject, between thine and mine?

In all the meanings of the adjective, sex was primarily the realm of tactile values. Stieglitz was to discover these values and intensify them in his photography even before Berenson had used them, too narrowly, as a key to the great painting of the Italian Renaissance. The blindness of love, debased as a mere figure of speech, is indeed one of the most characteristic of its attributes. It is blind in the fact that it reaches deeper levels of consciousness, below the open-eyed rationality of practical achievement. It is blind in the way that it often shuts out the outer world in order to concentrate upon the inner stimulus, blind as in terror, blind as in prayer; and finally, it has the beautiful compensation of blindness, for it learns to see with its fingertips, and to offset the closed eyes, reacts more quickly with the other available senses in every region of the body.

It was Stieglitz's endeavor, at first mainly instinctive, finally, through a better self-knowledge, with a fuller awareness of his actions, to translate the unseen world of tactile values as they develop between lovers not merely in the sexual act but in the entire relationship of two personalities—to translate this world of blind touch into sight, so that those who felt could more clearly see what they felt, and so those who could merely see might reach, through the eye, the level of feeling. Observe the work of Stieglitz's contemporaries in photography, moved perhaps by the same desires but deeply inhibited. See, in the many reproductions in *Camera Work*—which doubtless helped pave the way to the sun-bathing and easier nudity of a later day—see how they portray the nude body. However honest their efforts, they nevertheless surround the body with a halo of arcadian romanticism; note how resolutely they equip their naked models with glass bubbles; how they compel these naked girls painfully, for the first time in their lives, to pour water out of narrow-necked jugs; how they lash them to tree stumps or make them shiver at the edge of icy pools. Sex must be disguised as art—that is, as artiness—before one may peep at it without blushing. Undisguised, the girl averts her face from the camera, so that the self-conscious and self-righteous face shall not acknowledge the powers of the body. The efforts of these earlier photographers are not to be despised; but the tantalizing fear of sex, a fear of its heady realities, is written over their pictures, with their dutiful aversions, their prescribed degrees of dimness, their overarch poses.

It was his manly sense of the realities of sex, developing out of his own renewed ecstasy in love, that resulted in some of Stieglitz's best photographs. In a part-by-part revelation of a woman's body, in the isolated presentation of a hand, a breast, a neck, a thigh, a leg, Stieglitz achieved the exact visual equivalent of the report of the hand or the face as it travels over the body of the beloved. Incidentally, this is one of the few aspects of photography that had not been anticipated in one fashion or another by the painter, since the dismembered anatomical studies of the Renaissance, which casually resemble these photographs, are purely instruments of factual knowledge: they make no appeal to sentiments and feelings. In more abstract, yet not in less intimate form, Stieglitz sought to symbolize the complete range of expression between man and woman in his cloud pictures, relying upon delicacies and depths of tone, and upon subtle formal relationships, to represent his own experiences. Earth and sky, root and topmost branch, animal intimacy and spiritual expression—these things, which were so remote from the routine of the metropolitan world, or which there existed in such loud disharmony, were restored to their natural integrity in Stieglitz's life and work. What was central became central again; what was deep was respected for its profundity, instead of being ignored; what was superficial was thrust behind the essential.

Stieglitz was never a better son of the city he loved and identified himself with than when he turned his back on her desiccated triumphs and recalled, in word, in photography, in the tenacious act of existence, the precious elements that the city had excluded. With Whitman, with Ryder, with the handful of other men that each generation has produced in New York, Stieglitz has served his city, not by acquiescing in its decay, nor yet by furthering its creeping paralysis: he has served it by nurturing in himself, and in those who have witnessed his work, the living germs that may reanimate it, quickening the growth of the higher forms of life it has excluded. For, as Whitman said, the place where the great city stands is not the place of markets and stretched wharves and multiplying population and ships bringing goods from the ends of the earth: it is the city of the faithfulest lovers and friends.

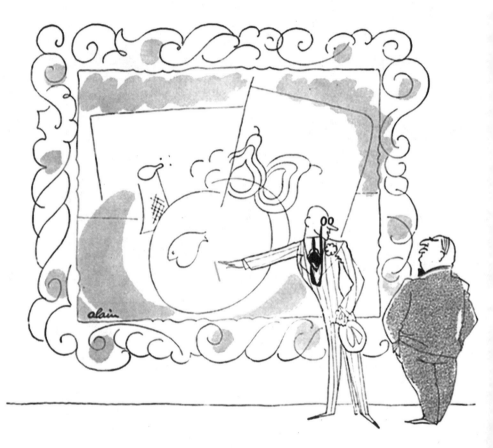

"In my opinion, Mortimer, that line says the whole thing."

When Lewis Mumford debuted as columnist for "The Art Galleries" on October 1, the nation was deep in the throes of economic depression, which had quickly become the defining issue of the fall presidential race. Nevertheless, his first column set a lively tone for the season, covering survey exhibitions at the Metropolitan Museum of Art and the Museum of Modern Art ("The Taste of Today," October 1, 1932). In a departure from the norm, his second column ("Shows Abroad," October 8, 1932) recounted exhibitions in the Netherlands, France, and Germany that he had observed while traveling on a Guggenheim Fellowship the previous summer. Mumford's review of Ernst Barlach's World War I memorial in Hamburg—soon to be denounced by the Nazi Party as "degenerate"— was especially prescient.

Subsequent highlights of the season included exhibitions of Berenice Abbott's photographs at the Julien Levy Gallery, which featured a portrait of Joe Gould, the idiosyncratic "oral historian" ("Mr. Bloom's Anniversary—And a Disciple of Atget," October 15, 1932); Mary Cassatt's pastels at the Durand-Ruel Galleries ("Seventy Years—The Work of Mary Cassatt," November 12, 1932); the first biennial at the Whitney Museum of American Art ("American Paintings," December 10, 1932); Georgia O'Keeffe's paintings at An American Place ("Paint and Stone," January 21, 1933); and Maurice Prendergast's paintings at the Kraushaar Galleries ("Impressionism and the Circus—Three Decades," April 22, 1933). In June, Mumford concluded successfully his first season in the dual roles of art and architecture critic, his byline having appeared in almost every issue of the magazine. Although normally off duty from both columns during the summer months, Mumford contributed a special "Art Galleries" in August on José Clemente Orozco's powerful murals for Dartmouth College's Baker Memorial Library ("The Summer Circuit," August 12, 1933).

THE TASTE OF TODAY

It is scarcely fair to let autumn burst in upon us without uttering a word of thanks for two public exhibitions which are soon to close: one at the Metropolitan Museum and the other at the Museum of Modern Art. "The Taste of Today in Masterpieces of Painting before 1900" is both handsome and ingenious. Any pretext that brings to the Metropolitan a painting like "The Mountebank's Family," by Daumier, has well served its purpose; but this was only one of an excellent array that has been hanging all summer. Convenience and historical logic usually keep one from seeing on the same wall three pictures like Brueghel's "Harvesters," one of the most precious possessions of the Metropolitan; a superb still life by Cézanne; and Delacroix's "L'Enlèvement de Rebecca," a scene out of Walter Scott. But what an admirable eye and instinct put them together! The paintings actually seemed complementary—each still as fresh as an apple clinging to the same tree, that tree which Mr. Albert Jay Nock lovingly calls the Great Tradition. Not the least advantage of an exhibition like this is that it sets one examining once more what "the taste of today" is, and, since that is a subject for endless disputation, it tempts one to compose an exhibition of one's own. El Greco was an inevitable choice; but was Titian? True, the particular painting, "The Adoration of the Kings," obviously was. In this composition, Titian treated the beams and posts of the barn with the same intensity of interest as the Holy Family itself—a thoroughly satisfactory design, provided that one acquiesced gracefully in this displacement of the subject. But Titian is not really very close to us; I should have preferred Piero della Francesca, or even Giovanni Bellini, whose landscape in "The Agony in the Garden," at the National Gallery in London, makes him seem curiously contemporary.

When all is said and done, does Rubens belong, either? He has never been out of fashion for any considerable period. How could he be, so long as sex and hunger continue to govern the world? But there is a touch of false grandiosity in Rubens. It was due not merely to the fact that the great palaces of the seventeenth century gave him enormous surfaces to cover, but also to the same erroneous conviction that influenced the righteously smug and noble Benjamin Robert Haydon; namely, that if you let out a great spread of canvas, you would somehow conjure up a big wind. Rubens' rhetorical floridness is just the opposite of our modern taste and temper. The very current that sweeps Rubens away from us brings Poussin in: we understand his studious mastery of design, because we, too, must achieve by intelligence what once might have been left to natural appetites and instincts, to the unconscious assimilation of tradition.

But one could go on with this endlessly. I should have taken out Renoir and put in Manet, and I should have hunted hard for a more modern Goya than the one which was shown; it scarcely required a hunt, since the Surréaliste landscape in the Havemeyer Collection would have done admirably. Nor could I have left out Rembrandt; for if the taste of today has any positive note, it is surely a keen appreciation of the art of biography and the science of psychology, and in these departments Rembrandt is likely to outlast the Stracheys and the Freuds. As for our sense of objectivity and that rich appetite for the actual which now disports itself in photography, no one in the Metropolitan's exhibition could represent this so well as Chardin, who was absent. And Ingres— But enough. Every intelligent person who went to the exhibition came away with a list of his own, different in some particular from the Museum's or mine; and if one could only recompose all those individual lists, one might begin to have a dim notion as to what the taste of today actually is.

Meanwhile, the Museum of Modern Art has the even more complicated task of representing the taste of today in the paintings of today—a hard and slippery road to follow, indeed. The summer exhibition of paintings and sculpture was full of excellent things; I cannot think of any city in the world where such a good round assemblage of contemporary work could have been done any better. But the taste of the Museum of Modern Art is still a little capricious. It has gone in for Burchfield, for example, and left out Thomas Benton, although Burchfield's paintings have little value, apart from their healthy pathos and sentimentality, whilst both as satiric commentator and as draughtsman Benton is infinitely Burchfield's superior. If the Museum wishes to be inclusive, it has not included enough; if it wishes to be aristocratic, its standards are not yet rigorous enough. To include Max Weber and leave out Walter Pach, to include Bernard Karfiol and leave out Harold Weston, to include Louis Eilshemius and leave out the whole annual show of the Independents—all this still shows a certain shakiness, not in the particular judgments but in the standards upon which the judgments are based. As for Eilshemius, I will say in excuse for the Museum that the canvas hung this summer is perhaps the best painting by him I have yet seen; but nothing will ever convince me that Marcel Duchamp was not playing a ribald practical joke when he first proclaimed the genius of Mr. Eilshemius. Sauk Center would have been a little suspicious of such a joke; it took a really sophisticated town like New York to swallow it hook, line, and sinker.

SHOWS ABROAD

The suburbs of New York have shared interest with the city itself in the matter of summer exhibitions. There was a good Rembrandt exhibition at the Rijksmuseum in Amsterdam, and an exhibition of Van Gogh at The Hague which held many of those precious early pictures of his in which, underneath the dark, smudgy colors and the awkward drawing, so much of the future artist plainly lay; more plainly, in fact, than during the indecisive middle period of Impressionism, represented in more than one example in the permanent collection at the City Museum in Amsterdam.

In Paris, the Picasso Exhibition, particularly the great red room which contained some of the very latest pictures, left the critics gasping and choking with vexed admiration: the Great Spaniard, high up on his trapeze, had executed another *salto mortal* and was gracefully thumbing his nose at the audience who had hoped, in 1922, that he would keep permanently in the classic poses of the Living Statues. Meanwhile, I must confess that nothing in the exhibition so profoundly moved me as the early pictures of the blue period, in which technique and accomplishment had not outrun a deep sense of humanity. He was still a Spaniard in the early years of the century, still close to El Greco and Goya, not perhaps as an artist but as a man; the language he spoke then was more universal than the cosmopolitan dialects he has invented every few years since and discarded in turn as soon as each became vulgar enough to be understood. Picasso's humanity is by now, I fear, permanently buried; and what is left of the essential *ornament* of the admirable Cubist period is its irrealism. Doubtless, I fail to do justice to the superb painting of the new pictures; but I am just old enough to have been irreverently touched by the fact that the figures resembled a little Gelett Burgess' Goops.

In Germany, the one ubiquitous artist in this centennial year was Goethe. As a painter and a draughtsman, he showed in miniature all his literary qualities except their greatness; but his classicism was more pedantic and arid in drawing than in any of the plays, and one would scarcely guess that the same hand could have done, with swift pen and brush, the fine romantic landscapes, some of which, in their quick lyricism, remind one of Rembrandt's etchings. As for German art itself, it is somehow at its best when it is furthest from French fashions. The exhibition at the Neue Pinakothek, in Munich, of the pencil drawings of Wilhelm Busch gave something that the woodcuts in his books sometimes a little lack: swift spontaneity. The sage, homely humor of Busch has no exact equivalent in any other country; to mention Hogarth or Daumier would be to misrepresent him entirely, although an American authority on prints, whose judgment I respect, has called him the foremost German draughtsman of the nineteenth century. German children know Busch as English children know Lewis Carroll; which is to say that they know him best when they are grown up.

The Barlach war memorial is alone worth a visit to Hamburg: a flat shaft that rises from a base below one of the most frequently used bridges. The German Ku Klux Klansmen have objected to the mother and child rendered in low relief on one side; their ground is that the figures look Slavic, a criticism even more absurd than the pious English outrage over the fact that Epstein's Madonna looked Oriental. What really troubles the Nazis is that the whole monument is so free from pomp and bluster; freer even than Tessenow's excellent interior of the war memorial in Berlin, with its metallic wreath and its top open to the sky. Barlach is a real *Nordgotiker,* essentially a hermit-artist, produced by what is still living in North Germany of the Middle Ages. In Lübeck, an hour away from Hamburg by train, one can see the first three figures of a series Barlach is doing; they occupy a special space in the old Katharinenkirche, now used as a museum. The strong Gothic interior, doubly strong by reason of the fact that it is painted a cold white, is just the right setting for Barlach's art: it needs the echo of that background to hold its reality, and to make one see that Barlach has not copied Gothic but *is* Gothic, perhaps one of the last creatures produced by that vanished world.

Incidentally, the Americans who confine their search for art in Germany to the big cities are overlooking their opportunities. The best museum of modern art is the Folkwang Collection in Essen, and perhaps the finest selective museum of medieval art anywhere is the St. Annen Museum in Lübeck, although the Germania at Nürnberg is more comprehensive. As for the triple-starred Pergamon Museum in Berlin, the less said about it the better; in more than one sense, it is ill-starred. The taste for that sort of large-scale reconstruction reminds one of the very worst flatulence of the Berlin of Kaiser Wilhelm II; which was in public life pretty much what Czar Nicholas' taste was in private. One wonders how the Pergamon Museum could have been carried out in the postwar period; before it was opened, it [was] dated. In archeology, a well-selected square foot is infinitely more rich and suggestive than a whole acre; for an acre, by its pretence to cover everything, just deadens the imagination without bringing one a step closer to the period or the culture. There is not a gallery in the British Museum I would exchange for the whole Pergamon Museum—Greek altar, Assyrian Hall, and all.

In Munich, the ultimate in contemporary exhibitions was on view. Ranged on the upper floors of the library of the Deutsches Museum were miles and miles of canvases representing the following groups: the Munich Artists, the Munich Secession, the New Secession, and the Juryless Group. The first were dead, the second were a little less dead, the third had signs of life; and it may be that a mere feeling for statistical curves made me discover better paintings in the last group than in any of the three preceding ones. One wondered what would happen when a new group broke off from that. If the return to Tradition keeps on making headway, perhaps the latest rebels will be Munich Artists once more.

MR. BLOOM'S ANNIVERSARY—AND A DISCIPLE OF ATGET

The two-hundredth anniversary of Mr. Sol Bloom is being appropriately celebrated at the Kennedy Galleries. Twenty etchings by twenty etchers record a series of episodes in Mr. Bloom's life: Sol Bloom as a young surveyor, Sol Bloom on his way to the Continental Congress, Sol Bloom at Valley Forge, Sol Bloom receiving Cornwallis' sword at Yorktown. These etchings are in every way worthy of the occasion, and in another two hundred years, when nobody remembers any more where George Washington left off and Mr. Sol Bloom began, our descendants will thank these artists for leaving the face of Mr. Sol Bloom—or is it George Washington?—so blank that their imaginations will be free to complete the portrait.

I will not say that the present show is worse than the great array of murals that was brought together in Washington to honor our hero—nothing could be much worse than that—but the theme apparently robbed the artists of even such special virtues as they have cultivated. Now, the etchers in this exhibition are the successful and representative exponents of American etching, chosen by a master in their own field, Mr. John Taylor Arms. They were given a definite job; namely, to portray scenes from the life of a particular historic figure, the sort of job that the vulgar draughtsmen and lithographers of the middle of the nineteenth century would have landed on with both feet. Why, then, is the result so insipid and sickly? Why is it that, despite the historical accuracy of the scenes, vouched for by scholarship, one scarcely has a breath of the eighteenth century in America; and why is there scarcely a chemical trace of Washington in the show, despite the fact that our hero is in every picture?

The answer is, I think, that our popular American etchers are specialists, each of whom has mastered a particular trick of the needle or has associated himself with a particular kind of milieu: one is known for his ducks, another for his nudes, another for his old buildings, another for his rare and elusive atmosphere. It happens, unfortunately, that none of these tricks includes George Washington. Perhaps the best print in the whole show, along with Earl Horter's "Washington at Braddock's Defeat," is the second stage of Mr. Robert Lawson's "Welcome of Washington": merely the bow of a great ship sweeping across an empty space. In the final stage, Washington on a barge occupies that space and he is lost in a mass of intricate detail.

The fact is that the narrow craftsmanship which has been cultivated by so many of our etchers has been attended by an atrophy of the other functions of the artist. They were plainly scared of Washington; they had no imaginative grasp of the fine, formal life of the eighteenth century, its crispness and its grand style, its brutality and its finesse; and the result is that the scenes themselves are as unsatisfactory as the portrayal of the subject himself in action. What justification can craftsmanship give for the bad drawing of so many of the figures, the feeble characterization, the hazy impressionism of detail, the compositions which lose their central motif in working out the subordinate parts—all qualities that characterize one or another of these etchings?

Unfortunately, the only possible excuse for craftsmanship that is so shaky, and in some of the prints so downright amateurish, is that the artists were "expressing themselves." If the representative of tradition is willing to make that defence, he is welcome to it; for it only leaves one with the uncomfortable task of judging these prints as works of art.

On going out of the gallery, my eye happened to light on a mid-nineteenth-century lithograph by D. Benecke: "Sleighing in New York." Here, too, was a craftsman, doubtless doing a job on order; but there was still in Benecke some of that skill in design which attends even the dwindling figures of a great tradition. Benecke perhaps had less talent than many of these distinguished etchers; but he had developed a general competence rather than a superficial technique; and I warrant he could have put Washington into one of those sleighs and not concealed the fact that he was there. Indeed, these etchings, like the more dreadful Washington murals, make one realize that, in comparison with some of our popular artists today, people like Benecke and Leutze, the painter of "Washington Crossing the Delaware," were masters of pictorial composition.

At the Julien Levy Gallery, Miss Berenice Abbott has been showing a series of photographs. Miss Abbott brought Atget, the master of French photography and the historian of antebellum Paris, over to this country; and some of the best photographs in the exhibition show strong and not unhappy signs of her discipleship: a dark harness shop with a shiny horse in front of it, an old "L" station, a waterfront street. But the white shaft of the Daily News Building, newspaper-thin, against a dark background of lower buildings is a photograph of another order; so, too, is a composition of small figures and a small statue of a horse against a background of open sidewalk—a very happy shot, indeed. Perhaps the best photograph of all is a tangle of black railings and cables of a bridge against the soft background of lower New York.

Miss Abbott uses the camera both for record and for commentary. She has caught the figure of Abraham Lincoln lying prone in Union Square, and in another mood she has debunked the Statue of Liberty by taking a foreshortened picture of the goddess from the rear. Unfortunately, the hardest part of any record is to deal objectively with human beings: they become artful and selfconscious when they are approached, or they make the photographer artful, too. Perhaps the only portrait by Miss Abbott which seems quite worthy of her New York scenes is that of Joe Gould—a horrifyingly good likeness. This picture should be used as a frontispiece to the history of Joe Gould and the Universe when that eccentric philosopher of men and manners, that ultimate product of Harvard individualism, finally publishes his great work.

SEVENTY YEARS—THE WORK OF MARY CASSATT

One would think from the newspaper comments that the only picture that counted in the exhibition of American art, 1862–1932, at the Museum of Modern Art was Whistler's portrait of his mother. It is bad enough that the Louvre itself has made a fetish of this amiable but much overrated canvas by putting it in embarrassingly good company in Paris; but the fact is that there are at least a dozen works of art in the present show that are superior to Whistler's painting; and this is the whole point of the tale.

Whistler, like Mr. Bernard Shaw in our own day, always had a flair for the headlines, whilst his contemporaries, Ryder, Eakins, Homer, were workmanlike, reticent artists, holding their peace dearly in a world that was becoming more vulgar and noisy and empty. With all of Whistler's fine assumption of his uniqueness and superiority, it is plain enough now that he was, unconsciously, the most distinguished member of a minor school that embraced men like Fuller, Tryon, Twachtman—that characteristically American group, dim, wistful, tender, very temperate in their emotional responses, a school that tapered off into nothingness in Dewing. Neither Ryder, Eakins, Homer, nor Mary Cassatt belonged to this school; they had something else to say and said it in a more effective idiom. Is it an accident that one of the most interesting Whistlers in this exhibition is that of Wapping Docks, halfway between the Pre-Raphaelites and Manet?

This exhibition is particularly happy because it presents the backgrounds and connections as well as the central figures; there is a landscape by Theodore Robinson which shows how directly Impressionism came into America, and there is a painting by John Twachtman, a green landscape, which shows how good a painter he was without the aid of soft atmospheric effects. There are some superb Winslow Homer water colors, which always shame the praise that has been too lavishly bestowed on his oil painting; and there is a still-life of a fish by John La Farge that gives a better measure of his talents than many of his grander compositions. Here are George Inness and Homer Martin and J. Alden Weir, men who look good in comparison not merely with Robert Henri and Ernest Lawson, who immediately followed them, but with most of the people we can show today.

The notion that American art is essentially only fifteen years old is one that is scarcely excusable today even on the lips of a fifteen-year-old. This exhibition demonstrates a good, solid, painter-like tradition which, beginning long before the Civil War, came to a maturity in the seventy years that followed its outbreak. American art, even in the hands of its most cosmopolitan painters, has had a definitely national flavor; but, like any art that is worth its salt, it has been subject steadily to examples, influences, and ideas that spread beyond the parochial boundaries of time and place. This was as true in the seventies as it was in the decade of the Armory Exhibition. What is merely American is not even American.

In this show, the representation of the older painters is fairly complete: if some of the more masterly Eakins portraits are missing, perhaps because the Modern Museum has itself made them familiar during the past year, the Ryders were very happily chosen. Among the painters of the Brown Decades who might have had a place, I can think of only Robert Loftin Newman and William Morris Hunt; one surely does not miss Elihu Vedder today. As for the choice of contemporary painters, there is naturally plenty of ground for debate. The Museum erred, if it erred, on the side of mediocrity; but, needless to say, some excellent paintings are here.

In sculpture, the American tradition is a little more uncertain. John Quincy Adams Ward, who worked on a heroic scale, too heroic to be included in a remodelled American mansion, is represented by a good small figure done in 1884; in this same decade, Saint-Gaudens did his bust of General Sherman, also shown here, as well as his tombstone for Henry Adams, and his Farragut monument. Between that decade and the present one, sculpture in America was in a precarious state: it was seduced by Impressionism, by archaicism, by didacticism; and even men of talent had difficulty in finding themselves. But the work of Lachaise and Epstein, and—among still younger men—Robert Laurent and Harold Cash, has restored the balance a little between sculpture and painting; and one feels that more good work is perhaps about to come.

In almost any company during the nineteenth century, Mary Cassatt could have held her own. The present show of her pastels at the Durand-Ruel Galleries only completes the demonstration in the Museum of Modern Art. She was a fine draughtsman, she was a marvellous colorist, she had a warm knowledge of human character: her stolid nursemaid, in this exhibition, is worthy of Toulouse-Lautrec, and her smudgily angelic babies have no rival anywhere. The notion that one can do the sort of painting Mary Cassatt did out of a mere technical interest in adjusting volumes is one of the superstitions of the recent past that should have been blown away with the powder smoke of the last war. For the obvious and staring fact is that Mary Cassatt loved mothers with children, and was precisely the artist that she was because she loved them and comprehended the special tenderness of this relationship.

Ruskin used to say that the character which differentiated the great masters from the lesser painters was their skill in composition; but unfortunately this was perhaps the only quality of a work of art that could not be defined. And composition, whatever it is, is not a mere arrangement—like the nice but patent arrangement of chair, picture, and curtain in Whistler's portrait of his mother—but a building-up from within. The external disposition of the parts is an art the photographer can practice; but the organic building-up of color and form belongs peculiarly to the painter and depends upon more ultimate matters than pure visual response. Mary Cassatt had this ability, alike in her paintings, her pastels, and her etchings; and her work proves that it is not the presence of a human or sentimental subject that makes a picture bad but the absence of art. Renoir knew this, too; that is why he dared to paint nudes which would easily increase the sale of a beauty cream. It is only the inferior artist who is afraid that his sentiments will give him away. He is right. They will. And his suppression gives him away, too.

MARIN—MIRÓ

The John Marin show is now on at An American Place. Need I say that Marin is the most significant and poignant and accomplished landscape-painter of this generation in America? In truth, Marin occupies a place similar to that which Ryder had forty years ago. He goes his own way and quietly keeps his own gait; no art is freer from echoes and fashions than his, with its curious inner feeling of the movement of buildings and mountains or the heave and push of sailboats, with its daring short-cuts and its emphatic complexities of statement.

In method, Marin is at the opposite pole from Ryder; instead of clinging to a single picture for a decade, like the older artist, refining, readjusting, laboring tenderly toward the last right stroke, Marin until last year worked in water color and carried to the limit its swift economies. When he does not completely hit the mark, he follows Manet's happy advice and tries again; for he is inexhaustible both in his capacity to be stimulated by landscape and in his ability to respond with appropriate invention.

Last year, Marin abandoned the medium in which he has no contemporary rival: he showed a series of oil paintings. While one sympathized with his impulse to master a new set of technical problems, in most of the paintings last year one could find nothing that Marin had not already said better in water color. One still felt in the treatment of the pictures the method of water color, but what was spontaneity in one medium was thinness and superficiality in the other. In oils, Marin was plainly a novice, and the question was: Was the change worth the effort?

Marin's oil paintings this year are a pretty complete refutation of one's doubts and distrusts; they have a quite different story to tell. He not merely demonstrates a mastery of the medium, but in his seascapes and his more or less abstract interpretations of New York he extends the range of his art by a couple of octaves; in these pictures, he uses color to achieve a depth and solidity that was possible in his earlier work only by linear emphasis. Is it an accident that some of these oils have, also, the special warmth and intimacy that comes through the presence of living creatures in the foreground?

A few years ago, Mr. Waldo Frank could write: "The fact that Marin . . . paints a world without men and women is a symbol." But now the symbol has changed, even as the medium has changed; the lyricist, filling his lonely mood with images of sea and mountain and skyscraper, no longer rejects man's presence: the foregrounds are populated. No one has given better than Marin the queer, dismayed excitement of being alive in the streets of New York; no one else has such a magical way of turning the passive remoteness of a scene into an event—something one not merely sees but lives through. There are three or four pictures in the present exhibition that seem to me at the very top of Marin's accomplishment—and I know of no one today in America who has climbed higher.

Mr. Pierre Matisse has followed his show of Maillol's drawings, pure examples of fine draughtsmanship and great beauty of line, with the drawings of Joan Miró. Miró's art stands in accidental but ultimate contrast to Maillol's. His paintings are arrangements in lines and rectangles of color; some of the drawings are teasing linear elaborations that haunt one, as the puzzles of one's childhood did, with faces that cannot quite be seen and suggestions of members that dissolve into something else. Miró's drawings are witty and amusing; and wit and amusement have their place in art. (For which reason a glance at Max Ernst's Surréaliste capers at the Julien Levy Gallery is in order.) But Miró's drawings are also a little repetitious; and repetition has small place in wit and amusement.

Such a refinement of abstraction finally brings the painter to the point where the Dutch artist, Mondriaan, has carried his art: a white rectangle cut in four by two black lines. When the last black line has been taken away, the art will have reached its final purity of form: It will be nonexistent. In the case of both Miró and Mondriaan, I am not ready to say, with the little boy in Hans Andersen's fairy story, that the Emperor has no clothes. I would merely remark, with an eye to the gray November sky, that the Emperor must be rather cold.

AMERICAN PAINTINGS

The first biennial exhibition of contemporary American painting at the Whitney Museum contains the work of one hundred and fifty-seven artists. All in all, the show is pretty entertaining; if there is no single breath-taking, hat-lifting, knee-bending canvas, there are a number of things that give one pleasure. And it is very doubtful if twenty years ago half the number of artists of equal merit could have been assembled so easily. This is perhaps the first time I have extracted any cheer from the thought of quantity production. But if artists keep on multiplying, we shall be well on the way to solving the problem of leisure in the Machine Age—of leisure and longevity, for painters are notoriously tenacious of life, and they breeze along on their second wind in their seventies. Meanwhile, either the lawyers and the bankers and the engineers will have to take to painting too or they will die off like flies, leaving the keys of the world to the graybeards of Provincetown and Montparnasse.

It was a happy stroke on the part of the Museum to represent the more liberal wing of academic painters: Redfield and Melchers and Lawson and Kroll, for example, are here, and one can compare their quality with that of people whom the National Academy would never dream of exhibiting. The joke about these two great schools becomes apparent as they meet in one building: first, that there are modernists who have evolved an academic formula quite as deadly as anything that is shown on Fifty-seventh Street; and second, that there are modern painters who have assimilated much more of the grand tradition than their more conventional brethren. Jan Matulka's nude is demonstrably closer to the classics than Melchers' gaudy red-haired lady, suspended halfway between the Mount of Venus and Virginia Beach; and I, for one, prefer Georgina Klitgaard's landscape to Jonas Lie's, and John Carroll's sweet, neurotic nude to Schnakenberg's studio goddesses.

This is perhaps as good a place as any to follow the example of the little girl in the story and mention the favorite pictures I hate the most. I am by now pretty tired of Surréaliste pictures, unless they are superbly painted and unless they bring an immediate conviction that the painter knew what he was doing. The formula is too easy; a winch and a leg and a scrap of sky and a thermometer do not by themselves constitute a work of the imagination, even if they are placed on a single square of canvas, and *even* if the thermometer is broken. I am tired of pictures on classic themes in which an artist imagines that Aphrodite, Hera, and Athene, three characters as different as Mae West, Mary Morris, and Eva Le Gallienne, are the same as the Three Graces, three beautiful blanks; by the same token, I am tired of groups of bathers who have come not out of the water but out of Cézanne. I am, finally, completely enervated by waxen landscapes filled with paper flowers and iron foliage, even though these landscapes resemble equally corpselike canvases done by other bad painters a hundred years ago. I saw samples of all these things at the Whitney Exhibition; but that, I hasten to add, only made it more representative.

But what do I like? That is a fair question, for no one who talks about art ought to hide his tastes behind generalities; and one hundred and fifty-seven American artists give as wide an opportunity to expose one's weaknesses and prejudices as one hundred and fifty-seven historic painters would. Unfortunately, half a dozen of my favorite artists are represented by pictures in the current show I do not warm to particularly—I must leave out, for example, O'Keeffe and Hopper—and furthermore half a dozen other artists whom I value were not represented at all. But I would include in the first twenty pictures paintings by the following people: Bouché, Isabel Bishop, Ben Benn, Boyd, Burkhard, Carroll, Curry, Fiene, Glackens, Hartley, Hartman, Kantor, Knight, Klitgaard, Kuniyoshi, Matulka, Pach, Schary, Speicher, and Weston. This indicates more about the actual pictures than it does about the artists, and more about me, I am afraid, than about the pictures. And after all, scorecards have nothing to do with art.

Having a gardener's objection to painted flowers, how was I to guess that the exhibition of French flower paintings from Delacroix to Lurçat at Knoedler was to turn out the most brilliant show, so far, of the year—and it has not been a particularly bad year at that. It was altogether a dazzling affair. There were Redon's superb flowers, including a pot of geraniums one could scarcely have identified as his; there was a bouquet of classic clarity and simplicity by Fantin-Latour and a vase by Cézanne so moving and melodious that one laughed to discover in the catalogue that he had remembered the shapes of the flowers themselves by looking at a seed catalogue—it is as if Wagner had listened to a hand-organ in order to compose "Tristan." There were Surréaliste flowers by Lurçat which only a very original mind could have composed; and there were geometrical flowers by La Fresnaye which were as charming as the more luscious and fulsome abstraction by Dufrèsne. There was a weaving of delicate patterns of wallpaper, cloth, and flowers into a remarkable unity by Vuillard; there was Renoir at his best and his worst; and Van Gogh, and Courbet, and Corot. For comic relief, there was a painting of roses by the great Picasso, pink roses, with a background of a wooded park at twilight, dripping with tenderness, sentiment, and the *Art Nouveau* atmosphere of the early nineteen-hundreds: a masterpiece one might preserve for blackmail, were the artist sensitive about his early work. Finally, there was a deadly metallic cabbage by Léger: a picture that followed Picasso's like a rap of brass knuckles after a sticky kiss. But all in all, the show deserved nothing but what it began with—bouquets.

The shows have been coming on so thick and fast that I must resort to mere prods at the elbow. Stefan Hirsch's exhibition at the Downtown Gallery was worth seeing and so is Guy Pène du Bois' at Kraushaar; but above all, Harold Weston's new paintings at the Montross Gallery are not to be missed. The Durand-Ruel show of Renoir's paintings since 1900 of course demands attention; while, if you are on Fifty-seventh Street and are very cold, and if you don't care whether you ever see another work of art or not, you will be richly rewarded by a tour of the Winter Exhibition at the National Academy: they keep all the galleries at a very even temperature.

PAINT AND STONE

The new paintings by Georgia O'Keeffe that Mr. Alfred Stieglitz is now showing at An American Place represent phases of her past work in different settings, and with differences of emotional emphasis. The colors are pure, the painting is as firm and suave as ever, the symbols embody genuine experiences; all one can say of the present show is that it is not the seventh wave, which goes all the way up the beach.

But Miss O'Keeffe is without doubt one of the most original talents America has possessed in painting; and her present work is consistent with that which she was doing six or seven years ago. Her paintings of New York skyscrapers and New Mexican pueblos and Southwest landscapes demonstrated that she has no mean eye for the outward scene it-self; but her special achievement was to invent a language for emotions and feelings, dumb ecstasies and nameless fears, even for sounds like the roar of gigantic wheels that throbs in one's head as one awakens from ether. The black-flower abstraction in the retrospective room remains one of the high points of her expression. No matter what Miss O'Keeffe's further development, one can already say pretty confidently, I think, that she will occupy a place in painting similar to that which Emily Dickinson has in poetry. The little Amherst witch knew what she was about; and so does O'Keeffe.

The new paintings and drawings by Henry Lee McFee at the Rehn Gallery show a very solid and accomplished artist, whose virtues lie not in any new vision of the world but in a beautiful craftsmanship. The vase on the table, the farmyard, the poll of a little Negro boy, the pattern of tree branches, all charm him; and his sober but subtle palette embraces these objects and makes them his own. Sometimes the vision is a little ac-ademic, in the sense of being arranged with a view to getting a subject to paint and of using too obviously the associations of other paintings to bolster up his own version; such, to my mind, is the large nude of the young Negress, against an elaborately draped background. But the work is sincere, dignified, competent.

It is a large leap from McFee to the recent paintings of Jean Charlot at the John Levy Galleries. Charlot is a dozen kinds of painter: now a fine impressionist, with a spray of snapdragons; now a melodramatist in his picture of Adam and Eve; now an exponent of *die neue Sachlichkeit* in the portrait of Mr. Gilbert R. Gabriel; now a caricaturist of Thomas Benton in his portrait of Mr. Lincoln Kirstein—only eventually to turn out a pious follower of Bouguereau in a very bad painting of that amiable poet, M. Claudel. Though doubtless an accomplished painter, Charlot seems here like some brilliant student who has settled down to the ca-reer of making a record for himself by taking *all* the courses in a univer-sity. A man might spend his lifetime in that effort without having very much to show for it.

Noguchi's sculpture and drawings at the Reinhardt Galleries remain in one's mind as one of the satisfactory exhibitions of the season. He is probably the best of the younger sculptors in America today; his portrait heads, such as those of Angna Enters and J. B. Neumann, have both dis-tinction and a recognizable kinship to the subject, while his abstractions are usually—I except the well-known flying lady—more than mere audacities of experiment.

As for the Maillol show, now on at the Brummer Gallery, it deserves to be seen again and again; for it is a rare opportunity in America to see Maillol sculptures on a scale very near that of the living figure. Is there anyone in France today, except Despiau, who can touch him? Serene, clear, unmannered; delicately modulated yet strong, Maillol's figures spring out of deeper foundations than the machine age. Are they peasant girls or earth-goddesses? The heavy calves and ankles, the soft round chins, the sturdy trunks all point to the farm; but the figures as a whole, despite these provincial attributes, are classic and timeless. Maillol proves again what every man in his heart of hearts knows: woman is still a fresh and practically untouched subject.

WORLD TOUR

The 1933 International Exhibition of Contemporary Art at Rockefeller Center is a very useful and instructive exhibition, a quick tour through the modern galleries of the world. It has filled me with a sense of confusion, ignorance, dismay, and hopefulness; and what more can one ask of 336 paintings by all the nations, languages, and kingdoms of the earth? The effect of such large exhibitions, as far as I am concerned, is the effect of any crowd: it reduces to a common denominator the most outstanding personality.

By and large, the International gives a pretty fair cross-section of the work of the larger countries: the main stress is on the work of the moderns, and the paintings of the younger men do not go unnoticed. Here and there are some pretty big omissions, as in leaving out that interesting Frenchman, the late Amédée de La Patellière, still practically unknown in America; and the Dutch section, for one, is too sketchy. The only honest thing to do, when faced by such a chaos, is to review the catalogue. I note, then, that Mr. Forbes Watson hails the return to nationalism as the basis for modern art; and the various people who introduce their respective countries are inclined to stress the same point. I came away with just the opposite impression. One could have mixed up the labels over each of the big sections without creating more than an occasional strain of puzzlement. These artists work in a common milieu. They respond to similar ideas. They express similar emotions or confess, in the same manner, to the lack of them. One need not doubt the reality of the local tradition, the local way of feeling, the profound stimulus of the immediate object; but what makes these things carry is the fact that the world of ideas is international.

Yasuo Kuniyoshi is an inimitable painter; perhaps that is why he has so many imitators who have attempted to take over his palette, to reproduce his lustrous, almost metallic-looking surfaces, emphasized by streaks of solid paint, and to assimilate his way of looking at the world. The flattery is genuine, and not undeserved. His present exhibition at the Downtown Gallery has some of the finest things he has shown during the past five years; and he easily leaves his imitators behind, because his charm and significance do not lie in any tricks of perspective or drawing but in his own individuality. His circus ladies have the tender fullness of Pascin, his landscapes the sombre poetry of Vlaminck; these poles of feeling are somehow harmonized in his work. His debt to Japan is less to its art than to a certain temper of mind: it comes out above all in his color, which binds him, one sentimentally fancies, to the bronze-workers, the lacquerers, and the swordsmiths of his own country.

Gallery 144 West 13 Street has been showing Louis Eilshemius' water colors and oils from 1885 to 1909. Here is Eilshemius at his best: tepid romantic landscapes, in which he occasionally captures some of the atmosphere of the horizon, some of the fluent line of forest growth, without the pretentiousness and desolately bad painting of what Mr. Valentine Dudensing has somewhat euphemistically called his "difficult" period. His work could be shown easily in the exhibition of Early American genre paintings on view at the Newhouse Galleries. This genre painting was not, strictly speaking, folk painting: it was an art that had fallen off from, or had fallen short of, a greater tradition; and, unlike folk art, it prepared the way for Ryder, Eakins, and Homer. The view of Griswold's Wharf by Charles Parsons connects directly with the almost equally literal river landscape by Eakins at the Milch Galleries. James Beard's astonishing head of a baby, which is even better than Eastman Johnson's portrait of Evarts, lacks completely the naïveté of folk art: it is, again, but a step from these pictures to Eakins. If people turn to Eilshemius today, it is less out of respect for him as a contemporary than out of a sentimental interest in him as an ancestor.

CABARETS AND CLOUDS

The show of George Grosz' paintings and drawings at the Barbizon-Plaza and the Raymond & Raymond Galleries offsets a little the sordid humorless insanity of the Nazis. After the war, Grosz was the most savage cartoonist in a country that, with *Simplicissimus* to set the pace, did not lack strong satire and caricature. Grosz pictured a bourgeois and Junker Germany that was in a state of almost liquid dissolution. His black-and-white drawings had some of the quality of a schoolboy's malicious scrawl, heightened by obscene marks like those that might be produced by accident on the surface of a maggoty cheese.

That Grosz could draw powerfully was obvious—no schoolboy could produce such *intestinal* effects—but that he could draw suavely and compose harmoniously, with something of the direct sensuous charm of Renoir, became apparent only in his water colors. He is still at his best, perhaps, with figures that correspond to those of his original milieu—obese, slobbering people, snoutish men, and women whose limbs billow with the suspicious softness of sausages; in "Toilette" and "In a Restaurant," he has them at their best. The tenderness of Grosz' painting—accentuated by the blurring of the strong colors as they are laid swiftly over the still-moist underwash—reinforces by contrast the grossness of his subjects. At bottom, like Hemingway and the other hardboiled babies, he is a sentimental soul: even his hatred of porcine men is blended with a certain fond respect for nice, large, pink, well-larded pigs. What he will do with America still remains to be seen: the part he has approached closest so far is the universal metropolitan environment of the cabaret and the burlesque show.

Among the artists who most completely defy an apt label one must put Arthur Dove, whose new work is now being shown at An American Place. A little while back, Dove was an experimenter with materials, in the fashion of Duchamp and Picabia, contriving exotic visual and tactile and symbolic effects out of weeds, fungi, stones, shells, and paint, or out of the contents of a five-and-ten-cent-store counter. Recently, Dove has stuck to pure painting, and he has approached subjects which only amateurs as a rule look upon as particularly paintable: sunrises and sunsets and clouds, or houses and boats that seem to wink enigmatical eyes out of the pages of an unwritten fairy book. In a world that has its share of slick painters who alternately adapt the current fashion plates to nature or trim nature to the fashion plates, Dove has said his own say. Even when the painting itself was not convincing, there was something behind it, eager, groping, at least alive. His talent is at its best, I think, in his water-color sketches, like "Barge at Evening" and "Gale." This is, one might say, his "real" medium, for the importance of a work of art is not determined by either the size of the canvas or the amount of labor expended on the job; and Dove's painting, which loses something by the elaboration of oil, is at its best in the almost instantaneous intuitions and decisions of his water-color sketches.

Sanford Ross, whose water colors are in the modern wing of the Macbeth Galleries, belongs to the school of Burchfield and Hopper; but he is something more than a gleaner after the harvest. His best pictures, in fact, are those like "Matawan, New Jersey" and "Shrewsbury Church" and "Empty House," in which he has got farthest away from his original models. With his decisive draughtsmanship, his firm color, and his more direct feeling, Mr. Ross seems to me to have the potentiality of pushing beyond the obvious impedimenta of the Brown Decades, and also beyond mere sentimentality and mere factual statement—the two bogs in which Burchfield and Hopper have tended, respectively, to get stuck.

IMPRESSIONISM AND THE CIRCUS—THREE DECADES

When the tumult and the shouting dies, it will become apparent that perhaps the most important painter in the generation immediately after Ryder was Maurice Prendergast. The exhibition at the Kraushaar Galleries is a representative one, and it shows Prendergast at the high level he so frequently achieved and so long maintained.

Technically, Prendergast's Impressionism came closer to Signac's than it did to that of the men by whom he must have been influenced. His canvases and water colors, similar in essential technique, are kaleidoscopic blobs of sun and color, which compose at a distance into serene, somewhat static masses. This man, whose physical life was as constricted and difficult as Ryder's, for he knew the harshest poverty, seemed to expand like a blossom under a summer sky, and like the proverbial sundial, he chose usually to record only the smiling hours: out of his abstemious life came a sort of Franciscan hymn to the sun and his fellow-creatures.

Prendergast was perhaps the most consummate decorative painter that America has yet produced. If his paintings have any special weakness, it is that the frieze of figures which stretches across them is repeated again and again with little alteration in the fundamental composition; and if one has any single regret about them, it is that they are not permanently attached to walls, for they lose something by their isolation in pretentious gilt frames. But the wealth and variety of Prendergast's forms within the quiet horizontal division of space he established for them are an additional mark of his resources as a decorative painter. Without doubt, Prendergast was the greatest mural painter of his generation; and the irony of it is that he never painted a wall.

While Maurice Prendergast's Impressionism was markedly a matter of temperament, one feels that at least a part of Claude Monet's Impressionism was the outcome of his technical interest in the use of divided color, and the very drive of this interest weakened the talents as a painter with which he started. Certainly, the finest canvases in the present Durand-Ruel exhibition date from the late sixties and the early seventies: the village scene in Holland, and the riverfront with a bridge on the Seine. These pictures belong to the same period as the strong and "untypical" boat on the green sea in the Havemeyer Collection at the Metropolitan Museum. In these earlier pictures, Monet had not submerged the structure of objects in the mere shimmer of color and light: a gray sky was originally as full of meaning to him as a sunny one. Contrast those pictures with the terrible vacuity of so many of his purely Impressionist canvases: in perfecting his technique, he had lost more than he had gained. The one massive triumph of his Impressionism was the decoration of the Orangerie in the Tuileries, a work bestowed on him by Clemenceau toward the end of Monet's career. As *background* those walls are superb—perhaps for the very reason that would cause them to fail as easel pictures.

John Curry's pictures of the circus at the Ferargil Galleries are the result of warm sympathy and comradely interest. The best of them—the acrobats in red tights on the high trapeze and the return of the performers down the runway—also are the most ambitious; while the simpler studies of elephants and individual characters, which lack the dynamic movement of the major canvases, lack also the expressiveness. Consciously or unconsciously, the return of the performers gains something from the slight allusion to Paolo Uccello in the treatment of the colored props of the tent; while in the high trapeze, Curry has interpreted the sense of space, movement, and the abyss below without any other aid than the lighting on the background and the movement of the figures. If the other pictures let one down a little, it is only because his best work is so much better.

The contrast between the taste of the Art Nouveau period of the nineteen-hundreds and that of today is admirably set forth in the new exhibition at the Museum of Modern Art. Here are the floral forms, the wavy lines, the billowy curves, the emphasis upon "freedom" and "growth" that marked the dominant style of the first period; alongside are the mechanical objects, neat, finely finished, mathematically ordered, of the best work today. One emphasizes the surface and the human interest, the other the structure and the mechanical function; one seeks to be distinguished and unique, the other prides itself upon its anonymity, its unobtrusiveness, its standardization—upon the fact that the thousandth piece would be exactly like the first. While the omission of examples of the work of Lalique in France and De Klerk in Holland weakens the exhibition from the standpoint of documentation, the use of the products of the Tiffany Studios as one of the earliest and most consistent expressions of L'Art Nouveau was a happy thought indeed.

Ben Benn has had a number of minor shows at the Gallery 144 West 13th Street, but the last was by far the best. This painter has a certain dash and playfulness and ease in all his work; and now that labored drawings, made with the respectable dullness of plaster casts, have become fashionable again, I would say an extra word in Ben Benn's favor. His elisions and short-cuts, his very casualness, gain by contrast with the wax-works school; "Plunge in the Sea," "The Meeting Place," "Reclining Nude" perhaps show him at his best. I have always held the heretical doctrine that *someone* should enjoy a painting; and one gathers from his canvases that this artist does, for he communicates some of his pleasure to the spectator.

RESURRECTION—AND THE YOUNGER GENERATION

By accident I stumbled the other day into the most interesting exhibition of the whole season. It was nothing less than the accumulation of art and history that began a whole generation ago at Mr. Alfred Stieglitz' "291." The floors, racks, and shelves of An American Place were quaking under the impressive mass of pictures and documents. It was a sort of Resurrection and Last Judgment on art in America during the past twenty-five years.

There was one of the very earliest Cubist montages by Picasso; there were the first Matisse drawings to come to America; a Diego Rivera of the Paris period; the mild audacities of color with which the late Alfred Maurer, the first painter to bring back modernism to America, had shocked and infuriated his contemporaries in 1908; there was a dreadful Steichen landscape which made one glad he discovered photography; some early Marsden Hartleys, full of Ryder and hope, and some late Hartleys, full of *je m'en fiche* and variegated banality; a brilliant picture in glass, "Rain," by Arthur Dove; two portraits in the best München style of a romantic-looking youth named Alfred Stieglitz; and heaps of *Camera Work*, a magazine which bears the same relation to the arts that Emerson's *Dial* does to our literature. As von Moltke said of London, "*Was für Plunder!*"

Emerging from the tombs of the storage warehouses and crowning the whole staggering pile were pictures by John Marin. They ranged from the first Whistlerian water colors, still bearing the mark of the architectural student, to the extraordinary paintings of the past twenty years—work whose wealth, variety, purity, clarity, and emotional fullness put it in a class by itself. Those Marins! There is no part of sky or sea or land that he does not seem to have revivified for us in fresh images: surely no one since Thoreau has expressed so adequately a living passion for the landscape. Were I writing a history of American civilization and did I want a symbol of the utmost economy and organization we had achieved, I should select not a Ford factory but a Marin water color. One regrets to add that this impromptu exhibition is not open to the public; and one's regrets are all the more genuine because An American Place, with its present contents, is potentially the finest small museum in America.

Perhaps the most difficult duty in art is to deal fairly with undeveloped talents, or with that vast fund of mediocrity without which talent and genius would have no foundation from which to arise. There is in America at the moment an unusual supply of *respectable* painting and sculpture, but what shall one say about it in detail? The problem has been plaguing me all year, in relation to the groups of painters I am just about to mention. Contemporary Arts has held a series of shows presenting the younger men, and some of these artists are surely worth watching—Charles Logasa, Francis Criss, Clifford Pyle, Michael Rosenthal. Criss and Logasa have, I think, gone farthest in their development; the others are still emerging from that embryonic form in which one is more conscious of the ancestral stages they are recapitulating than of the personalities that are to emerge. This is likewise true of An American Group. In the present show at the Barbizon-Plaza, Wheelock, Ribak, and Hobson Pittman seem to be the outstanding men; but all of the work is pretty competent and honest and straightforward, and in a healthy society such paintings would pass quietly into circulation without critical censorship or adulation. At the first anniversary show of the Eighth Street Gallery there is still another interesting group. Apart from Harold Weston, the most promising painter in this collection is Joseph de Martini: he has bite, a certain clumsy sincerity and directness, a grim freshness of feeling. But I could not have predicted from Marin's commonplace water colors that he would turn out the most talented and original painter of his generation; certainly I could not have done so without knowing the man. And why should I pretend to be more omniscient about the younger people today?

THE SUMMER CIRCUIT

Summer is here and the galleries are dead: it is a good time to look at art. By a mere perversity of the market place, the galleries are going at their strongest precisely during the months when people are bouncing with energy, stuffed with too much food, distracted by too many engagements, and in general too full of fresh barbarian impulses to devote themselves to the quiet visceral art of looking at pictures. Is it not silly that all our potential appreciation of art should be exhausted in the summer on our bathing beaches? Not that I have anything but praise for the priapic torsos and voluptuous bronzes one finds there; they have perhaps done more to revive sculpture in America during the past decade than anyone yet suspects. But something should be done about pictures in the summer. The propagandists and the publicists and the pedagogues are all recuperating from their winter's chores; even the College Art Association is asleep, stretched on the couch of a beauty parlor. It is a fine time to sneak into a gallery if one can find an open one.

Fortunately, the Museum of Modern Art has given us another good European exhibition, chiefly French. On the ground floor, Bonnard and Rouault have been placed in happy juxtaposition: one so tender, refined, perceptive, the other dark and mystical, like some belated Gothic glass-painter turned atheist and set loose in the twentieth century, a man close to the earth, such earth as one finds in Paris itself, moldy, full of rotting garbage, but fertile and kind. Some of the Picassos and Matisses are classic, there is a landscape by Derain with feathery trees and a sun-flecked meadow that has great distinction and beauty, and for once there are a couple of canvases by Léger that rise above his usual assertive dullness.

At the Metropolitan Museum, the somewhat pointless show on Plant-Forms in Ornament—pointless because it has too many points and so none is clearly brought out—continues through the summer. Living plants are shown here alongside the textiles and carvings and jewelry they inspired; and somehow the sight of any living thing in a museum—a custodian who can wink his eye, a spectator who can smile, or a curator, like Mr. Ivins, who can burst into epigram—is still unusual enough to be pleasant, no matter how trivial the occasion. Moreover, the sound of dripping water in the fountain in the centre of the room is just the right note on the sort of day when even the ancient cabbies at the Plaza loosen their stocks, take off their coats, and dissolve into waxen lumps.

If I were arranging a busman's holiday, I could think of nothing more pleasant than a motor trip through the Connecticut Valley, stopping only to look at the pictures. At Westport, Mr. Frederick Fairchild Sherman has a gallery with a handful of fine Ryders in it; at New Haven, there is the exceptionally fine collection of Italian Primitives—*pictures,* not merely names, some of the most exciting in the country—thanks to the perceptiveness and originality and initiative of James Jackson Jarves; at Andover, there is another good museum; and at Northampton, Ryder's "Perette" is alone worth stopping for. The final goal of such a trip might be the new frescoes that Orozco has done for Dartmouth College in the reading-room of the Baker Library.

The Dartmouth murals are, I think, the finest work Orozco has done in the North. The first movement of his symphony is the migration of the Aztecs: powerful, brutish men with faces set between a sneer and a defiance moving in a compulsive unison toward their new habitat. Drunk with the mystic terror begotten by their own fantasies, the Aztec priests sacrifice by disembowelment the young victim who represents their chief god. But Quetzalcoatl, the white god, awakens the people from their tortured sleep: his figure dominates the older gods, and, dawning over the sea, he predicts his return five hundred years later: on the very edge of the wall, where there is a break, the grim iron mask of the Spaniard, bearing a spiked cross, marches into the picture—a hint of the white man's might and his own sinister forms of barbarism and terror. The other half of the room, still to be painted, will deal with the history of the new civilization in America, its disasters and its promises.

In contrast to the New School murals, these Dartmouth frescoes have a strong rhythmic movement back and forth across the walls. The familiar reddish browns are heightened by the clear metallic blues, which are relieved, in turn, by the mystical white robes and translucent blue eyes of the new god. Orozco has not hesitated to create deep space in the foreground in order to make more overwhelming the scale of the great symbolic figures that dominate the upper levels of the wall: an excellent device which breaks the monotony of a single plane, while it avoids the ordinary system of visual perspective. In short, a grand piece of orchestration. But the point to remember is that the visual means were the outcome of the necessities of expression: it needed this mixture of history, myth, religion, prophecy, interpretation, hope, to bring into play the technical resources of the painter. The power and organization of the painting has a direct relation to the significance and dignity of the subject. Herman Melville said of literature that no great work was ever written about a flea. That holds for painting, too. The appearance of this sombre drama on the walls of Dartmouth's library at a moment when the country at large is complacently throwing art and literature and education to the pursuing wolves marks in itself an act of courage worthy of the painting that it has begotten.

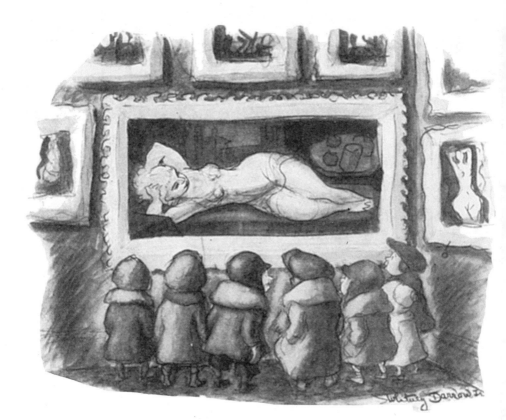

"How did you happen to find this place?"

The 1933–34 season began quietly with Mumford's overview of shows outside the metropolitan area and his ruminations on the important role of the emergent regional museums ("West, South, and across the Harlem," September 23, 1933). An October review of an American folk art exhibition at the Downtown Gallery prompted Mumford to muse on the evolution of this indigenous movement and the vagaries of its critical reception ("Miniatures and Heirlooms," October 21, 1933). He reviewed two unusual exhibitions later in the month: paintings by the critic Roger Fry at the Ehrich Galleries and paintings by the architect Le Corbusier at the John Becker Gallery ("Extramural Activities," October 28, 1933). Fry earned Mumford's derision, while Le Corbusier earned his approbation; this last response is especially noteworthy when one considers how coolly Mumford regarded the architect's buildings. Dual reviews of works by John Marin at An American Place and Edward Hopper at the Museum of Modern Art, respectively, juxtaposed an artist who experimented freely with one who pursued a solitary path ("Two Americans," November 11, 1933).

High points of the new year include reviews of Diego Rivera's murals at the New Worker's School ("Rivera and the Workers," January 13, 1934); the landmark Machine Art exhibition at the Museum of Modern Art ("Portrait of the Mechanic as a Young Man—Newcomers in Retrospect," March 31, 1934); works by Thomas Hart Benton at the Ferargil Galleries ("Benton of Missouri—A Galaxy of Goyas," April 21, 1934); and sculpture by Alexander Calder at the Pierre Matisse Gallery ("Toyshop—Reflections on Mediocrity," April 28, 1934). Mumford concluded the season with another visit to Dartmouth's Baker Memorial Library and a tempered assessment of the Museum of Modern Art's commitment to covering the contemporary scene ("Tips for Travellers—The Modern Museum," June 9, 1934).

WEST, SOUTH, AND ACROSS THE HARLEM

My notes on the art shows of the summer are a little meagre, because I am unable to report on some of the brighter but more distant points. The grand collection of paintings at the Chicago Fair—have I said this before?—is probably alone worth the trip, and among the purely record-breaking events at the Fair is the colossal mural Thomas Benton painted for the State of Indiana, which is almost as if Mr. H. L. Mencken should have been chosen to write the official history of Alabama. Benton did his work amidst the lofty protests of the exponents of Good Taste who wished the State to be represented by a native son, Mr. Eugene Savage, the Meredith Nicholson of murals; but what the upshot of this turmoil was I can judge only by photographs, and they give no foundation for gauging anything except the political results. On those terms, Benton won. And that in itself did honor to the State of Indiana.

I missed the show of modern American sculpture in Philadelphia, too, but people who have been there tell me that it was a very handsome exhibition, because it was composed in the open grounds about the Museum and profited by the parklike background. If detached sculpture belongs anywhere, it belongs in a Renaissance setting of park and garden. Indeed, this tradition is deeply embedded in American folk art. Did not the Earlier Americans let cast-iron deer browse on their lawns, and do not their descendants—equally avid for art—litter their suburban greens with painted puppies? The modern sculptor cannot look to architecture for salvation, for the forms of modern building are not those of masonry, and there is no reason they should be perverted into masonry in order to please the sculptor. The formal park remains the best habitat. Old Olmsted set an excellent precedent in the Mall in Central Park, but the lesson was spoiled a little by the divertissement of Robert Burns about to throw his pen at a sparrow and by the slightly rhetorical figure of Walter Scott being Walter Scott. With our present talent in America, we could easily compose a double row of statues that would entertain the multitude as heartily as a Bathing Beauty Parade—and why not?

The other day I wandered into the Berkshire Museum in Pittsfield in time to see a dismantled exhibition that was going out and a new one that was not yet hung on the walls. Both of them, even with their hair down and the cold cream smeared over their faces, were very attractive. The first was a show of four young moderns: Alexander Calder, George Morris, Calvert Coggeshall, and Alma Morgan; abstract, non-representational, with no hint of the Neo-Romantic reaction, these works of art simply could not have been shown in a provincial gallery ten years ago. Whether they were mad or admirable, dull or inspired, their presence here was an indication that the windows were open and a fresh breeze was stirring the must and dust.

As for the new exhibition, it represented a triumphant pillage of the garrets, drawing-rooms, and family parlors of Berkshire County. It included almost every manner of painting that America has produced or possessed, from a very adolescent Copley to a water color by John Marin, from the still unappreciated Robert Loftin Newman to a fake Whistler, denounced on the back with waspish amusement by the artist himself. The naïves and primitives in this exhibition were among the finest I have seen, and some of the mere provincial painting, forgotten by later critics not because it was bad but because it was not fashionable, was likewise excellent. (Perhaps one of the justifications of our now morbid interest in merely quaint Americana is that it has disclosed so much solid stuff too.)

The fact is that the tide has turned and the regional museums are now beginning to set the pace in showmanship and interest. In back of this revival—and the Berkshire Museum is now one of the best examples— is a new type of director. These new directors have no desire to make their museums mere repositories for sentimental bric-a-brac, mere exponents of a backwater aestheticism, thirty years behind the taste of the metropolis, nor do they seek to make their museums hopelessly minor Louvres and Metropolitans. With admirable zeal and taste, they are dismantling the bleak galleries of the past and painting them in vivid colors that reinforce the objects they hold, they are dusting off the pictures every month or two by the simple process of shoving them into the cellar and putting on a fresh exhibition, they are laying profane hands on insipid but unbreakable statuary labeled "Sappho" and "Aspasia" and renaming them, in the interests of historic accuracy, "A Victorian Lady" or "A Maiden's Prayer." In short, they are out to invent, to experiment, to stir up. The development of these healthy provincial centres of art is the best remedy I know for the functional disorder called "museum fatigue." And the museum at Pittsfield is not alone. When the new Springfield Museum of Fine Arts opens on October 7, we shall have still another reason for leaving New York to see how much better things are done on the other side of the Harlem.

MINIATURES AND HEIRLOOMS

Perhaps the best preparation for the very comprehensive exhibition of Islamic miniature painting and book illumination at the Metropolitan Museum would be the purchase of a small magnifying glass. For in the main, the great charm of these pictures resides in the delicate and subtle and dexterous detail; and no one can appreciate them who will not linger over them, and take them piece by piece, line by line, gradation by gradation. Following the intricacies of one of these brilliant little illustrations is like picking out the figure on a carpet. This sort of craftsmanship on the part of the artist, this patient attention on the part of the spectator, are different exercises from those most modern pictures demand. It is something of a game to see how much one can get through methods so foreign by means of a sensibility schooled to react to such different things.

One is furthest away, I think, from the elements of most obvious appeal: the story upon which the artist often counted for his effect, and the brilliant enamel-like clarity of color which turns the picture into a tiny crazy quilt. One is nearest to the drawings and to the magnificent arabesque of the manuscripts. There is the tiny head of a nobleman in one of the cases, beautifully placed within a rectangle; there is "Picnic in the Mountains" in a Persian miniature of the sixteenth century; there is a superb Turkish monogram; there is line upon line of splendid text, winging over the page like a flight of pheasants—these things are ultimate symbols of refinement. Tintoretto could probably have finished the wall of a palace while one of these miniature-makers was covering a space four inches by six. But the point to remember is that the very quality of the Eastern work depends upon its scale; just as the drop of dew hangs together by reason of its surface tension and would become a puddle if it were a thousand times bigger, so this art is shaped by its smallness and has its special scale of values.

The exhibition of "American Ancestors" at the Downtown Gallery (which has been extended to October 21) leaves me with that mingled feeling of respect and alarm with which such exhibitions have always left me in the past; respect for some of the art itself, and alarm for the probable effect of it upon a people so addicted to crazes over periods and antiquities as our fellow-countrymen. For once one has got over the notion that all folk art is funny, one may very easily embrace the equally fallacious belief that it is all worthy of serious attention. Passing from the contumely, neglect, disdain, and outright scorn with which we treated our folk art during the period when we were piously ransacking Europe, we are on the point of assuming a posture of dangerous adoration; meanwhile, contemporary artists of infinitely greater merit than the best of our folk painters may starve.

At all events, the possibility that our folk art would molder away under leaky attic roofs and become extinct has passed; already ladies in Oneonta and Mechanicsville and Pottstown, having heard of the fabulous prices that the neglected masterpieces of Grandfather Ebenezer are bringing, have begun to put equally dramatic values on the crayon portrait of Aunt Sally, done from a photograph in 1892; and heaven knows what will be labeled folk art and trafficked in as such before we are through with it. Look at what now passes for a hooked rug of ancient vintage on more than one New England roadside stand! So it is time to establish a few clear distinctions.

Our folk art divides roughly into three groups: first, the genuine product of unlearned artists, who had perhaps seen and heard about grander achievements, but who, from the standpoint of current tradition, were still clumsy if not illiterate; such a one is plainly Pieter Vanderlyn, grandfather of the more famous John. Like the itinerant painters a century later, Vanderlyn's portraits are done according to a useful formula: tend to first things first. The body, arms, and hands, even the posture, are all standardized as much as possible, in order to concentrate effort on the face; the simplicity, the naïveté, the honest banality of these portraits all spring out of a healthy desire to do something better than the artist is technically capable of doing. Education and improved training undermined this type of folk art by enabling the painter to do even minor things passably well; the result was a sort of diffused mediocrity which did away with the primitive's natural principle of selection.

The second kind of folk art sprang more or less directly out of practical life: the figureheads of ships, the horses and steers of weathervanes, and—to speak of something which rarely reached the level of art—the cigarstore Indian. The figurehead of Ceres in the present exhibition is an astonishing piece of carving; the folds of the drapery make one feel that the sculptor must somehow have seen fifth-century Greek sculpture and have learned a good deal about it, but the head, so far from being "ideal," looks like a cruel portrait of a living woman—a portrait whose veracity is not lessened by the fact that the painter made the lady cross-eyed. These figureheads were never sufficiently appreciated by the learned and the educated; many of them must still be rotting away in forgotten lumberyards. Here was probably the last ember of the great wood-carving tradition of the Middle Ages.

The third type of folk art was that of the amateur: the glass painting, the mourning pictures, the samplers, the moony landscapes and wooden portraits which stood among the "accomplishments" of a genteel female education. With our eyes sharpened for formal abstract merits and with no special bias in favor of realistic conventions, we can often find spots of aesthetic interest in this amateur work; but let us admit the facts—most of these pictures are copybook exercises, to be treasured only for the same reason that their makers often preserved human hair in lockets. Aesthetically speaking, by far the solidest art belongs to the second group. And so what? And so it behooves one to keep one's sense of humor, and to realize that when our immediate forefathers thought that these neglected heirlooms were funny, three-quarters of the time they were probably right.

Scattered Items: The drawings of Eilshemius, some of them dating from the eighties: tender, wistful, sometimes competent, sometimes amateurishly weak, striking minor notes of feeling without that disconcerting resemblance to the Italian restaurant painting of the nineteen-hundreds which characterizes so much of his later work. . . . Photographs of Mexico by Anton Bruehl at the Delphic Studios: straightforward competent work which nevertheless comes as an anticlimax after the magnificent stills which open "Thunder Over Mexico."

EXTRAMURAL ACTIVITIES

It is a truism to say that every good artist is an excellent critic, for criticism is an integral part of the process of creation. But when the artist is a man like Roger Fry, the critic so far overshadows the painter that one expects prodigies of either talent or self-discipline, and one makes the mistake of asking of the art all that Fry himself would demand were he not, unfortunately, also the painter. The thirty-seven paintings on show at the Ehrich Galleries do not, like the occasional paintings by Fry one has seen before, leave any loophole for escape. One rubs one's eyes as one picks one's way gingerly around the gallery, but the fault is not in one's own Vision but in Mr. Fry's Design. Two or three paintings, notably "A Stream in Suffolk," show a certain mastery of the elements, but the greater part of these canvases are blank mediocrity. Every year, Burlington House is filled with such canvases. That they should be the work of the most intelligent expositor of modern art in Great Britain is almost a joke, but a sad one.

The key to the joke lies in the fact that there is somehow a complete breach between Mr. Fry's knowledge and his painting; except for a feeble reminiscence of Cézanne or Constable, these paintings are not influenced by Mr. Fry's admirations, still less are they enriched by any depth of experience; nothing has been sharply felt, strongly organized, boldly grasped, or subtly related. Mr. Alan Clutton-Brock, who has written an introduction to the show, suggests that Mr. Fry has studied the nature of his own sensibility and set himself only such problems as fell within his special talent, but the point is that the author of "Vision and Design," the author of a supremely acute criticism of Cézanne, could not look upon these paintings without blasting them with a mere shrug of the shoulders. Alas! Fry the critic and Fry the painter have never met; or, rather, it was only by murdering the critic that the painter has had a chance to live.

The show of Le Corbusier, at the John Becker Gallery, provides the opposite kind of surprise. In architecture, Le Corbusier has been undoubtedly one of the most original minds in Europe during the last fifteen years, but it is now plain that if he had not achieved eminence in architecture, he would easily be a candidate for an almost equally high place in painting. Although a dozen years ago, with Ozenfant, he founded the school of Purism, a sort of post-Cubist return to the concrete image, divested of its Impressionist subtleties and reduced to its architectural form, he has developed since then on a line similar to Masson and Léger. But I am inclined to think that he is a stronger talent than either, for he has a better sense of structure than Masson, although he has just as brilliant a capacity for invention, and he has a far more interesting mind than Léger's. The olive green that Le Corbusier uses in one of his big canvases would never, for example, have occurred to Léger. Here is all the sensuality, the animal feeling, the gay unrestrained gestures that are eliminated in Le Corbusier's architecture; in fact, the painting and the architecture are complementary: they are both at that extreme point of sophistication which is already halfway round to the primitive once more. From the mauve nudes to the bloated horses, from the refined abstractions to the excellent portrait done on the South American journey that gave us "Précisions," Le Corbusier discloses an individuality which both belongs to a great school and transcends it. Moreover, the artist and the architect are joined like Siamese twins, and the same bloodstream feeds both of them, even when they perform different functions.

Stojana, at the Julien Levy Gallery through this Saturday, comes to us from California, ushered in by Diego Rivera and Walter Pach; and one hopes that even without such distinguished help one would have recognized the unique and interesting vision of this artist. His pictures and sculptures are a sort of epitome of his racial inheritance, which is Latin and Slav; the country of his birth, which was Africa; and the places in the Far East and our own Far West, where he has spent much of his time. The paintings show a sort of effortless eclecticism: one recognizes the deformation of a Picasso in an essentially Chinese line, the abstractions of a Klee in what might be a Japanese painting, or a touch of the Congo in a derivation from Brancusi; but the surprising thing is that these influences have been assimilated, and Stojana appears as a sort of living bridge between the art of the West and the East. The two most interesting pictures, I think, in their fusion of Eastern and Western concepts and modes of feeling are the large unfinished abstract canvas in light greens and a panel in three sections with figures. What Stojana has done in these pictures could not be accomplished by a pure effort of will, as MacDonald Wright attempted to do it in the pictures Stieglitz showed last year; it could come only by the direct absorption and the powerful digestion of the necessary experiences within the unconscious. The sort of fusion that has taken place in Stojana's consciousness may be a commonplace in the world at large a few centuries hence, unless cosmopolitanism is finally beaten by the current fashion of autarchy.

Henry Varnum Poor's quality as a painter has been too long obscured by his excellent craftsmanship in pottery. Looking at his show at the Rehn Galleries is like going out into the garden after having watched a peony gathering buds through the spring and suddenly discovering that overnight they have all burst into flower. His landscapes are excellent; he recaptures the melancholy delight of gray days, bare spring hills with their cold browns and moist grays, he demonstrates in the view over Nyack the hard excitement of bleakest winter, and in another mood he gives us the fine autumnal skies of the Upper Hudson on a day that might still be late in summer: the smell of the earth and the touch of the wind are in these pictures. His still lifes are almost equally good, and two of his figures, the "Man in the Brown Jerkin" and "The Pink Table-cloth," are richly and solidly painted, even though an arrangement of two figures in "Morning" seems too artfully artless to come off. Here is a painter whose interpretation of America gets no adventitious inter-est from mere Americana, a painter with the tang and juice of russet ap-ples in November. Men like Poor and Biddle give fresh meaning to the phrase Hudson River School.

TWO AMERICANS

Two important exhibitions can now be seen side by side; at least, they are on the same street. One is that of the John Marin water colors at An American Place; the other is that of Edward Hopper's paintings and etch-ings at the Museum of Modern Art.

Both artists are Americans, their work spans almost the same period, they have roots in the scene around us, they even share a few of the same limitations. But the work of Marin has been a continuous creative act, and each year has brought fresh surprises and pleasures; that of Hop-per has settled into a definite phase of commentary, like the prose and criticism of Mr. H. L. Mencken. Marin is a great protean spirit who stands on the level of the best of his contemporaries in any country; Hopper is a fine and capable artist whom one may characterize fairly ac-curately, and certainly without disparagement, as a second Winslow Homer.

John Marin is not a second anything. He is simply a first Marin, and in visual awareness, sensitiveness, and sheer creative volume we have not witnessed his like before in American painting; in originality, he is touched only by Ryder. Both Marin and Hopper have been interpreters of America, but while Hopper has utilized our limitations and made the most of them, Marin has demonstrated our possibilities. In literature, one would place Marin with Thoreau and Hopper with William Dean Howells. Comparisons are slippery as well as odious, but no one will mistake my meaning if he concludes that while I think Hopper a *good* painter and immediately enjoy his dust-swept colors and his inverted open-eyed sentiment, I think John Marin a great painter, an artist who has not merely recorded the common experience but added dimensions to it. Visually speaking, one may follow Hopper on the pedestrian level; following Marin, one must risk one's neck in an airplane, and abandon comfort for speed and danger and unexpected bumps and sudden splendors through a hole in the clouds.

Marin's earliest paintings in this show date back to 1908, and they strike the simple lyrical note that Maurice Prendergast, in some ways a similar talent, was to repeat with minor variations through a long and happy career. In this period, Marin produced exquisite water colors, of which "Tyrol" (1910) is one of the finest. The necessity for growth broke this small mold; by 1918, he had learned to reorganize his visual experience. Here is a sinking sun and a headland, done in a few simple contrasting masses; here is the crazy pattern of moving New York seen from the top of the Woolworth tower; here is the skyline of Manhattan, a superb interpretation in unexpected greens and yellows. The actual shapes the camera's eye would see are rearranged or refocussed; here concentrated, there suppressed. The sureness of stroke, the mastery of design, the powerful ordering of the picture into a living organism—all these elements are at the service of a fresh experience. There is no Marin style. Each picture is a new phrase in a strange language; he has an apparently inexhaustible gift for creating new symbols that match the fresh permutations of sight, feeling, attitude; and no painter, not even Picasso, works with fewer clichés. Like Whitman's traveler, Marin no sooner reaches his destination than he starts off again: So long! The perpetual freshness and vitality of Marin's painting is one of the best consolations I know for these somewhat dreary days; symbolically, he indicates one of the roads out.

Hopper began at another point. His early drawings of French types are jaunty and assured; Gavarni, Manet, possibly Degas, left their mark. This was back in 1907 or thereabouts. After that came a period of sterility, dedicated to magazine illustration; in revolt against it, he began a series of etchings, fresh, tender, not yet flattened out into a style. The girl in "Evening Wind" still has as much life as the curtain. After this first unsteady trial of his legs, Hopper began to walk steadily in a single direction; he became an interpreter of the American geography, climate, architecture. He delights in the hard lemon intensity of winter sunlight, the relentless clarity of a cirrus sky, the stiff shapes of our uglier mansard-roofed mansions; he finds value here in the very things people usually turn their eyes from. Indeed, he stares at these battered facades and crass interiors with eyes open and unabashed, till the people in them must want to pull down their shades.

So Hopper, in the work of the last decade, has caught one phase of

America, its loneliness and its visual exhilaration: the loneliness of even occupied houses, the exhilarations of even mean cottages and sordid tenements when the sun slices through the crystal air and makes one welcome the horrid form for the color it reveals under Hopper's skillful hand. An early Sunday morning's emptiness against a row of two-story, red-brick banalities, or night on the corner drugstore with a big Ex-Lax sign screaming across the front—it is precisely these "unpaintable" subjects that Hopper appropriates and triumphs over. So good is Hopper at transfiguring our visual sins and crimes into graphic virtues that he looks for nothing else. The result, for one thing, is that he has lost his hold on the human figure; the people in his restaurant interior, his hotel bedroom, his barbershop are not as real as the furniture. His limited vision is good, but it is not enough. This fixed focus and this special choice of subjects have limited the painter who was still latent in the Hopper of fifteen years ago.

Is the air too rarefied? Let us descend to the lowlands. No, to the morasses—to the fashionable portrait-painting that has been spread on the walls recently. If I have ever said any harsh things about Sargent, I take them back; for though he painted the Wyndham sisters, he also painted the unforgettable Asher Wertheimer at the Tate Gallery. His successors specialize in the weak-sister side of the tradition: plausible surfaces and cotton stuffing behind. Occasionally a superb touch, as for instance a scarlet fingernail in the De László show, and a rectangular brooch of precious stones in the much inferior show by Penrhyn Stanlaws. Take my word for both of them. There is better fun among the young. Ellertson's water colors, which were at the Delphic Studios, are betrayed by his love for the medium; he sacrifices too much to mere juiciness. Maldarelli's sculpture at the Midtown Galleries is post-Brancusi and post-Lachaise, perhaps pre-Maldarelli. But he will bear watching. So, too, will Martha Simpson and Dorothy Eisner, at the Argent Gallery; likewise Eugene Ludins, who was recently shown at Contemporary Arts.

NEW YORK UNDER GLASS

The show of paintings and prints of New York at the Whitney Museum leads one into all sorts of profound reflections—as, for example, what a big and wonderful city New York is. But to a captious Old Inhabitant, who can remember the days when Little Coney Island was at 110th Street and when there were roadhouses mid green fields on the way to

Woodlawn and Fort George, the astonishing thing is that the artists have done as well by the city as they have. They have left out much, and they have swarmed to a few good spots; but perhaps that was to be expected. Some of the pictures in this show are terrible, like Joseph Stella's razzle-dazzle-Luna-Park-Expressionist version of Our Great Metropolis; some of them are feeble and even apparently misnamed, like Du Bois' "Fifth Avenue," whose shadowy buildings resemble those on Park if they resemble anything; but the level is fairly high and the attack and interest are varied.

Roughly speaking, there are two kinds of artists in this show: those who plainly love or loathe New York, and those who have just been looking at it. I am all for the first kind, although some of the best painters belong to the second group. The lovers include, to begin with, the inimitable John Sloan, who never sacrifices the life of the streets for the sake of magnifying the buildings; he apparently cannot believe that buildings matter that much. There is McSorley's saloon once more, and I wondered again why Sloan had forgotten to paint the bowls of onions which always used to be in the middle of the tables; they went fine with the ale. But the painting that made me want to sit down on a park bench and weep over joys recollected in tranquility was Sloan's "Spring Green"; in this, he has caught the marvelous rosy-lavender sunset light that comes after rain on a spring evening in Washington Square. Robert Henri's landscapes had another virtue: one showed the East River under snow, the other derricks on the North River—scenes which will be real and importantly part of New York long after the last chromium plate has fallen off the Chrysler Tower. Among those who have caught the wild romanticism of the skyscraper, I think Bertram Hartman stands out; his pictures come off better than the late Glenn Coleman's. Hartman's best work in this show is a snow scene of Central Park. Why is it that the small casual touches of nature—like Saul Berman's "Rainy Day"—seem much more essentially New York than the buildings by themselves? Is it possible that what we really like about New York are the things we see between the crevices—the clouds between St. Patrick's steeples or a patch of water at the end of a dull street? Among the haters, Marin easily stands first. It takes intelligence to hate not too obviously; and in his water colors he gives precisely the feeling of being disrupted and shattered that New York produces when one comes in after a long sojourn in the country.

But there are good painters on the other side who merely see, not hating, not loving. O'Keeffe has caught the hard outlines of the Radiator

Building at night and Howard Cook has geometrized the skyscraper masses; Stuart Davis has treated Jefferson Market playfully, as if it suggested something exciting and unreal; and Kantor's two interpretations of Union Square, with and without roses, are very good. But what a lot of things have been missed. Leon Kroll saw, but muffed, the grand view of St. John's from Central Park; but why has no one done the vast murky masses below the Brooklyn Bridge; why has no one seen how exciting the deserted warehouses on the Brooklyn waterfront are at night; why has no one dwelt on the astonishing vistas along East Forty-second Street; and why have the great gas tanks found no adequate painter? I missed Walter Pach's excellent study of the crowd in a subway train; why have there not been more studies of New York faces? Kenneth Hayes Miller and his school have caught a few of them; but the types John Sloan painted have already changed, and no one except Thomas Benton has tried to take in the wealth and variety of the contemporary face.

While we are in the neighborhood, let us look at Aaron Goodelman's sculpture at the Eighth Street Gallery. His figures display a search among forms for something that will finally, perhaps, serve as a basis for a consistent expression: there is a torso in brass, obedient to the laws of mechanics; there is a figure, of a Negro boy with a noose around his head; close to the African wood carvings, there are two figures of a man with a wheelbarrow, in which the brute strength is overlabored, all the more because the barrow inadequately expresses resistance. But, as with so many of the young sculptors, there is an honest effort to recover that form which was lost when anatomic fidelity— *pace* Michelangelo!—disrupted the architectural and symbolic function of sculpture.

At the Reinhardt Galleries, Edward Biberman leaves one with mixed feelings. His landscapes are abstract without being empty: his paintings of the Manhattan pinnacles cut off by a high roof line, of a pier with a springboard, and of tall corn take advantage of an unexpected palette, and they have the virtues of clean statement and internal coherence. The figures seem to me a little doubtful. The large canvas of Katharine Cornell looks like an incarnation of Sin as a Baptist preacher in Evansville might conceive it: one touch more of carmine on the lips and she would be a caricature by Peggy Bacon. As to the other ladies, the dress seemed too slickly fastened to the underlying form, as though it were applied wet: the blurring, the suppression, the accentuation of the eyes, all tended to create a dollish unreality. In "Adolescent Girl," the theme itself was overstressed: the hands were too, too obviously not merely hands. One does not need a clout on the head to realize that adolescence has something to do with sex. After looking at Biberman, I wanted to eat nails, drink vinegar, and look at Dürer, Teniers, Chardin, and Eakins. Perhaps he ought to do that too.

THE FROZEN NIGHTMARES OF SEÑOR DALI

Among the many paradoxes that modern art presents is that offered by the Surréalistes. For the method of the Flemish realists, precise dry painting as labored as a miniature, has come back in association with symbols that are as far away as possible from the objects people see with their open eyes and touch. Painters like Salvador Dali, whose exhibition just closed at the Julien Levy Gallery, have paid the compliment of imitation to the old Flemish masters like Bosch. He is far closer to them than the Pre-Raphaelites were to the Italian Primitives.

By now it is plain that there are two main schools of Surréalistes. In one, the school of Miró and Masson, the painting is as mad as the symbol; in the other, that of Roy and Dali, the painting is rigorous and complete in its verisimilitude just to the extent that the artist himself is cuckoo. Both schools, fortunately, have a sense of humor, which saves them from ultimate madness, while it gives them all the licence necessary in the intermediate stages.

These pictures by Dali are as inexplicable as a dream; they may mean nothing and they may mean everything. Unlike the sentimental painters who represent dreams as misty and delicate, Dali shows them as hard and as severely realistic in surface as dreams often are. But the wild images of dreams cannot be represented in language, because they are too completely distorted and declassified: a landscape flows into a naked form which disappears into a pedestal that becomes a stream tending toward embryonic entrails. In the best of Dali's painting, such inexpressible images achieve a superficial coherence; the madness is, so to say, domesticated. Whether this is worth the effort is another question, and one not lightly to be answered.

Fortunately, Dali postpones the final reckoning by his emphasis on craftsmanship: the clarity of his color and the fineness of his execution stand him in good stead. He is most happily astonishing in pictures like that of the gigantic watches, wilted and drooping, as though time were taffy and had melted in the sun, or in that of a creature on an imaginary architectural bracket holding out a chalice-like white hand—or is it a hand-like chalice? His more deliberate humor, the satire on Böcklin's "Toteninsel"—as if that were not funny enough in itself to be set down as an unconscious precursor—or his play on Millet's "Angelus," is not quite so good. But his best pictures have the accurate nastiness of the sort of dream one can neither describe at the breakfast table nor recall, without a mild touch of disgust, during any other part of the day—which is to say, they are excellent transcriptions of a world hitherto described only in clinical analyses. This dream world was never unreal, but it was always evanescent. Dali does not permit the dream to dissolve; his pictures are, as it were, frozen nightmares. It would be intolerable to look at them if one could not also smile, and if one did not suspect that the madman who painted them is grinning at us, too—a little impudently, like a precocious boy who has mastered a new obscenity.

Mr. Eugene Higgins is an artist with large and generous intentions: he has endeavored to paint the lives of simple laboring people, miners' wives, turf-diggers in Ireland, sheepstealers, and rustics; and he has sought to invest the scenes that surround them with the poetry that is so often naturally theirs. Why is it that these pictures do not, somehow, come off? It has always been my misfortune to see Mr. Higgins' paintings in stuffy old-fashioned galleries, with dark walls and dim lights; and the cavernous gloom of the Grand Central Galleries' branch on Fifth Avenue certainly does nothing to help these pictures. But it is not this alone that makes Mr. Higgins' paintings seem old-fashioned, nor is it his romanticism or his story-telling. Ryder, who told stories, does not seem old-fashioned, and only snobs or people who are unable to throw off the effect of dead lithographs would underrate J. F. Millet as an artist—although his interests were similar to Mr. Higgins'. But somehow these paintings seem deliberately softened and poetized; even the large calm rhythms of movement, which are sometimes handled well, seem unconvincing.

After the darkened palette and the twilight tones now spreading everywhere in the neo-romantic reaction, there is a special pleasure in coming once more upon strong juicy colors and pure daylight; it is like escaping from an old-fashioned country parlor into the open air. The direct simple pleasure in bright flowers, bright landscapes, strongly modeled objects is one's first reaction to Jerome Blum's work at the Delphic Studios. His painting plainly expresses a delight in the tactile and visual quality of things; it states, with utmost clarity, this flower is red and velvety, that pear is green and metallic, yonder landscape can play a duet with a bowl of flowers in the window. These pictures have life, in the special sense that they are at the other end of theoretic, programmatic, and literary painting; the feelings and sensations they convey are those purely visual ones in which painting itself must periodically bathe and renew itself. The vigorous coherence of these landscapes and still-lifes exhibits a health and a lustiness and a firm grip that promise well for Blum's future work.

A few years ago I had the duty—doubtfully called an honor—of looking through some two or three hundred prints in order to select an estimable fifty. Among those that I recognized immediately as the work of an artist of talent were some etchings by an entirely unknown person, E. Pressoir; and though in the unaccountable accidents of the last hour's juggling Miss Pressoir's etchings were not in the final fifty, they remained vividly in my mind. I discovered the artist again at the Cronyn & Lowndes Galleries; and I stand by my original intuition. Her water colors and her prints are still in an experimental stage, but they all have that indefinable touch which merely well-groomed mediocrity never acquires. After beholding acres of academic competence during the last two months, I am grateful for these water colors and prints, as one is grateful for a witty quatrain after reading a stodgy epic in blank verse.

ACROSS THE HUDSON—JEAN LURÇAT'S DOUBLE BILL— PAINTS, PASTELS, AND THE PARTHENON

The current exhibition at the Museum of Modern Art filled me with vague foreboding. Painting and Sculpture from Sixteen American Cities: or what has regionalism done for art? One's chickens were coming home to roost. Being a good regionalist myself, I have deplored the absorption of the rest of the country by New York. Are we merely a sponge? I have scoffed at the notion that life was any sweeter in a Fifth Avenue jam than on Main Street. I have said that the moonlight on the Wabash was just the same moonlight that catches the metallic bands on the top of the Empire State. I have held that America wouldn't be worth living in until there was as much art and good conversation and intelligence in Peoria as on Park Avenue—which, after all, isn't asking much. But suppose I was wrong? Suppose people had to tread on each other's feet before they could think, or stare all day at a dirty wall before they could enjoy art? Then what?

The show at the Modern Museum still leaves me a little uncertain. It has good spots in it, promising spots: a fine seated figure by John Storrs from Chicago, and an amusing painting by Rifka Angel of a little group of female art-appreciators; a good portrait of the artist's mother by Grant Wood (with, however, a feeble background), and an interesting composition by Paul Travis of Congo Negroes. And it is good to think that people can paint in Dallas without taking to the Catacombs. But what exactly did the whole show prove or illustrate? After much pondering, I am finally pretty sure of the answer. It proved that local art committees are not to be trusted. The Detroit committee was intelligent enough to select John Carroll and the Buffalo committee to show Burchfield—who spent most of his life in Ohio—but neither pictures are really first-rate examples of the artist's work. If Chicago could show Storrs, why should Philadelphia not have shown Harold Weston, and why were Stojana and Valenti Angelo left out of the California show? (Angelo's current work at the Ferargil Galleries shows him to be a serene and well-balanced painter.) Were the provincial committees trying to show only the stay-at-homes? It is a pretty delicate question to decide when an artist belongs to a particular region. I suggest that the real test is that the region should like him and be proud of him and want him—as we in New York claim Lachaise, say, for ourselves. By this test, some of the results look pretty bad. That St. Louis should not have claimed Thomas Benton as a native son of Missouri shows a low degree of either regional or aesthetic consciousness. Indeed, a few more painters like Benton, with a similar sense of the earth and the people and local manners, would have given this show real distinction—and relieved my mind. As it is, a good regional artist will probably have a better time of it by coming to New York. Every good artist we grab from the backwoods adds to the prestige of *our* local committee; and in New York, the aunts and the other relatives are somehow canceled out.

Jean Lurçat opened in two galleries at once: a show of oils at the Valentine Gallery and one of gouaches at the Pierre Matisse Gallery. In the first show, he is obsessed by a single theme: a sailing ship going down with its sails flying. The best of these pictures is the large Battle of Trafalgar canvas; but although the canvases are called "Disaster at Sea" and "Battle of the Derelicts," one somehow doesn't feel that it is more than a toy tragedy in an imitation universe. Lurçat has also invented a race of microcephalous giantesses who, in some obscure way, seem to mark a step away from Surréalisme; but on the whole, neither the imaginative design nor the color of the oils seems as effective as his work in the smaller gouaches. The smallness of the latter seems more on a par with the themes themselves, although one of them, with human figures, might well be enlarged into a mural; then, too, the flatness of Lurçat's painting, which seems a little empty at times on a large canvas, adds to the clarity and sharpness of the smaller pictures.

I have looked several times at Jo Davidson's sculptures at the Knoedler Galleries without coming to any very positive conclusions about them. The terra-cotta polychromes of the ladies' heads are a little inane; that of Dr. Wellington Koo is the best in this medium. As for the bronzes of various men, they seem honest portraiture; but in the case of Gandhi, one doubts if Davidson has caught even the surface, to say nothing of feeling what was under the surface. I should have to look at the heads a little longer before I could be quite sure whether my lack of any strong impression at first is due to their banality or their subtlety.

The Silvermine Artists at the Montross Galleries are, as you might imagine, as strangely assorted a collection of animals as ever walked into Noah's ark, from John Vassos, whose pictures are almost a compendium of the things I dislike in art, to James Daugherty, an artist whose pictures suggest a vitality that is too often imperfectly realized in the painting. The best of his work there seemed to me a pastel of two figures, which was uncatalogued. The Gifford Beal water colors at Kraushaar's and the Childe Hassam etchings—a lifetime's work—at the Leonard Clayton Galleries are perhaps as good in their way as anything the old school can show. In back of both men are craftsmanship, a quiet response to outdoor scenes, a feeling of health. This health is never a satisfactory guarantee of art, but it is sometimes a nearly acceptable substitute. The photographs of Greece and Crete by Charles Harris Whitaker at the Architects' Emergency Show at Rockefeller Center make one wish to take a tramp steamer immediately for The Piræus. The things that Mr. Whitaker has photographed are, in a way, stereotypes of the imagination; yet so good is his photography, and so good were the original monuments themselves, that they send one into quite legitimate raptures. The Parthenon *was* a beautiful building, and it wasn't seventy stories high, either.

RIVERA AND THE WORKERS

On Fourteenth Street, which was foreordained to sordidness almost from the moment it was built, there stands near Sixth Avenue a dirty building with a black sign at the top that says New Worker's School. In the front room of the top floor of this ramshackle building there stand in specially constructed steel frames around the wall a series of murals. They are the latest paintings done by Diego Rivera and, next to the buried treasure in the Rockefeller Center, perhaps the most discussed pictures he has painted. Opinions on them are very discordant, for they reflect everything from the state of the owner's pocketbook to his love for Mexico. But the only opinion on the subject that really annoys me is that these pictures are not murals.

Let us get that little matter settled right away. A mural is merely a picture that covers a wall. It may be done in tempera, in oil, in charcoal, in glass, or in some still undiscovered medium; it may emphasize the wall or it may efface it; it may be subordinate to the architecture or it may supplant it; it may be decorative and self-effacing, or it may be dramatic and strident. In any case, if it covers most of the wall, it is a mural; and the only reasonable point of inquiry is whether it is a good picture or not. The dogma that a mural should be primarily decorative was probably invented by jealous architects, who likewise invented the other dogma that a mural must be part of the wall; both notions are nonsense. If a painter is good enough to make us forget the architect, that is just so much to his credit. Fortunately, the New Worker's School doesn't boast any "architecture," good or bad; the panels stand in an oblong room, and instead of being treated as decorations tending to create a fictitious ornateness, they should be appraised for what they actually are—illustrations, a sort of universal history of the working classes, with the emphasis upon America, by one of the most intelligent minds among our contemporaries.

Rivera's murals here are not to be taken in with a sweep of the eye. They are crowded from top to bottom like a page of Karl Marx's "Das Kapital," with a main thesis, like the bold text, in the foreground, with quotations and bibliographical references, from Jefferson, from Calhoun, from various other worthies; and then there are further footnotes and illustrations, such as Marx scatters through his work, on the upper part of the panels. Portrait and story, biography and history intermingle. The symbolisms used are direct and graphic: Hitler bawls with open mouth a small hospital scene of sterilization [sic], and wears a modest pansy in his necktie; and though one of the panels is a sort of apotheosis of Lenin, he is shown surrounded by the real men who assisted him, not by an ideal proletariat. One naturally misses the clarity and the serene large masses of Rivera's earlier murals, and one must not look for these qualities; this is something different. These murals constitute a book, crowded with Rivera's comments upon Capitalism and Communism, upon Fascism and Revolution; it is his "Comédie Humaine," or, rather, his "Inferno" and "Purgatorio" of the working classes; it is meant to challenge, disturb, exacerbate, exhort. But this is propaganda? Of course it is propaganda, like Christian art from the earliest origins onward. As painting, its weakness does not spring from the propaganda but from the lack of precision in small details of the background. But the portraiture is often excellent; and if one reads the pictures, instead of merely looking at them, one will find that Rivera accomplished what he set out to do.

The second annual exhibition of American genre paintings at the Newhouse Galleries should not be missed by anyone who is interested in American history or who wishes to see more of the work from which the lithographs of Currier & Ives, which for twenty years represented a fairly high level of genre painting, were to emerge. Very little of the painting in the present group deserves attention on aesthetic grounds. There is, however, a fine view of the Astor House and Broadway, by William Henry Bartlett, that has some of the dry precision and a little of the grace of Canaletto, and there is a small picture called "The Circus Is Coming," by C. C. Ward (1871), which in its Flemish exactness and more than photographic realism outdoes anything that Señor Dali showed us recently; within its limitations, it is almost perfect. One wishes that the Newhouse Galleries had found more vulgar paintings like the "Sporting Club," by P. Miartani, which seems to date from the seventies; the tough mugg waiting for his turn in the ring seems carefully observed. But though it is worth while to exhume and decently preserve these memorials of our buried past, I trust that the interest will not lead to a premature neglect of our far more talented contemporaries. The contemporary genre painting of Frank di Gioia at the Marie Harriman Gallery reflected the tradition of Sloan, with a special touch of lightness and delicacy that is di Gioia's own. These tempera drawings are as entertaining a collection as I have seen this season; di Gioia was brought up on the East Side, knows his people well, and caricatures them tenderly in the shops and the markets, entering church and congregating in a vocal furor in the parks. Work of this sort deserves a wider circulation; one wishes it could be reproduced in a portfolio.

Whether one understands Miró or not, he can paint a handsome canvas; his new show at the Pierre Matisse Gallery shows this, perhaps more clearly than before. He knows how to create life in lifeless objects and to suggest blood in fleshless abstractions; one picture of a red, parrotlike almost-gentleman pursuing a white-shift-of-perhaps-underwear is as amusing as it is tantalizing. Even in the larger, and to me usually less interesting, canvases in which the chief symbols look like billies and puppy biscuits, the background has a charm that only an adept painter could give it. His smaller canvases tend to be richer in color and, in addition to being named, are usually more intelligible. Thus my companion immediately said "Antony and Cleopatra" when she beheld one of them; it turned out that Miró had called it "Les Amoureux." And similarly, "Femme en Extase" is easy to read. Nevertheless, as pure painting, the most satisfactory canvases seemed No. 4 and No. 5, which do not depend for their success on their allusions and suggestions. In general, these paintings are done with a light touch and a firm hand; and, unlike the products of Paris' Peck's Bad Boys, they do not depend upon the 'orrors for their effects.

PORTRAIT OF THE MECHANIC AS A YOUNG MAN— NEWCOMERS IN RETROSPECT

No old Stuyvesant boy can be turned loose in the exhibition of Machine Art at the Modern Museum without his conjuring up memories of a New York childhood. At the first sight of the circular saw at the entrance, I smelled the pungent, charred sawdust of the old shops, and I wandered in a delighted daze through the fairyland of mechanics that enveloped my adolescence. Once upon a time, my life was bounded by Eimer & Amend on the north and Hammacher Schlemmer on the south. I fell in love with a young lady and a new type of variable condenser at precisely the same moment, and made the variable condenser as a solace for the loss of the young lady. When an old modelmaker near Seventh Avenue gave me a battered Wimshurst machine, a box of old binding posts, and a half-inch spark coil, I felt as Leonardo must have felt before he assembled his flying machine. And I was no more daunted than he by the fact that none of the contraptions worked. I have choked with emotion at the sight of a new electrode standard, designed without the usual knurls and curlicues, as I took it out of the lathe, and the faint reek of a coal fire in a forge brings back as tender memories as any perfume bottle. That was New York!

The emotions awakened by machines and machine-made objects are, perhaps, a little elementary, but they are the stuff out of which complexer types of art are made. The machine has become a second nature to all of us, whether or not we are ex-Stuyvesant boys, and it lies at the basis of many of our reactions to modern art, even as nature itself lay at the bottom of Renaissance painting. If you like ball bearings and springs, you are prepared for Brancusi, Moholy-Nagy, Jacques Villon, and Kandinsky; or, if you like these artists, you are prepared for Machine Art. Perhaps the very best example of Machine Art is the exhibition as a whole; complex in design, it is extremely simple in effect. Mr. Philip Johnson has used color, as in the pinks and blues at the entrance; texture and light, as in the employment of black velvet to show off polished steel and glass; and texture and color and pattern, as in the use of cedar shelving. The total result shows how little need there is to associate monotony with the most standardized mechanical forms.

For the greater part, the objects shown are exemplary. When one compares an old-fashioned kettle with the handsome and correctly designed modern one done by Lurelle Guild, or an old-fashioned perfume bottle with those now turned out, one is conscious of a great advance. Perhaps the most disappointing instruments are the clocks and watches, for clocks that do not show divisions for the minutes and that do not point to them accurately are just the opposite of instruments of precision. I regretted to see that an old Stuyvesant boy (who is otherwise a credit to his school) designed one of them. One of the other interesting points is that some of the best work was in traditional departments of technics. Not alone the Early American dessert spoons and forks but the greater part of the glassware were products of handicraft. They prove that good Machine Art is the outcome of a special habit of mind rather than a purely automatic result of using mechanical instruments.

Contemporary Arts, during the past three years, has been giving one-man shows to a series of newcomers. Now, in a retrospective show, which closes on March 31st, the various painters who have been sponsored may be seen side by side. With one exception—Francis Criss—most of the best people brought out belong to the Neo-Romantic school. The most important of these is, I think, Charles Logasa; he has a good landscape, "New England Church," in this exhibition, and he has done some interesting portraits. He paints with a dark, bituminous palette, a heavy impasto and oily surface that sometimes, it seems to me, get in the way of what he is trying to express. Elliot Orr, another Romantic, is closer to Ryder. With him I would put Martha Simpson, who has a fine pastel of a mother and child at the present show. At the other extreme at almost every point is a painter of undoubted talent—Francis Criss: instead of darkness, there is light; instead of confusion, there is clarity; instead of brooding and yearning, there is the crisp vision of midday, with the colors laid on thin, not a brush stroke showing. One or two other members of this group have promise, but they have not carried their work far enough.

The series of water colors Jacob Getlar Smith is showing through this Saturday at the galleries of An American Group is a great advance over the oils he showed last year. There is a decisiveness and an economy in them, a freshness of feeling, a competence in taking hold of his subject and making something out of it by sheer good painting, as in "Clouds Over Summer Meadows," and a very fine direct sense of the landscape, as in "Christmas Thaw" and "Golden Hills." These pictures are as American as goldenrod, without resort to any of the pat symbols of Americana.

Still another water-colorist merits more than a passing attention— Nathaniel Dirk. His work, lately at the Eighth Street Gallery, exhibits a growing sureness of color and a happy animation of design. The rectangular patterns of the water in one of his paintings form a type of composition of which Marin, in our day, is the master. In his new oils, Dirk has been more " experimental." His arbitrary selection of color and his emphasis of pattern do not always come off, but one of them, a still-life with a fish, is up to the best of his water colors.

At the Downtown Gallery, Joseph Pollet shows a few modest landscapes and figures, and three canvases of composers—Mozart, Bach, and Beethoven—done on a colossal scale, in the fashion of the historic painters of the first half of the nineteenth century. The comparison, alas, is too close for comfort on every point; it would take genius of the very first order to escape the banal effects of this association. Indeed, at first glance, one is tempted to look upon Pollet's canvases as caricatures of the Victorian effort to carry on the "grand style." But there is no satiric intention behind these large canvases. They are just large canvases.

CIRCUS TIME—STATUES AND PRINTS—AMERICANA

Art has been full of mysteries during the past week or two. There was the mystery as to why the Whitney Museum suddenly closed the day before the exhibition of Philadelphia artists was supposed to go on. The dark hint that some person or persons unknown might assault the pictures surely gives more credit to the stimulating effect of the Pennsylvania school of painting than it deserves at the moment. One sympathizes with the scab taxi-driver who had his car loaded with stones and said the strike was O.K. by him because it broke d' monotony. Bad art might profit by a little mayhem. (This is not to be taken as a solicitation in states where mayhem is prohibited.)

Then there was the perennial mystery as to why the National Academy opened its doors again for a spring exhibition. I have seen that same show, man and boy, nigh onto twenty times, and as a result I no longer believe in the resurrection of the dead. The Academy, of course, has no monopoly on dullness, but it has some of the best vintages in its cave. Then there was the mystery of the golden slippers that heeled their way into the Ferargil Gallery, and the mystery of the whole stableful of horsy prints that found a sumptuous home at Brooks Brothers. Putting all these signs together, one can be sure of only one thing: the Circus is here.

At a long distance from the Circus stands the group of sculptures that the Weyhe Gallery now has on. The show includes Barlach, Lehmbruck, Kolbe, Mataré, and Sintenis. Ernst Barlach is probably the most important sculptor in present-day Germany. Certainly his work is closest to that of the great northern woodcarving tradition, and while his forms are not archaic or sentimental, there is something strong and spare and austere, in both silhouette and mass, that reminds one of the great churches of Lübeck. His war memorial at Hamburg is one of the few pieces of monumental art which do not simply add to the disasters of the occasion they commemorate.

The present show has one of Barlach's finest woodcarvings, that of a peasant woman, with a slow-witted face, and a body whose animation seems to increase as it approaches the earth. The curve of the belly beneath the folded arms could not be improved. The elementary planes that define the "Avenger" have the same simplicity as the wood carving, although the figure is cast in bronze. Here the main interest is not in the quiet sense of life but in movement as the embodiment of an idea. Barlach's humanity, his humor, his masculinity, and his early-medieval sense of freedom have all, doubtless, conspired to make him anathema to a large camp of Nazis. But one does not need that extra reason for liking his work. The roots of his Germanism are so deep that they become part of the heritage of the world; one need be neither Protestant, Christian, nor North German to embrace his art.

At another pole of sensibility and feeling are the sculptures of Lehmbruck. His work has not been widely shown in America and Mr. Weyhe has some of the very best examples of it. The statues in the present exhibition are particularly interesting because they range from the tender, quietly modelled, almost Maillol-like head and trunk of a girl, a superb piece of work that belongs to his early period, to the mournful, elongated head of a mother with a ghostly starved baby at her breast, which he did toward the end of the war, before he committed suicide.

As for the other sculptors, I confess to a sentimental liking for both Renée Sintenis's own head and the little figurines of calves and colts that she does so admirably; and the drawings and prints of Kolbe and Mataré, like those of Sintenis, share the interest with their sculptures.

At the same time, the Weyhe Gallery is showing fifty modern prints, which cover "almost everything except etchings of dogs, ducks, patriarchs, and picturesque foreign architecture." There is much good work, a few new artists from the South and the West, and three or four things that stood out specially for me—Raphael Soyer's "Girl at Table," Doris Rosenthal's "Nude on a Sofa," John Marin's "Sailboat," and Adolf Dehn's "Waves," from which anyone who wishes is welcome to conclude that I like tables, sofas, and the wild waves. The lithographs are not as exciting this year as in the past. One of the reasons for this, perhaps, is that some of the best printmakers have taken to using the lithograph pencil as if it were a spray brush, eliminating the pencil stroke entirely and shading and blurring all the planes and defining lines into velvety surfaces. It is a treacherous trick, and it is capable of taking the edge off the firmest draughtsmanship.

While I am playing the aged uncle, let me say a word about Sanford Ross's show at the Reinhardt Galleries. Following hard on the trail of Burchfield and Hopper, he has acquired the same sort of hardboiled aplomb in digesting, with a positively goatlike appetite, the tin cans and rubbish and concrete roads of the more humanized parts of the American landscape. So far good, but not so good. For one thing, his color is still bleak, and there is nothing to show that he can handle more complex harmonies. His compositions are uncomfortably close to photography. His range is still narrow. Some of the themes within his range are excellently handled, and one of his landscapes at the municipal art show is very fine; but unless he departs from his present path, he is bound to get caught as badly as Burchfield and Hopper have been by their own aptitude for specialization.

The show of the late George Luks's paintings and drawings, which will be at the Rehn Gallery through April 7, troubled me. He was patently a likable man, and his earlier work was done with joy and gusto. But he seems to have undergone the same degeneration that overtook Robert Henri, and his later work—except for a few water colors—was pretty empty and academic. Even the earlier paintings, like the black-and-white series of barrooms of the nineteen-hundreds, seemed thinner than one had hoped they would be: they almost needed Benjamin de Casseres's dreadful wisecracks to supply some raw color that was missing in the drawing itself. What was lacking in Luks, in Henri, in Bellows? Why did their growth take place in reverse? Will someone page Mr. Van Wyck Brooks?

MEMORIALS AND MODERNS

Two memorial exhibitions are on at the moment, and alas! it is impossible to work up very much excitement about either. The minor painters who did most of their work between 1880 and 1910 were amiable but undistinguished. Charles H. Davis, whose exhibition is now at the Macbeth Gallery, struck a pretty fair average among the academicians. Little of his painting is downright bad. In some of his canvases, as "In Early May," he captured the atmosphere of an Eastern spring with considerable subtlety and feeling. But it was with him somewhat the way it was with his senior, Inness, in all but the latter's best work: his painting did not bite, and for all his habit of composing in the studio, his imagination remained limited. When we are as far away from the minor moderns of our own generation as we are from those of the past, we will observe that they have just the opposite failing. They rely upon the imagination—usually that of someone else like Cézanne—without ever having successfully looked at anything.

Elliot Daingerfield's full-dress show at the Grand Central Art Galleries was, I confess, an even greater disappointment than that of Davis. Daingerfield was one of the deliberately noble painters of his period. When he painted a landscape, he went to the Grand Canyon or sought to rob the sunset of its glory. When he did a religious theme, he turned to the Italian masters. His palette was sometimes brilliant, but somehow never very convincing. He was at his best when he followed closest to

Ryder, as in the marine at the Metropolitan Museum and in the painting "Midnight Moon" at the present exhibition—or perhaps he merely seems at his best when he reminds one of something greater. Much as one may respect the high-mindedness and decency of men like Davis and Daingerfield, one cannot pretend that they have much to give us today. In recovering our buried past, they are not among the treasures.

"Manhattan Patterns" is what Charles G. Shaw has called his exhibition, which is at the Valentine Gallery through this Saturday. That is exactly what these pictures are. Shaw has taken the setback towers of the city and emphasized their two-dimensional quality; he has treated them as if they were cut out of cardboard by a lot of ingenious children designing scenery for a puppet show. There is much to be said for this treatment, but perhaps his best pictures are those done on the street level, where he has added a touch of the third dimension.

The show of new members at the galleries of An American Group is not as distinguished as the last group show was. But there are some interesting things in it: "Palm Trees," by Yack Pell; a mysterious fence and a dark, suicidal-looking house, by Paul Mommer; a crisp study of pomegranates, by Helen McAuslan; and a girl tying a sash, by Isami Doi.

The Industrial Arts Exposition in the R.C.A. Building must face comparison with the Machine Arts show at the Modern Museum and with the Fashion Group show on one of the lower floors of the same building. For me, it wins by a good furlong over the Fashion Group show because it contains less cellophane. In presentation, it is a mere also-ran alongside the Modern Museum show, for the background is not so carefully worked out, nor were the objects themselves selected with anything like a comparable rigor of taste. But just for this reason the Industrial Arts Exposition gives one a representative cross-section of the arts today, and the result is not as hopeless as you might imagine.

The pre-fabricated weekend house at the show is done in asbestos blocks, a material whose possibilities Mr. Lee Simonson explored in a Macy show three or four years ago. The metal joints and cornices are tasteless, but the house as a whole is worked out well. There are two excellent pieces of furniture attached to it. One is a wooden-slat lounging chair on a delicate metal frame, for outdoors; it has a leather cushion at just the right set for the head. And there is a copper lampstand, with a shade that folds back completely for indirect lighting, by K. Versen. Except for its lack of vertical adjustment, the stand seemed to me perfect. The Pierce Foundation kitchen unit is perhaps too compact even for weekend use—cooking on two burners saves equipment but wastes time—but the bedroom is very neat.

In general furniture design, the best work was that of Gilbert Rohde. His nursery for children is a straightforward and intelligent application of the unit principle, and it was free from the singular adult hallucination that children like pictures of Mother Goose and Red Riding Hood on their furniture. Rohde is one of the few designers who realize that "modern" is something that you are, not a theatrical effect you try to achieve. His adaptation of the morris chair to metal showed the same intelligence. Then I must say a good word for Russel Wright; his two radio sets are the best I have so far seen. Wright has a good feeling for materials, particularly for wood, and if this sometimes leads him into extravagance—as in using aluminum containers instead of glass for groceries—he avoids the sordid little advertising marks of the "modernique."

Egmont Arens's later designs for A. & P. packages are even better than his original efforts with canned salmon; the coffee bags, and the cans for applesauce and cocoa, are particularly good. The low-water mark in design was struck by Mr. W. D. Teague, who has doubtless many good things to his credit, but what he has done to such fine modern objects as the camera and the thermometer and the barometer scarcely bears thinking about. To say that he has spoiled them aesthetically puts it mildly; they *were* modern until he tried to make them so. As for the show as a whole, one notes, with a robust sigh of relief, that the dreadful Victorian note that was sounded at the Metropolitan Museum a couple of years ago has died out. Even the Empire twist of the Macy exhibition last fall is missing. The stage is set for decent, straightforward design. The one thing that spoils our industrial art at present is the notion that modern decoration has anything to do with ornament. Ornament does not belong to us; positive modern design is dramatic, but not ornamental. Every attempt at ornament in the present show underlined this. Even Ruth Reeves's superb designs for the Hudson River prints were valid as individual *pictures,* rather than as ornament: the part was better than the whole. Ornament is dead. So, thank Heaven, is Victoria.

BENTON OF MISSOURI—A GALAXY OF GOYAS

The work of Thomas H. Benton, at the Ferargil Galleries through this Saturday, has rarely been appreciated for its own values—perhaps not even by the painter himself. Benton's reputation rests chiefly on his murals at the New School, the Whitney Museum, and the World's Fair. After crying for a decade for a wall big enough to carry the historical epic he desired to paint, fate ironically granted his request. Like most such fulfillments, there was a catch in it, for the entire work had to be finished in two months. His preliminary sketches for this Indiana mural are now on view: the abstract plan, the photographs of the clay models in which he established the relations of his masses, and his preliminary sketch. The whole feat was a marvel of intellectual organization, and there are few painters with either the moral decision or the stamina to carry through such a job. The one element missing was time: time with its new experiences, its happy accidents, its fresh growths, its reconsiderations. I have still to see the finished work, and the sketches and photographs give only a clue to the process.

Benton appears to most people, possibly even to himself, as a graphic historian and illustrator; hence his deliberate use of anecdote, and a positive desire to shock by emphasizing the literary content of his paintings. But the fact is that he is a poet, and about some of his best painting there are a poignancy and sweetness that fly in the face of the literary content of the picture. Take the moonlit landscape with a girl lying prone in the foreground and a black figure stealing into a car in the middle distance. The patent content might come from a tabloid headline about a wild party and a midnight rape; the real content, however, is the virginal moon, the mysterious landscape, and the form of the girl. It would be a good picture even if the girl had not been raped; in fact, it might have been a better one. Benton is no more a realist than Vachel Lindsay was: he is wild, high-spirited, melodramatic, as fiery and abandoned as a country fiddler whose realism is only the touch of cow dung clinging to his shoes. The free, lyrical design of "The Jealous Lover" is matched by the luminous colors and the tender romanticism of "Homestead" and "Lonesome Road." In these pictures one sees how little need his paintings have for any other content than the direct emotional one. Similarly, in the handsome little picture he mockingly labels "Twelve Planes and a Silver Egg," one sees what a superb painter of abstractions this hater of abstraction is. In some degree, Benton has hidden his gifts. Assuming a belligerent attitude toward the fashions and frauds of his contemporaries, he has also carried over a distrust for the living elements in our culture that are neither fraudulent nor fashionable. If I am not mistaken, this has hindered his growth. Like Mark Twain, another son of Missouri, he has remained defensively lowbrow. Like Mark Twain, too, he is still a little ashamed of tearing loose, because the boys might laugh.

The Goyas in America are so well scattered that the Knoedler show, which brings together many of the portraits, does a valuable job. (It, too, closes this Saturday.) There were two elements in the eighteenth century, the wild uprising of the spirit of man, symbolized by Rousseau, and the cynical, worldly, polished society of fashion and letters, against which the revolt was directed. Goya inherited both moods in equal measure; in a sense, he carried the courtly art of Velásquez and the solitary democratic art of Rembrandt, his two masters, to their final conclusion. The present exhibition emphasizes his courtly side: the best of the adult portraits were those of Señora Sabasa Garcia, with its touch of El Greco, and that of Isidro Gonzales; but none of them seem to touch the portrait of his wife in the Prado. The famous little boy with his animals, Don Manuel Osorio, is here; perhaps Goya, who was a father many times over, was—like Diego Rivera—at his best with children. But the greatness of Goya does not lie here; what one finds in the portraits is the greatness of his tradition. For the man himself, one must turn to the magnificent horrors of the "Caprices" and "Disasters of the War."

Looking back over the shows of interest recently, I find I have said nothing about the water colors of John Whorf, lately at the Milch Galleries. They are perhaps the finest example of current realism one can find anywhere, not excepting the water colors of Hopper. While Whorf has mastered all of Sargent's and Homer's lessons, he is most interesting in the paintings where he has gone beyond them and has begun to approach his own idiom. The painting is remarkable as clean craftsmanship.

One may say the same, incidentally, about Katherine Schmidt's paintings at the Downtown Gallery; the still-lifes with the Chinese tigers in porcelain are consummately done. Nagai's gouaches at the A.C.A. Gallery were worth more than a passing glance; so, too, were Renee Lahm's oils at Gallery 144 West 13th Street; and Joseph Solman, a very young newcomer at Contemporary Arts, has at least—I trust the word does not seem cowardly—promise.

The annual show of the ancient and honorable Society of Independent Artists (not to be confused with the Salons of America) is now on again at the Grand Central Palace (not to be confused with Rockefeller Center). The Independents are always worth the price of admission, and unless I am mistaken, the show this year is worth the price of two admissions. What has given it this extra touch of vitality is more than five minutes' careful reflection enables me to fathom. Perhaps it is merely the fact that there is an unusual amount of good painting. There are, indeed, more nudes than usual, possibly because there are more free models lying around in convenient meadows; but most of these studies are low in aesthetic vitality, and must be put in the class of sunsets and spring blossoms, subjects that only masters can touch. No, the strength of the Independents lies in another place: partly in the healthy indignation and resentment that stir in the proletarian sections, and partly in the work of some of the newer painters who are reënforcing the Old Guard—Minna Citron, David Dovgard, Dorothy Eaton, Charles Logasa, and a Californian painter of landscape, Warren Newcombe. The best of the proletarian paintings were, it seemed to me, Iskantor's "After a Life of Misery" and "The Trial of the Bread Thieves." Good and bad, effective and amateurish, profound and silly, the total effect is that of an April day. Healthy people usually enjoy April.

TOYSHOP—REFLECTIONS ON MEDIOCRITY

A few years ago Ralph Steiner showed some moving pictures of the elemental parts of machines in action. Wheels rotated, pistons slid, eccentrics turned and shoved, screws wormed, and an intelligent audience had a very good time at what was in fact, though not in effect, a scientific demonstration of the various types of motion and transmission. Some of this naïve pleasure in things that turn and swing and twist and jiggle has gone into Alexander Calder's exhibition of mobile sculpture at the Matisse Gallery.

In general, Calder makes two types of apparatus. In one, he balances the moving parts on a pivot against a heavyweight arm, and by giving the weight a push one imparts motion to the free-hanging parts, and they continue in motion for a long time. In the other, he more elaborately rigs up a toy motor and pulleys and provides for both continuous and discontinuous motion. Straight lines, helices, red and black circles are the chief formal ingredients of the latter type, while the simpler mobiles are sometimes wiry and wavy, like the magnified feelers of gargantuan insects. And what on earth, you ask, has this to do with sculpture?

Well, one of the leading experimenters in this type of art, Moholy-Nagy, has written books to prove that the static sculpture of the past no longer expresses our age and that our present concepts of form must be worked out by the use of lighter metallic elements which will define the mass by the passage of a line or a surface through space. If you take any comfort in that sort of explanation, it may be a help at the Calder show. There is, however, a less sublime way of approaching this sort of crafts-manship, and I suspect that Calder himself follows it. His talents have always been ingenious and playful. His wire figures and animals of the static period did not require any elaborate philosophical justification be-fore one could enjoy them; they were just amusing.

That is equally true of the sort of purist mechanical toyshop he erected at the Matisse Gallery. If this were really a mighty intellectual attempt to abstract and formalize the spatial relations or the mechanical concepts of a world that has become vaguely emotional over the more incompre-hensible parts of Einstein, if these mobiles were to be taken *au grand sérieux,* one would have to quarrel with their happy amateurishness. To tell the truth, they lack mechanical rigor and perfection. But the fact is that Calder is a sort of abstractionist Joe Cook, and he preaches a lesson unlike the scientific philosopher's—not the importance of being earnest, but the blessedness of remaining young.

The show of Early American Folk Art that has been on view at the Na-tional Committee on Folk Arts' headquarters makes one reflect a little on what a long way we have to go before we learn to fill up our leisure— or unemployment—as happily as our ancestors did. These sad reflec-tions were deepened when one contemplated the exhibition at the Met-ropolitan Museum of fine and applied art done in the adult art schools in New York City. Those drawings from life and nature, which consti-tute about ninety-five per cent of what is called art education in our schools, have no meaning whatever in themselves—not even as efforts at self-expression. The total effect of this kind of art instruction is the mass production of minor academicians. Contrast this with the art that was being produced in every little village in this country before 1875 by the people who were carving decoys, cutting out weathervanes, making cloth, or piecing together quilts. There was some relation then between capacity and achievement, and the arts themselves were of such a nature that when a person of genius appeared, like the inspired designer or de-signers who did the coverlet hanging in the secretary's room at the Na-tional Committee on Folk Arts, she accomplished something superior to almost all the paintings of the period, even when judged on the purest aesthetic grounds. Our adult schools of painting, if they are not to be-come a menace to genuine art, must bring their adults up to the level of the best children's schools in the country. They should seek to turn out healthy amateurs, not tenth-rate professionals. What they need both in craftwork and in painting is a touch of childhood. Otherwise our adult art education will be another name for organized boredom, led by the bigger and better bores.

And speaking of the mediocre, the Brooklyn Museum celebrated its centenary with one of the most dreary collections of "competent" contemporary painting I have seen this season; one doesn't have to go further than the Grand Central Terminal to see such painting any day in the week. They might have cooked up something heartier for a centenary exhibition of art; indeed, they did a little better by their historic display of Brooklyn. (The one striking painting in the show, incidentally, was by Eugene Higgins.)

The Contempora New Art Circle's show (closing this Saturday) has as fine specimens of Beckmann as we have seen in America. With Hofer, he will probably wear as well as any of the contemporary Germans.

Virginia Berresford's show at the Montross Gallery, which closes on the same day, is hard to describe. One particular mood of nature, a tropical sky and sea with a tornado brewing, she has captured more than once; but at times she is overpowered by her subject, as in her desert landscapes, and at times she is overpowered by her method, as in the weakly Japanese water colors. But her skyscraper has merit, and every now and then a drawing of real distinction makes one look forward to her further development.

TIPS FOR TRAVELLERS—THE MODERN MUSEUM

Before the summer shows in Manhattan claim your attention, it might be a good notion to jot down the main events out of town. Whether the International Art show in Venice is worth dropping into, I have not the faintest notion. From the fact that the American exhibit was drawn from the Whitney Museum, I should tentatively say "Maybe." If you are near Colmar, in Alsace, you must not forget to see the Grünewalds there; you have doubtless always meant to. Despite the Nazis, I understand, some of the public museums in Germany still show degrading, meaningless, defeatist, foreign, non-Aryan art. You will probably enjoy it all the more keenly in such a hostile setting. (In certain circumstances, a bowl of fruit by Braque might feel like the Statue of Liberty.)

The Van Goghs at The Hague and Amsterdam should give you an extra excuse, if you need it, to visit Holland. The truth is that those fine lowlands are sprinkled with dark-haired, long-limbed girls and passionate, inarticulate men like Mynheer Peeperkorn in Mann's "The Magic Mountain." A few days in Amsterdam help one appreciate Van Gogh.

As for the shows nearer home, the museums at Hartford, Springfield, Pittsfield, Northampton, Andover, and Worcester are likely to have something to relieve a dull hour or point up a bright one. Even if no special shows are on, the new interiors of both the Springfield Museum and the Wadsworth Atheneum at Hartford are worth a look. (Museums, even modern ones, retain some of the cool, dusty tranquillity of the tomb. Artificial ventilation cannot be compared with marble slabs for taking the edge off a summer's day.) Frankly, the little art colony shows, from Lyme to Ogunquit, from Woodstock to Westport, usually do not warrant a detour unless you are in a sociable mood. Occasionally you may be pleasantly surprised. For those who like folk art, the New Bedford whaling museum has some bone jagging-wheels, shaped like gulls, that surpass much of the stuff in recent exhibitions.

The one work of contemporary art worth making a special pilgrimage to is, I think, the series of Orozco murals at the Baker Memorial Library in Hanover, New Hampshire. Aesthetically, it is a superb orchestration of plastic forms and color; intellectually, it is one of the most penetrating criticisms of ancient and modern civilizations that anyone has made; the stillbirth of higher education is alone worth the visit. No other painting of the same range and intensity and vitality, with the same emotional drive and intellectual force, has yet appeared on this heroic scale north of the Rio Grande. Incidentally, the grand figure of Christ, who has chopped down his own cross, a fresco which was destroyed in Mexico, reappears as the climax of these new murals. As with many great works of art, there are occasional weak spots of painting, but the whole is magnificent. Do not forget to see the first mural Orozco did at Dartmouth, to demonstrate the fresco process for the art students. While it preceded the other murals and is not organically connected with them, it forms a sort of final chord, carrying one into the second movement of a symphony which Orozco will still create, perhaps, on some other wall.

With the Lizzie Bliss collection now permanently installed in the Museum of Modern Art, this gallery has achieved the outward sign of stability and continuity. There are a few duds in the collection, notably a painting by Arthur B. Davies, but one must remember that it was owing to Miss Bliss's admiration for this American artist that she went on to her Cézannes. The Cézanne pictures, oils, water colors, and lithographs form the foundation of the collection, and it could have no solider bottom. Chicago is richer in Renoirs and the Barnes Foundation, according to rumor, has a finer lot of Matisses, but Cézanne is Cézanne. One would have to travel far to find a better representation.

Is it not time that some friendly eye cast up accounts with the Museum, now that its existence seems assured enough to satisfy Miss Bliss's executors? As one who has never received anything but kindness from the Museum, I feel that the lot of uttering harsh words apparently falls to me.

So far, in the realm of painting, the Modern Museum has done for modern art what the older museums have done for historic art; its best efforts have been in the intelligent presentation of well-established judgments: the shows of the early French moderns, of the German moderns, and of the older Americans—Eakins, Ryder, and Homer. The more positive sort of pioneering has been done in departments other than painting. The exhibition of modern architecture, of machine art, and of the art of the theatre has been exemplary both in matter and presentation. Taken together, these are not small achievements, but they do not completely overbalance the errors and omissions, some trivial, some colossal.

The hasty mural show, for one thing, was an error; the neglecting to follow up Rivera with Orozco was another. The pushing forward of Maurice Sterne and Edward Hopper, and the failure to single out John Marin for the honor of a contemporary one-man show, verge on the ridiculous; it is the same kind of provincialism as Mr. Craven's putting Barnard and Epstein above Maillol, Despiau, Lehmbruck, and Barlach. When the definitive Picasso show came to America, it was the Wadsworth Atheneum, not the Museum of Modern Art, that put it on view. As for the ballyhoo that attended the odyssey of Whistler's "Mother," it had less to do with modern art than a circus parade, and was almost too raw to be funny. (It deserved the postage stamp, with the bowl of flowers thrown in to please the florists' associations, that it finally got as reward.) Add to these lesser and greater enormities the fact that the Museum has not yet, in four years, given a photograph show—this with the world's greatest living photographer established on the same street as the Museum.

In short, except in architecture and the industrial arts, the Museum has not yet given a clear lead. In its presentation of contemporary painting, it has been neither catholic nor impeccably restricted. To an outsider, its judgments are unaccountable except on the purely hypothetical ground that its decisions have been warped by the small considerations of patronage and politics. The result is that the Modern Museum has been drifting into the same sort of discreetly ambiguous attitude toward contemporary work that has been taken by the Metropolitan Museum. Since the Modern Museum was conceived originally in order to perform a function that the Metropolitan refused to assume, it has in painting lost much of its reason for existence. That is a pretty high price to pay for success. Or isn't it?

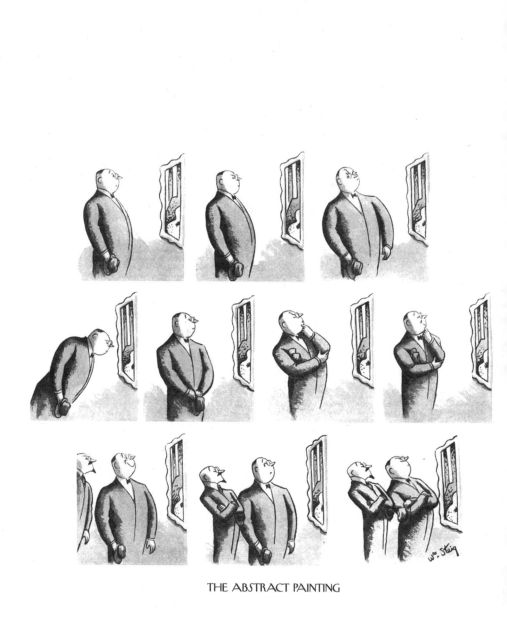

THE ABSTRACT PAINTING

Mumford began his third season on a generally light note, as he hopped from the usual galleries and museums to the Washington Square outdoor art show. His mixed assessment of George Platt Lynes's photographs at the Julien Levy Gallery is especially notable in that Mumford was himself one of the portrait subjects on exhibit ("A Catalogue and Homer," October 20, 1934; see frontispiece to this volume). In November, Mumford wrote eloquent, posthumous appraisals of two American artists, Alfred Maurer (1868–1932) and George Luks (1867–1933), who were then the subjects of memorial exhibitions at the Uptown Gallery and the Newark Museum, respectively ("In Memoriam," November 17, 1934). Later that month, Mumford spied an early work by Jackson Pollock at the John Reed Club ("Marin and Others," November 24, 1934). Alfred Stieglitz was the subject of a glowing review a few days before Christmas; in a reminder of the Depression's enduring miseries, Mumford ended his column with a plea to his readers to consider patronizing needy artists during the holiday season ("A Camera and Alfred Stieglitz," December 22, 1934).

Some highlights of the second half of the season included Mumford's simultaneous reviews of Gaston Lachaise's sculpture at the Museum of Modern Art and Georgia O'Keeffe's works at An American Place ("Lachaise and O'Keeffe," February 9, 1935); mural painting at the Grand Central Galleries ("Paints, Palettes, and the Public Wall," February 16, 1935); abstract painting at the Whitney ("New High in Abstractions," March 2, 1935); and George Grosz's watercolors at An American Place ("The Dark Continent—And George Grosz," March 30, 1935). The painter Bryson Burroughs (1869–1934) was the subject of yet another memorial exhibition at the Metropolitan Museum of Art, where he had been the curator of painting; Mumford's review is uncharacteristically harsh ("Mirrors and the Metropolitan," April 6, 1935). Thomas Hart Benton and Grant Wood, recognized widely as America's premiere regionalist painters, were the subjects of separate columns later that spring ("The Three Bentons," April 20, 1935; "A Group of Americans," May 4, 1935). And Mumford, in his end-of-season summary, awarded special praise to the social realist painter Joe Jones ("In Capitulation," June 1, 1935).

CRITICS AND CAMERAS

On the summer shows of painting I have nothing to report. The only one that might have tempted me to leave my gaillardias and broccoli was heavily sprayed with the sort of publicity that is used to put over a movie palace. I wish I knew where one could get that spray in small quantities; it would keep even the worms and squash bugs and Japanese beetles away. If any surprises have been concocted at Woodstock or Gloucester or East Hampton, I am not the man to tell you about them. In Dutchess County, we run heavily to giant cucumbers, clematis, honey, pot cheese, and Presidents. We leave the arts of painting and sculpture to the city folks, who don't know the difference between the Holstein milk we export and the Guernsey milk we drink. Our local high school has even escaped a PWA mural. That's luck for you.

My one chance to look at pictures this summer was a private collection that contained many paintings by Maurice Prendergast. At least four of these were the very top of his work, and in each case I was puzzled by the fact that I did not remember seeing the picture at the Whitney Museum memorial show. Imagine my surprise when I found that these pictures had been submitted and had been turned back, while poorer ones were hung. I do not know whose judgment was at fault, but I am satisfied that someone blundered and did a disservice to Prendergast's memory and reputation. As with Monet, some of his best pictures were in his less characteristic style.

While calling attention to the selection of PWA art now at the Museum of Modern Art, let me pass on a word that came my way since I reported the larger exhibition at Washington. It seems that the big show last May was deliberately pitched toward mediocrity and sweetness and light for what are called political reasons. Nothing was shown that might ruffle the tender skin of a Congressman; the aim was to "avoid criticism." The artists, according to my authority, really gave a better account of themselves than the exhibition indicated. If this is true, one is not awestruck by the amount of intelligence it indicates. But it accounts, perhaps, for all the dull, painful press releases from Washington about the great service to art and the great eruption of public interest; whereas a little more life in the exhibition itself might have awakened enough discussion to spread the show spontaneously into the news columns.

If you are aching for a good book about modern art, before the galleries break loose, you will have to go on aching, without any help from the publishers' medicine chest. The best they can do for you is Herbert Read's "Art Now," published last spring, and James Johnson Sweeney's "Plastic Redirection of Twentieth Century Painting." Both are serious, effortful attempts to say something intelligent about modern art. Read's book has an admirable lot of illustrations; Johnson's has the virtue of brevity. Both of them are written in the terrible jargon that curses art criticism: a dialect more obscure than the paintings it is supposed to explain—all wind and darkness and the patter of rain on the rotten shingles of an empty attic. The fact is that art criticism is now in about the stage that grammar was in the early Renaissance. The analyses that are now fashionable deal, as it were, with the grammatical structure of painting: they are centuries away from that understanding of the reality of art which gave us the literary criticism of a Goethe or a Coleridge.

Like any other segment of life, art represents things as far apart as mathematical equations and primitive magic, as gasoline motors and the dreams of a hysterical patient. What purely aesthetic formula can bring Rouault and Braque, Feininger and Barlach, Dali and Arp, into the same aesthetic pen? And what value is there in a pure aesthetic approach that does not venture to point out, for example, that Hélion, as a painter, has an extremely uninteresting mind, or that Miró, who is far more witty and intelligible, nevertheless borders on triviality, and that each of them bears about the same relation to Tintoretto or Rembrandt that a crossword puzzle does to a sonnet by Wordsworth? Is this to undervalue abstract and non-representational art? On the contrary; it is to emphasize that the more abstract the picture is in form, the more it depends upon imagination and the less upon the practical conventions of seeing, the more important becomes the quality of the painter's mind. A dull or empty mind means an even duller or emptier abstraction.

The show of commercial photography held under the auspices of the National Alliance of Art and Industry at the R.C.A. Building includes all the neonized names that glow in the advertisements. If you have been looking at the magazine advertisements carefully, you have a pretty good notion of both the black-and-white and the color photography. When one examines the color work by itself, one is reminded of the technical progress that has been made during the last few years. There are still, however, blemishes. Unless only my "cold" eye was working the other day, the values of the greens are still unsatisfactory, and the pigment itself is somehow thin; also, as soon as the focus is not sharp, as in backgrounds, the color is a dead loss. While the process is not selective enough to have the aesthetic possibilities of black and white, it can do some amazing transcriptions of fruit, loaves of bread, dishes, soapsuds, at close range. Within this department, the form of slavery known as realistic painting is bound to disappear. And when they are not posing simpering young Hollywood beauties, registering health and joy and success, some of these photographers can do a straight, honest job: a wire basket of eggs, or the prow of an ocean steamer, or the inside of a factory. At that, the influence of painting is visible, even in the most factual photographs: it was Mr. Edward Hopper, for example, who first discovered the value of Mr. Anton Bruehl's handsome lighthouse.

Living in Paris, Man Ray has become slightly legendary. Those who wish to preserve the legend should not look into the book of photographs by him, 1920–1934, published by James Thrall Soby at Hartford. If they should get past the terrible color lithograph on the cover, they will find an extremely adroit technician, who has done almost everything with a camera except use it to take photographs. Man Ray's repertory is large. There is the usual study of stone texture; a flat shadowgraph of a flower; a pocket cigarette-lighter juxtaposed to a walnut that looks like some opened brains. There is the oval head of a lady, placed horizontally on a table in the manner of Brancusi; there is a schoolboyish imitation of O'Keeffe, with the aid of an apple and a metallic screw—perhaps it is meant to be funny. There is a Renger-Patzsch forest, an Eisenstein statue, a Paul Strand rock formation. Man Ray can make a photograph look like a water color (No. 27), or a crayon drawing (No. 32), or a charcoal drawing (No. 51); he can even produce the brush effects of an oil painting, as in the hair of No. 47. I cannot think of a single trick anyone has done during the last fifteen years that Man Ray does not show in this book, and for all I know, he may have done the trick first. But, considering Man Ray's capacities, it is a pretty sad performance, for in some of his male portraits, particularly in those of Derain, Schoenberg, Joyce, and Lewis, he shows honest gifts as a photographer, and he need not have smirked and gyrated so often to call attention to his talents. A photographer who can deal intelligently with the human face should not waste his time photographing calla lilies so that they will look like a drawing by a second-rate academician.

A CATALOGUE AND HOMER

The open-air art show in Washington Square is over now. But it will be worth while remembering when the leaves start to bud again if you have not yet seen it in action. There, on the south side of the Square, facing the cruel north light, were acres of pictures, hung on the billboards and the railings. They even formed an L by swinging over to the west side. True, they were mostly bad pictures, but what the show lost in art it gained in entertainment. Here were oleos that might have been shipped down from the picture-frame stores on Fourteenth Street; here were the crayon portraits, done to life, rubbing against the latest news, the burning of the Morro Castle, with all the flame coming out of the masts; here were little minor twists of abstract art, to say nothing of that curious purple "mysticism" in which shallow painting is covered by mock-profundities.

With a little patience, one might have found an artist of promise here; I know for a fact that a real painter sold a picture last year, and perhaps that always happens at least once. But the holding of an art show in the open demands courage, and at least for their moral qualities these artists deserve our respect. How many pictures on Fifty-seventh Street do you think could afford to go forth in the open air, without the protection of a gallery, soft light, the catalogue, the blurb in the catalogue, the learned description by the College Art Association? It will be a healthy moment for art again when the picture market rivals that on First Avenue and Eighth Street for color and vitality, when people buy pictures with the same untortured gusto with which they buy pickles and persimmons and pumpernickel. Mr. Moses, how about more public markets for pictures?

The season has opened with so many group shows that one can hardly name them without the aid of a catalogue, or talk about them without making another catalogue. What do you see, Walt Whitman? I see the pictures on Fifth Avenue shaking the dust off the burlap; I see the water colors at the Morton Gallery soberly dancing on the walls; I see the primitives and provincials at the Ferargil Galleries reminding one of how well the Early Americans painted the sky; I see the Hamilton Easter Field memorial collection at the Downtown Gallery matching painting with modified philanthropy, offering American Art gratis to American Museums, tempting American Museums to encourage more American Art. Health to you! Good will to you all—from me and America sent. What do you see, Walt Whitman? I see the Eighth Street Gallery; I see some water colors by Dirk; I see a "Quarry with Bathers" by de Martini, the grim, the mordant, the capable; I see the water colors of John Lonergan and the still life of child's toys by Harold Weston. I see the old doorway in a Greenwich Village tenement that I faced each morning a dozen years ago; in the name of sentiment, I salute the painter, Mark Datz; I salute the luminous color and the glamour, and I will never know whether the painting itself is a good or a bad one. I see the A.C.A. Gallery; I see Joseph Biel's "Hurdy-Gurdy," his "Lights," his French peasant, the painting thin, the face genuine. Hail again to luminous paint, the shimmer of color, the breath of humanity. I see vapors exhaling from unexplored countries, and I salute all the inhabitants of the earth, even the Hottentots and the neglected persons who have not become painters.

If the whole business could end on this slightly poetic note, it might be all right, but there remain the two hundred and fifty pictures at the American Regional Art Exhibition of Contemporary Painting, at Wanamaker's. There is a certain amount of excitement in the mere bigness of this exhibition, and if one could only look at it innocently there would be spots of real enjoyment. It is, I think, more interesting than the PWA exhibition. Is this because of the touch of social criticism here and there? Certainly one of the better pictures was the chastely titled and nicely balanced "Composition" by Refregier, with its simple contrast between wealth and poverty; and another was "The Struggle," by Abraham Harriton, which unfortunately was spoiled a little for me by the rocking-horse innocence of the horse's face. Some artists were included who had not been specially invited, and this was fortunate, for it brought in paintings as good as Carman's "Setting Fence Posts," Gunn's "Central Park," Klein's "Dawn," Pantuckoff's "Dark Day," and Orr's "The Wreck." Among the other pictures, I was particularly impressed by Bouché's "Hope Cove," Boyd's "Early Spring," Ault's "New England Landscape," and Schreiber's "Clowns"—but there goes the catalogue again, and I can't haul Old Walt out of the grave to help me.

The Museum for the Arts of Decoration at Cooper Union has bashfully begun to call attention to its buried treasures. I say "buried" with bitterness; it is a blow to my pride as a New Yorker to realize that three hundred Winslow Homer sketches have been on view there for twenty years without my even knowing that they were in existence. They include his Civil War jottings at the battlefront, the basis of his *Harper's Weekly* drawings; and there are also some sketches for a few of the important later paintings. If you are interested in the early Homer—and in the young man one finds the beginnings of the great water-colorist of the final years—you could do worse than spend an hour with this collection.

I cannot mention the Fifty Photographs by George Platt Lynes that opened the year at the Julien Levy Gallery without feeling a little like the shepherd in "The Way of All Flesh" who always blushed modestly when the choir sang "Shepherds, with your flocks abiding." About all but one of the portraits, however, I am entitled to have a judgment.

It comes down to this: When Mr. Lynes does straight photography, he usually does a very able job; his prints are delicate and finished, without loss of definition. The portrait of André Gide, the "Green River Mill," and the "Sleeping Beggar" are entertaining straight photography. The more artful photographs, relying upon a composed subject or little tricks of distortion, leave me as bored as the conversation of someone who fences for a whole evening for the opportunity of getting off a witty remark he has composed beforehand. What would be fine if it came spontaneously looks even more synthetic than it is after so much preparation. It is just at this point that the difference between the painter's imagination, which reorganizes experience, and the photographer's natural opportunities spreads widest; and the disadvantage is demonstrably with the photographer. He should never challenge that comparison.

IN MEMORIAM

A few years back one would occasionally meet on Lexington Avenue a small, black-haired man with a plump face and a little dark mustache and kindly eyes, mellow with sweetness and pain. He might be chatting at Weyhe's, where a few pictures by him would be on view, or he might be eating in Buchler's, where I saw him last, not many months before he died. His name was Alfred Maurer. History knows him as the first American to return to this country animated by the new vision that was plaguing the Wild Men of Paris. (Before that time he had been in the line of Whistler and Dewing.) In 1908 Mr. Alfred Stieglitz showed Maurer's new work at "291," and at that moment American art began to move at right angles to its previous course.

In point of time, Maurer led the whole movement toward modernism. But the quiet, restricted life that this gentle man lived was not the sort to produce a "leader," which so often means one who knows how to manipulate the arts of publicity. So even after Cubism and Expressionism became acclimated here, Maurer's work never held a central position. People knew that Maurer had talent. His flower pieces were charming, often brilliant; his elongated female heads, though a little perturbing when repeated too often, were good. But though the notes were clear and the pitch true, the melody itself seemed limited. Had Maurer nothing else to say?

∙ ∙ ∙ ∙ ∙

The Memorial Exhibition of Maurer's work at the Uptown Gallery is an event not to be missed: it is the first opportunity we have had to judge the man's energy and variety and mastery, and it is now apparent that he had a great deal else to say. Of all the painters who developed abstract art during the last twenty years, struggling for new symbols to express new states of mind and feeling, Maurer was one of the handful of genuine moderns who really felt these abstractions as experiences. His Cubist paintings are exciting and effective canvases; and if they were seen in the early days, one wonders that they did not attract greater attention. Nor was his success with these abstractions a matter of a momentary fresh vision that died out with repetition. The man kept on growing as a painter to the very end of his life: perhaps the finest paintings of all are the beautifully ordered still lifes, Nos. 17, 18, and 19, that he produced in the last year of his life—superb pieces. His original sense of color, often as bold and inventive as Matisse's, lost nothing with age.

Maurer was not an untutored primitive. The drawings in the present show—unfortunately, not hung for lack of space—show him to be an excellent draughtsman who subjected himself to a long apprenticeship to the outer appearances of things before he sought to draw forth from himself a subjective equivalent. How good a draughtsman he was one can tell easily from the swift, economical modelling of the neck and collarbone in his water colors. His gigantic heads, or his faces in which the eye absorbs all the character from the rest of the features, were not accidents; they were founded on knowledge and necessity. All in all, then, this is a moving and terrible exhibition. In some of the haunting faces of the latter period of his life, heads with ghastly, blotted eyes and haggard cheeks, one participates in Maurer's misery, and one shares the spirit that brought about his end. But whether Maurer painted a pure still life or two faces whose planes resolve into a single form, he painted from within, and sought—and again and again achieved—an expressive, objective symbol for his state. Far from being monotonous, these paintings run a great gamut of feeling and formal invention. Though it is too early to place Maurer—if only because acquaintance with his work as a whole comes so tardily—one can hardly doubt that he will count among the leaders of his generation rather than among the camp followers.

To the credit of the Whitney Museum, one should note that it promptly made an effort in 1932 to arrange for a memorial exhibition. Unfortunately, the Maurer family, which possesses this treasure hoard of unknown and unsold pictures, did not see fit to give its gifted black sheep the honor of such a public show. This only adds one more touch of irony to the tragic fate of the man himself.

By a curious chance, another memorial show is being held now, that of George B. Luks at the Newark Museum. The contrast between the two men is that persistent one in American life between highbrow and lowbrow, between tender- and tough-minded. Thirty years ago Luks was considered a radical artist. His radicalism consisted in the fact that he had worked as a lowdown illustrator for the *World* in New York, that he preferred depicting tough kids and street scenes to pallid, ethereal ladies, and that he painted in a broad, free manner. Actually, his radicalism was little more than a defiance of late-Victorian decorum. As late as 1905 he painted "The Pawnbroker's Daughter," which might easily have been done by George Fuller a generation before. This year, incidentally, was perhaps the high point of his life as a painter. It included "The Little Milliner," a fine portrait that has been improved a little, it may be, by the ravages of time; one of his best landscapes, the "West Side Docks"; and above all, "The Spielers," a painting of two little girls dancing that has some of the glad spontaneity of Hogarth's "Shrimp Girl." After this his work was sometimes richer in color, for, like Glackens and Lawson, fellow-members of The Eight, he partly threw off the influence of Düsseldorf by becoming Impressionist. In 1917 he utilized his richer palette in a market scene on Houston Street, perhaps the best of his later paintings; but he did not surpass his earlier work, and when he lost the stimulus of the street he sometimes sank into the shallowest sort of academicism.

If Maurer, like Ryder, did some of his best paintings in his last years, Luks—like Sargent and Henri—did some of his worst. As a genre painter, he stands below Sloan, and as a landscapist lower than Lawson, but the lovable and human spirit who did "The Spielers" will perhaps be remembered as long as his more accomplished fellows.

Among the offerings at the moment—and there is the usual November avalanche—I would note the Annual Exhibition of the American Water Color Society, with a total effect of too much bluing in the wash, but occasional minor spots of interesting painting, such as the water colors by R. F. Mead, Dorothy Harrison, and Jay Roland. Among the musts at the moment, apart from the Maurer show, are the Marin exhibition, the early Degas paintings, and the Despiau retrospective exhibition.

MARIN AND OTHERS

John Marin is both the most consistent and the most varied painter America has produced in the present period. Now in his sixties, Marin actually looks like a wrinkled, weather-beaten Pan, and no one in America, surely, has captured more of the spirit of the land and the sky than he has. Why, then, has his body of admirers remained so small? As one would expect of Pan, his wild pipings are far from the sentimental songs that the popular crooners in water and oil serve up for us, but this still does not account for his limited reception. Is he unpopular in the way that Thoreau was in his own time, because he is an original? Because people must acquire his vocabulary before they can understand his sentiments? People always look at the unfamiliar in terms of what they already know, and there are no other Marins in the bushes. Every new painting of his is still a fresh experiment, but none of the experiments are in the line of the current fashions and manifestoes and propagandas. His own growth has been a steady progression—from color as seen to color as felt and revalued, from form as given to form as reorganized in exciting arabesques. Marin, in his best paintings, has the gift of being able to formalize without impoverishing the contents of the picture; it is a great power. Life, quick, shrill, intense, is at his fingertips. He does not paint placid cows, nor does he paint the sort of scene committees of placid cows like to graze on.

The present show, at An American Place, is well up to that high level he has established for himself over so many years. Look at No. 7, "Roque Island Beach," or No. 13, "Fishboat." The way in which Marin catches hold of a subject is part of the quality of the scene: each of these paintings is a quick stab at the heart of the matter, done with a careless freedom that comes only with long practice and effort, like the flick of the wrist that hooks a trout. Most landscape painting is as inert as an architectural rendering. Marin's landscapes are alive and actively doing things: one not merely sees the scene but feels the wind on the face; there is pressure and intensity behind every line. Sometimes the shot misses and the bird flies away, but when the shot goes home, as it does, for example, in the two studies of trees on Cape Split, the result is supremely satisfactory. Why must the appreciation of Marin's genius be confined to a handful of Ancient Mariners?

None of us who remember the shout of delight that was caused by the first exhibition of Despiau's sculpture, in 1927, will be quite as happy over the present show at the Brummer Gallery. For the first exhibition consisted of finished work, in its ultimate medium, stone or bronze, while the present exhibition consists largely of plaster casts, in the state in which they left the foundry. Plaster, of course, is a horrible material which turns living sculpture into a death mask, and these delicately modelled women's faces, with their quick bloom of animation, need the finish of their final form to show the difference that raises Despiau above the more literal sculptors who stand near him. That so much of him can survive even plaster is a tribute to his mastery.

There are a hundred ways of being original. One of them would be to walk backward on Fifty-seventh Street honking an auto horn and flapping a pair of purple wings. Two of the other means are now visible in the same neighborhood. One is Reinhardt's Green Exhibition, in which all the canvases were selected on the basis of their color content. The only thing that really commends the idea as such is the fact that Alexander's "The Green Gown" was left out of the show. If you can forget the Grand Idea, however, the assortment of pictures is worth looking at.

The other way to achieve originality is to paint canvases in which one body shall be superimposed on another, like a double exposure on a photographic film, so that the spectator may see the face of the young lady reading a book though the book is between them. This is the present method of Francis Picabia, momentarily on view at Valentine's, who was one of the more witty Cubists of the period before the war. I would have no objection to the method if the results were more interesting, but with a couple of exceptions, the pictorial idea is extremely banal. Once one has got over the surprise of seeing an X-ray machine make love to a Surréaliste, or conceiving a world in which all the objects in the foreground are composed of Cellophane, one becomes a little bored. The result is a species of graphic tattooing. Maybe I have missed the Serious Purpose; at all events, I prefer the older Picabia, who did a careful mechanical drawing of a carburetor and called it "La Jeune Fille Américaine."

Arnold Friedman's paintings at the Contempora Art Circle are the work of a minor but genuine talent. This kind of talent, like that of Leon Hartl, is too easily neglected by those who forget that an alyssum may be just as important in a garden as a dahlia. His portraits are particularly good, no less for the tender handling of the dress than for the face itself. Nothing here is overpowering, either in manner or feeling, but there is a quiet sensitivity in these pictures, with their delicate suppressions and their

chaste line, which is capable of giving genuine pleasure. . . . Sidney Lauf-
man's show at the Milch Gallery has three or four good sketches, and at
least one landscape—No. 4—that rises above the modest but honest
competence of the rest of the exhibition. . . . David Burliuk, at the Eighth
Street Gallery, is one of the Russian moderns; he is naïve and playful,
with a rich and somewhat arbitrary palette that he also uses playfully.
But his seacoast and his city façades touch me more than his more archaic fancies. . . . At the Downtown Gallery there is a good collection of
water colors and drawings by various moderns, ranging from the free
and spirited Kuniyoshis to Sheelers, that are more photographic than
photographs. . . . Finally, at the John Reed Club, there is a showing of
"Revolutionary Front—1934." The work has been pretty rigorously selected, and if it is a little monotonous in theme, there is plenty of variety
in method, from the distorted but almost classic volumes of Harriton's
"Death of a Proletarian Hero" to the Bentonesque "Chicken in Every
Pot," by Pollock. Perhaps the best painting was "East Side Landscape,"
by Nicolai Cikovsky, but many of the black-and-whites have bite, in
every sense of the word.

A CAMERA AND ALFRED STIEGLITZ

In 1921, the old Anderson Galleries contained a notable show of Alfred
Stieglitz's photography. It was one of a handful of exhibitions that one
remembers years after they took place. Up to that time, Stieglitz had been
for me just a name; now he was visible—a wiry body, a pompadour of
gray hair, a nose with a broken ridge, a sharp, sardonic face warmed by
smoldering brown eyes, and—this was part of the total impression—an
enviable red vest. His photographs altered all the dimensions of that art;
they had depth, intensity, delicacy, and strength.

The new show of Stieglitz's work at An American Place comes in his
seventy-first year; if anything, it is more positive and climactic than the
exhibition of 1921. Stieglitz's head is crowned with a vague, yellowish
cloud of hair and the red vest has given way to gray; but the incredibly
refined technique, the deep, relentless energy, and the steady vision of life
are still there. Neither his friends nor his enemies have done justice to the
man. One does not have to think of Stieglitz as a prophet to see that his
work is prophetic, nor does one have to decide whether or not photography is an art to realize that Stieglitz is an artist who might under other
circumstances have built bridges or written poems.

There is an astringent quality in Stieglitz that has escaped his admirers. He has been nourished by his hates as well as his loves; he has never cultivated that harmless good nature which is responsible for half the stupidities of American life. Stieglitz's demonic negations are part of his deepest vitality; they play the same part in his personality that the blacks do in his prints. As well think of Stieglitz without these dark elements as think of Melville without "Moby Dick" and "Pierre." Indeed, Stieglitz is closer to lonely Captain Ahab than perhaps to any other figure in our life or literature. I emphasize these personal qualities of Stieglitz because his photographs are not alone his work but his life.

In contrast to the restless cameramen of our time, Stieglitz does not go out of his way to get a print. He takes the world as he finds it; the grass at his feet, the sky over his head, the office buildings he sees from his city hotel are equally good. Nature, Man, the Machine—these three form the major chords of his work; upon that triple theme he plays a bewildering infinity of variations. He does not look for subjects—"aesthetic" subjects, or "*photogénique*" subjects—because his subject is life, and for him, as for Whitman, a blade of grass is a miracle. Some of the clever photographers who admire his technique even find him empty; but when they observe that he has nothing to say, they really mean that he has nothing they can copy. The secrets of his art are not in his camera, his papers, his developers; they lie in his mind.

Stieglitz's work shows consistency as well as growth. One wall in the present show presents a series of prints from the eighties and nineties that had lain neglected in his Lake George attic. Every element that one finds, abstracted and clarified, in Stieglitz's later prints is present in these early prints in embryo: they include a sky over the mountain tops which points directly to the masterly cloud "Equivalents." Modern photographers, who play with the effect of arbitrary blacks and whites across an image by means of an arrangement of slats, will find that Stieglitz did the same thing, with consummate skill, in 1889. And though Stieglitz is a master of straight photography, he has done a double-exposure print, "Dualities," that is almost diabolic both in its symbolism and its technical perfection.

Among his latest prints, the series of photographs of grass—not single stems, but a tangled foreground—show the topmost point, perhaps, both in execution and in realization of the object. But it is unfair to single out any particular set. Except for his incomparable studies of the nude, every phase of Stieglitz's work is present in this exhibition. The prints are all of the first order, and he who touches them touches a man. Stieglitz has done, in his photographs, what only the camera could do;

and he has said, in this mechanical medium, what only an affirmative and vital spirit could say.

Miss Angna Enters, the dancer, has returned from Greece with dozens of spirited line sketches of the figures she encountered on ancient vases and urns. (They were at the Ehrich-Newhouse Galleries.) These drawings have the clean decision of the originals, plus some of that extra excitement that a modern feels in beholding the originals under the sky of their birthplace. Neither Miss Enters' water colors, in which the painting usually does not do justice to the witty idea, nor her oils are on the level of the sketches. A mistress of line in her professional medium, she has a natural affiliation with those dead craftsmen who mastered it graphically.

The annual show of American Print Makers at the Downtown Gallery is, as usual, healthy and handsome; I can recommend it heartily. . . . Fitsch's paintings of New York at night at the Midtown Galleries are promising; those with figures are particularly good. . . . Arbit-Blatas, at the Matisse Gallery, has good moments; not original, but sensitive and charming. . . . If there are echoes in Sir Francis Rose's work at the Marie Harriman Galleries, he nevertheless communicates some of his immediate pleasure and interest; that he is a young baronet who has been patronized by Gertrude Stein is beside the point. . . . At the Rehn Galleries, two painters of the new Hudson River School, Henry Varnum Poor and George Biddle, command attention. Both men are doing distinguished work; and Poor's pottery—I except the Victorian genre pieces, which are neither flesh nor fowl—remain as handsome as ever. . . . At the Weyhe Gallery, there is a selected exhibition of prints that must be put alongside those chosen by the American Print Makers.

And now, if you have planned your Christmas stockings this year without including art, this is a last warning that you are omitting an opportunity to be patriotic and philanthropic and unusually canny all at a single stroke. Never has so much good American art been available so cheaply; for more than a handful of our very best painters and sculptors should be included among our thousand neediest cases. There are bargains all over town—as well as a lot of undeserving art that should be patronized only by those whose charity is boundless. If I must pick out a single place outside the galleries you are acquainted with, let me name the special relief exhibition of the College Art Association at their headquarters on East Fifty-seventh Street and Lexington Avenue.

ANNIVERSARY—POST-CENTENARY WHISTLER—
MR. CURRY AND THE AMERICAN SCENE

At least a dozen people have asked me what I think about the fifth anniversary exhibition that has been on at the Museum of Modern Art. I had just as lief be asked what I think about the beauty of American girls. (Do you mean Katharine Hepburn or Mae West?) Mr. Barr got together a pretty representative selection of modern paintings, some owned by the Museum and some, perhaps, that ought to be owned by it. The only thing that puzzled me a little is why, if Cézanne was included among the painters, Rodin was not included among the sculptors. It is the fashion to treat Rodin shabbily at the moment; but to ignore both his art and his influence is like leaving Trotsky out of an account of the Russian Revolution.

When one brings too much modern art together, unfortunately, all one's clear ideas as to what it is and isn't disappear. One is left clutching the naked word "modern" as meaning some part of the chaos explored by the artists who painted and modelled after 1870. Looked at roundly and squarely, modern art resembles architecture much more than I had suspected. It is eclectic. It has begged, borrowed, and experimented; but it has still to show something that defines a fresh movement in culture— a principle of restriction. Like Browning's unfortunate Duchess, it likes whate'er it looks on, and its looks go everywhere. The structure of things and the surface effects of color, the immobility of Seurat and the rapid flux of Matisse, the dull, grimy outer world and the crazy, disjointed inner world—all are part of it. It has shown a tremendous appetite for knowledge without a sufficient power of assimilation and growth. Perhaps never before has the artist had such a rich choice of means and such a poor notion of what to do with them.

A year or so after the Whistler Centenary it is too late to announce that Whistler was a fine etcher. The late Joseph Pennell discovered that he was a long while ago, and even made the mistake of putting him in the same class as Rembrandt. But the exhibition of Whistler's etchings at Keppel's, at the Metropolitan Museum, and at the New York Public Library are all worth a visit; the last even has a rich collection of caricatures and memorabilia in its permanent junk shop, the Stuart Room. (Is there any law, by the way, that keeps the Library from turning over its art collections to the Metropolitan, or is it just institutional inertia? The inmates of the Library are already piled three deep and those two big galleries would give them a little breathing space.)

The best part about these Whistler shows is that one does not have to stumble over a delegation from the Ladies' Club of Canarsie putting a pink wreath at the foot of Whistler's Mother. The Library exhibition begins with Whistler as an engraver of Americana; namely, a "View of the Eastern Extremity of Anacapa Island," done for the U.S. Topographical Survey. Some of this stiff engraver's technique remained in his early prints, such as "The Pool," "Eagle Wharf," "Limehouse," and "Billingsgate"; and I prefer these studies of London River to the crummy suggestions of his later style in the Italian series. "The Little Lagoon," on the other hand, is a fine example of elimination; one could count the number of lines in this etching, and each one of them does its work.

There was a picture in the parlor, when I was a little boy, that used to fascinate me. When the light shone strong on it, one could discover one or two little blurs of color in an otherwise impenetrable wilderness of black. There was mystery for you. One hung over that dark scene for hours at a time, hoping that the sun would rise and show what was there. The paintings of Logasa and Mommer at the New School recalled to me this Victorian masterpiece; some of them made me think that, like the Victorian artist, they might be overdoing the obscurity a little. I still do not know what Mommer's "The Supper" is about, and the face of Logasa's "Athlete Resting" remains undecipherable too. Logasa is sometimes a very adroit painter—for example, in his "Regatta"—and sometimes an unaccountably careless one. Both Logasa and Mommer will have to work hard before they catch up with the older romantics, like R. L. Newman and Eugene Higgins.

Mr. Guy Pène du Bois' paintings at Kraushaar's bear something of the same relation to our metropolitan world that Rockwell Kent's do to the Eskimos. His satire fails to come off the way that Kent's noble symbols fail; yet the fault is not due to any lack of technical facility as a painter. Mr. du Bois has a recognizable style; but his effects depend much more upon one's liking for the original subject than upon his own capacity for altering one's feelings toward the subject. Unfortunately, I am not titillated by his slightly depraved-looking young ladies with pulpy underlips, and his big picture, "Mr. and Mrs. Middleclass," a study for decorative panels, seemed a great deal of painting, reckoned in square feet, for a small result. Usually his drawings strike home more directly.

· · · · ·

At the Ferargil Galleries, Mr. John Steuart Curry reveals a great variety of things. In this new show, his Kansas studies outnumber his circus pictures, and yet I cannot help thinking that the circus has a hypnotic effect upon him that focusses his powers better than any other subject he has explored; there is a decisiveness in the "Clown and Bareback Riders," and even in the "Fire Diver," that is lacking in his other pictures. "The Line Storm" is perhaps the best-painted landscape in this show. Unfortunately, the part of the picture upon which a large share of the dramatic effect depends—the light thin clouds at the top, in contrast to the sinister solid bank beneath—is unconvincingly painted. So, too, the intention in "The Fugitive"—a treed Negro with the bloodhounds on his trail—is excellent; the ominous, flamelike red butterflies in the foreground are likewise well chosen; but the painting does not convey the terror and suspense. It remains an illustration which needs the extra power of words to make it real. Compared with the other Middle Western painters of the American scene, with Thomas Benton and Grant Wood, Curry lacks firmness. He is not always sure of his third dimension, and when he tries too hard to achieve it, he becomes waxen. But in the long run his faults may prove his salvation. If they now leave the observer dissatisfied, they may also leave the artist with a stimulus to growth.

LACHAISE AND O'KEEFFE

In the Lachaise exhibition at the Museum of Modern Art, the Museum is doing for the first time something that I had, perhaps erroneously, thought to be its chief mission. It has taken a distinguished modern artist, whose originality stands in the way of his easy public acceptance, and given him the space that is lacking at the private art dealer's gallery. While not exhaustive, the present show is at least fairly ample. The Museum has, it is true, countered this act by presenting at the same time the Americana of George Caleb Bingham, a mid-nineteenth-century worthy from Missouri, but that is a matter I prefer to turn over to the Raised Eyebrows Department, although it may easily belong to the Obituary Column.

But after all, here are the Lachaise sculptures—the billowy nudes with enormous breasts and flanks, the restrained buttocks, the almost Chinese delicacy of hands and feet. This sculpture was nothing less than a revolutionary gesture of protest during the happily bygone decade when everything about a girl was boyishly bobbed, and when the female backbone stood out in evening dress like the ridge of a razorback hog. Here are the early figurines, with the modelling of the lower draperies a trifle realistic and fussy, but already with the upper part of the body emerging in characteristic fashion. Here are the splendid drawings, in which grotesqueness becomes suave and elegant—drawings such as only a very good sculptor can produce. Here are heads that range all the way from a smooth archaism just a step above Manship to the strong, realistic portraits of Cummings, Kirstein, and Van Vechten. (Of the portraits, perhaps the most expressive is that of Evelyn Gerstein, No. 48, although the head in the "Portrait Figure," No. 59, ranks close to it.) At the other pole from these are Lachaise's monstrous distortions, as in his gigantic man with puddingy hands, his floating woman, his latest and largest version of "La Montagne." In these abstractions, the life of the figure seems to me partly sacrificed to the idea.

It is mostly in the realm between his realism and his abstraction that Lachaise has superbly triumphed. Among the smaller pieces, I would mention the torso, No. 42, and the beautiful marble breasts, No. 53; and though the buttocks of No. 55 are by themselves a little overpowering, the figure as a whole is very fine. (Was it a silly prudishness that caused this piece to be placed so close to the wall? The ironic result of confining the spectator to one plane is to magnify its obscenity.) But Lachaise's integral conception of woman dominates the show. She emerges in maturity, soft, ripe, ample, sometimes a little overblown. She is least interesting when Lachaise perversely contracts the space between breasts and flanks, and she is at her best in a series of standing figures, done during the last ten years: Nos. 25, 28, and 29. His art is consummated, in so-far-final perfection, in No. 16, a standing woman done between 1912 and 1927. This creature is wholly his own, from the proud head to the curved-back fingertips and the light feet, poised as in a quiet self-contained dance. Lachaise's Woman is worthy of a place beside Maillol's Woman and Lehmbruck's Woman. Can one give higher praise?

The retrospective show of Georgia O'Keeffe's work at An American Place completes that which was held last year, for it contains the flowers, the leaves, the East River landscape, and two interpretations of the skyscraper, one abstract, the other closer to representation. In addition, there is a very handsome series of charcoal studies (of banana flowers) rich in feeling and firm in draughtsmanship. The combination of austerity and exuberance, of clarity and warmth, of remoteness and intimacy, of an intensity of feeling and an almost mathematical capacity for abstract statement runs through all her work. It culminates in her abstractions, such as the very delicate pencil drawing in the little room—abstractions in which she gives herself most fully and at the same time exercises the maximum of restraint. Her pigment is thin, for she seeks the purity of sky colors rather than the heavier texture of the earth colors, but when she demands volumes, she achieves them: the forms themselves are not thin. The white carriage sheds, the gray-and-blue East River scene, the brown skyscraper at night, and the taupe and red and olive-green leaf paintings are perhaps the central pictures of this show. O'Keeffe's paintings are deeply and specifically American, even in the limited sense in which Hopper and Sheeler are American; yet they are probably as universal as anything we have produced in this generation. And they deepen with familiarity.

At the Marie Harriman Galleries there is Isamu Noguchi's exhibition of sculpture. The best things seem to me the three monuments: the abstract symbol of the hosiery workers' tools and machines, for the Carl Mackley Housing Development in Philadelphia; the kite, lightning, key, and insulator for the Benjamin Franklin Memorial; and the austere monument to the plough, set on a broad-based pyramid. His portraits show great facility and skill, but they still do not seem as satisfactory as his abstractions and his drawings. The dominating piece in the exhibition is the monumental dangling figure of a lynched Negro, conveying in its bluish glitter of steel and its bunched flesh the message of contortion, paralysis, death. But it raises a hard question: Does the physiological result on the spectator contain a germ of moral effect? Granting the horror at the sight of the body, does it convey horror over the human fact of injustice and cruelty? In short, is sculpture a useful instrument of propaganda? I applaud Noguchi's motives, but I distrust the medium and doubt the results.

Apart from these, the important exhibitions at the moment are the Kenneth Hayes Miller show at the Rehn Gallery, the large selection of John Kane's paintings at the Valentine Gallery (he could paint, finally, even when he forgot to be naïve), and the Maurice Becker show at the Eighth Street Gallery. The last is particularly interesting. Becker attempts to catch the luminosity of the sky in the solid figures of the earth, and though the form sometimes disappears in the shimmer of the color, when he succeeds—as in "Virgin Islanders"—he is good.

PAINTS, PALETTES, AND THE PUBLIC WALL

The fine show of mural paintings, contemporary and retrospective, at the Grand Central Art Galleries has a touch of the heroic about it. If you have ever paid the express charges on a mural, you will know what I mean. To be a mural-painter, you must not merely believe in yourself but be full of hope for your country: you must want to understand it, be part of it, have the desire to affect it directly, and seek to give painting itself a certain political dignity. In short, you must be either a paranoiac or a virtuous person. I am happy to report that most of the painters in this show, even those who lean toward oversized figures of overstuffed platitudes, are virtuous persons. At its very least, this show has sincerity and moral weight, and at its best it has a grand splash of good painting, too.

Indeed, the exhibition would have been worth arranging if it showed only how much better some of our good painters are than we had reason to suspect from their drawings or easel pictures. Perhaps the happiest surprise of all is William Gropper. One realized that he has been developing these last ten years into an incomparable draughtsman in black-and-white, with a quick, vivid line and an aptitude for caricature, but who knew until now that he was also a painter with a fresh and apposite palette, and a powerful sense of spatial composition, a master of effortless balance as well as movement? The ultimate source of such good painting may be Gropper's sustaining belief in the proletarian revolution; the proximate cause of it, however, was the repeal of the prohibition amendment and the opportunity to decorate a private bar for the Schenley Corporation. The final result is so good that one almost begrudges this panel to the people who commissioned it.

I have never held that filling public walls was by itself any cure for the ills of contemporary art, or that true fresco would turn a Bastien-Lepage of oil into a Giotto; nor do I think that a second-rate easel picture gains by high magnification. The earlier mural painting in America, inaugurated by Richardson with the help of William Morris Hunt, and carried on by La Farge, Alexander, and Blashfield, filled the theatres and courthouses and libraries a generation back to very little purpose; even the best of La Farge's murals did not equal his stained-glass windows. But the fact is that the mural has excited the imagination of contemporary American painters by holding before them two helpful illusions—the illusion of an audience, and the illusion of a destination. The result is that some of them have begun to work with an energy and vision that had remained undeveloped in their easel pictures. Look at Edward Biberman's fine mural panel, surely the best thing he has done so far. Does not Henry Billings's "Fascism" surpass both his abstract machine decoration and his Surréaliste flirtations, although it retains the virtues of both sets of experiments? Has not Stefan Hirsch's "Dispatcher" just that strength and inevitability that his smaller canvases have sometimes lacked? George Biddle's design for the murals in the auditorium of the Carl Mackley hosiery workers' housing project shows his art at its best, while Henry Varnum Poor's heads in fresco disclose a native talent for fresco painting that has been waiting for the stimulus of a public work and a public wall. These are but a handful out of a whole series of examples one might cite, while younger painters like Joseph Vogel and Marion Greenwood, who have grown up in the mural tradition, have already some of the powers of maturity. To release this concentrated vitality, we shall have, I am afraid, to put up with acres of weak and tepid and merely amiable painting; but that is the sort of price one has to pay for vitamins and radium, too. It may be worth it.

Mr. Kenneth Hayes Miller's paintings at the Rehn Gallery present a problem I have been struggling for years to solve. How is it that such a capable painter can succeed in being so dull? There is not merely craftsmanship in the canvases but good painting, as in the lower half of No. 4. This would be an excellent still-life if one could only guillotine the heads. The faces, however, turn it into literal *nature morte*. The point is that most of Mr. Miller's subjects depend, because of their commonplace associations, upon keen observation of character. Lacking the gift of Daumier, he turns his lady shoppers and saleswomen into conventionalized types, as bare of human interest as the noble ladies once espoused on canvas by Kenyon Cox. The far-off gaze, the round face with full lips, even the repetition of certain colors—in short, the complete absence of the unexpected—add to the waxen quality of the modelling or the pewter tinge of the flesh tones. His earlier paintings, if they lacked some of his solid virtues, held more interest. And the worst is, in the case of such an inspiring teacher as Mr. Miller, that his students have acquired a fuller share of his faults than they deserve.

The unexpected success of the mural show probably makes me a little overfavorable to two other group shows. But I liked the tenth annual exhibition of the New York Society of Women Artists at the Squibb Building, if only because it was so much better than the show of the National Association; the paintings of Hourdebaight, Pach, Schofield, and Weinrich stood out in it. As for the Weyhe exhibition, it was not, perhaps, better than those of the past—indeed, it was possibly a little more commonplace—but it contained such good prints as Cikovsky's "Portrait of a Girl," Dehn's "Stuyvesant Square," Victoria Hutson's "Lower New York," Raphael Soyer's "Two Girls," and Agnes Tait's cat picture.

NEW HIGH IN ABSTRACTIONS

During the last year a wicked fairy godmother—there is no other way to account for it—wove a spell over our two young museums of art. As a result of her malice the Museum of Modern Art has begun to act as if it were a haven for the preservation of American antiquities. Meanwhile, the Whitney Museum has taken over the business of presenting modern art. For the handful of people who haven't visited the Whitney exhibition of abstract painting in America, I will say at once that it is probably the best all-around show the Museum has put on. My catalogue is so marked up with arrows, asterisks, and exclamation points that I hardly know where to begin or whose paintings to single out.

We are accustomed to date abstract art in America from the Armory show in 1913. But it all began five or six years earlier with the little whirlpool of interest that revolved around the new work of Alfred Maurer and Walkowitz and Weber, who came back to America filled with the excitement of having something new to say and having discovered a new way of saying it. About the same time a young adept in Whistlerian impressionism, John Marin, found the beginnings of a fresh idiom of his own. Then the procession lengthened and the fun began.

What the new painters of abstractions were searching for were symbols that would present a fresh account of the noise and movement and order and experiment and raw emotion of modern life. Sometimes the method of symbolism was old: the use of a concrete form, as in O'Keeffe's "Pool in Lake George," to suggest an entirely different experience. Or, as in Stella's "American Landscape," the painter selected a single aspect or experience, in this case the formidable steel structures of a metropolis, and stepped it up to a higher voltage. Still another kind of abstraction, such as Stuart Davis's handsome paintings in this show, emphasized the playful, constructive arabesques of the artist; these pictures led directly into new patterns for textiles and floor coverings. Breaking up habitual associations with commonplace images, the abstract artists invented a new language and renewed the whole vocabulary of expression.

The paradox about this series of experiments with abstract forms is that it brought life back to contemporary American art. It enabled us to appreciate more keenly the important but neglected elements in our own past—the paintings of Eakins, for example, and the work of the early limners and lithographers. So far from leading the artist into a desert of geometrical forms, it bolstered up his self-confidence and gave him a better control over the materials of his own day. Let us bury the phrase "meaningless abstractions." The fact is that meaning is possible only with the aid of abstractions, and all art, in so far as it conveys meaning, is abstract. What abstract art turned its back on was not meaning but the old stage properties of realistic illusion. (The decline of David Belasco belongs to the same period.)

Obviously there are bad and feeble abstractions as well as effective ones. The point is that the abstract artist liberated the imagination in much the same way as the mathematicians who were playing with non-Euclidean geometry. As for imitation, the American school stands with remarkable solidity on its own feet: Billings' mechanical painting in relief does not remind one of Léger, nor do Demuth's austere constructions recall any European painter. Indeed, the one other point to be emphasized about the majority of these abstractions is that they are more specifically native than a good part of the illusionist painting of the glorifying-the-corner-grocery school. These abstract paintings link up with the good hooked rugs and quilts of our eighteen-forties, which were equally abstract and equally bold in design. All in all, abstract painting has probably had more to say in America during the last twenty years than any other kind of painting.

The present exhibition contains such happy and unusual items as the little-seen synchromist paintings of McDonald Wright (forerunner of the color organ), the cubist paintings of Walter Pach, the fine Hartley abstraction called "Provincetown," some of Dove's best work, and some interesting things by younger artists who are continuing the tradition. The chief omissions I am conscious of are the excellent abstractions of Benton and Orozco. Unfortunately, the representation of Alfred Maurer is inadequate. But I don't wish to carp. It is a fine show, and it speaks as directly to the viscera as a bass drum.

One didn't lose the theme of abstract art at the recent show of Guatemalan textiles and the new textile designs of Ruth Reeves at the R.C.A. Building. For obviously pattern and pure symbol have always had a place in such aboriginal art, and it is equally plain that the primitive machine process of weaving called into existence designs which speak more directly to us than the flowered brocades of the Renaissance. Miss Reeves, with an intelligence and spirit that have been all too rare among textile designers, has used this Guatemalan handicraft in exactly the fashion that the work of another culture should be used. (Let our museums of art gather round in a circle and take out their notebooks.) She travelled among the natives, ate with them, cajoled them, learned from them, and climbed about the ruins of their old civilization. Then, instead of copying their patterns, she took some slight suggestion as a starting point for her own imagination, itself raised to a higher pitch by her travels. The result is a series of hangings and dress fabrics that leap out in their distinction and in their fitness to *our* environment—probably the most interesting work any designer has offered for commercial production today. The adroit puppet figures by Bufano on which the original costumes are mounted and Miss Honor Spingarn's jolly illustrations of native costumes likewise deserve a good word.

If your eyes have been fixed on the newcomers these last three years, you have probably been conscious of the rise of Joseph de Martini. The show now on at the Eighth Street Gallery puts his star well above the horizon. His paintings have a sort of architectural firmness about them, and this architectural quality includes an ability to handle simple masses and to suggest deep space. There is the "Outdoor Fight Arena," for example— a yellow ring in the midst of blackness, nondescript hunched figures in the foreground high above the stage, and the earth and sky and a big building mingling in the distance. His portraits have a quiet force and decision, too; and in some of the small recent paintings there is a happier note in his color, a note that begins to break through like spring blossoms on bare boughs. His "Rocks and Sea," his "Tree and Cliff," and his "Quarry Bathers No. 5" are perhaps the best of his landscapes.

THE DARK CONTINENT—AND GEORGE GROSZ

The exhibition of African Negro Art at the Modern Museum is the most exhaustive one that we have seen in the United States. Mr. James Johnson Sweeney has done an admirable job in collecting and arranging these pieces. Like the exhibition of pre-Columbian American art two years ago, the present show puts on the map a section of the world that the conventional art museum still hesitates to acknowledge. Hence the specimens come either from private collections or from ethnological museums. May we still live to see these fetishes and masks and stools and weights and sceptres in the Metropolitan! And may they be not too far away from the Cretan and the early Greek sculptures!

Till only yesterday, these products of the various Negro cultures of Africa were dismissed as crude, barbarous, and horrible—as if the "Lesson in Anatomy" or the "Massacre of Scio" or the "Disasters of the War" were the expressions of a gentler race. During the last generation, however, our whole scale of values has undergone a change. We primitives of the machine world feel our kinship with the earlier phases of other cultures; the Romanesque is closer to us than High Gothic. If we have a special kinship for this African Negro art, it is perhaps, too, because we live under a similar spell of fear and death, stunned by spectres of calamity, cowed by arbitrary assertions of power. Worringer has shown, in his "Form in Gothic," that an absolute art, geometrical and perfect, is the answer of primitive peoples to the uncertain chaos of actual existence.

The word "primitive" is, of course, ambiguous. This African sculpture is primitive chiefly in the sense of being close to the elemental sources of emotion: sex, fear, death. The forms themselves are the products not of untutored fingers making their first essays in plastic expression but of experienced artists who must have had behind them a firm tradition. The animals are remarkably fine; there are a couple of antelopes and a mule and a bird in which life has been arrested and formalized—almost in the way in which Duchamp-Villon or Brancusi arrested it—without losing its essence. The Benin bronzes are remarkable, and two of the figures, Nos. 321 and 476, have faces in which the sorrow and weariness of slavery are expressed in the mouth and eyes as well as in the posture.

But one cannot describe all the variety and wealth of this show in a paragraph. It is very fine, and if one remembers that it is something more than the plastic values which brings these masks and figures so close, one suddenly becomes aware of the great gap that spreads between us and the hardy explorers and traders and soldiers who first opened the Dark Continent. Inside their sons, we have discovered a darker continent. Mr. Sweeney's introduction to the catalogue is helpful, but perhaps D. H. Lawrence's stories would be more helpful; and before we are done with digesting this African art, we may even have to call in Dr. Jung.

George Grosz's new water colors at An American Place show, for the most part happily, the result of his steady acclimatization to his new home. They cast a light both on his own development and on the American spirit itself. During the war, he made his debut as an artist. Between 1915 and 1922, he did the terrible series of drawings and water colors published later in "Ecce Homo." In these pictures, with a line that crawled like a maggot over a dead body, he revealed the death and putrefaction of the world around him—a world of snout-faced, lecherous men and plump, rapacious women in whom the sexual organs and the stomach had taken on, as it were, an independent life, absorbing every other human potentiality.

Grosz's technique, with his scratchy child's lines and his smeared, interpenetrating forms, was extremely original, though in their faces there was more than an accidental reminder of the spirit expressed centuries earlier in Grünewald. (To a German, one might say that it is the brutal antithesis of the spirit expressed in poesy by Walter von der Vogelweide and Wolfram von Eschenbach.) During the false dawn that happened in Germany between 1925 and 1930, Grosz's satire became a little more benign. He did a series of "*sachlich*" portraits, and his water colors, though often of porcine women or voluptuous butchers' stalls, had a warm glow of health. Life was not the hopeless sink of bestiality he had felt it to be during the years of the war and the inflation.

Coming to America three years ago, Grosz had to penetrate and express a new world. Has he succeeded? Most remarkably. His satire is now alive again; witness a remarkable series of studies of the American woman of society, wilted, wrinkled, but zealously youthful, with an anticipatory touch of the corpse already hovering around the eye—Grosz's moist-paper technique is excellent for revealing this in water color—despite the undertaker's zeal of the beauty parlor. Well do we know that false youth, that age without dignity or self-respect, that perpetual childishness of spirit; with unerring instinct and a merciless brush, Grosz has gone after this American idol. His landscapes of New York are clear, and sometimes deep and resonant. Only the color has become a little monotonous in its blues and reddish browns, as if the artist were working within the limits of the reproductive process and quenching some of the richness of his personal response.

Compared to Grosz's earlier work, these new paintings, even the more sardonic ones, have a quality that is relatively pure and clean. I have often remarked on the virginal element in American life as revealed in painting, from Whistler and Fuller to Demuth and O'Keeffe and Grant Wood, and it is interesting that even in the midst of the metropolis Grosz has caught a whiff of this clean smell, coming from fragrant meadows and spotless barns and scoured milk pails and cool, tidy porches. That Grosz's instinct should lead him not toward "Tobacco Road" but toward "North of Boston" does not mean that he is less of a satirist; it means that his appetite for reality is sound and that his unconscious has already begun to anchor itself in the country of his adoption. He has much to give us.

Hasty Notes: The Academy show is a little better, and the moderns are no longer segregated as if they were a contagious disease. The newly done-over gallery at Brummer's, showing some sound but not overwhelming animal sculpture by Mateo Hernandez, presents probably the handsomest ensemble of the year: blue walls, black granite sculpture, gray columns and pedestals, dark parquet floor, and tall gray-green cactuses.

MIRRORS AND THE METROPOLITAN

For the last three centuries, the dullest painters in the world have been the mirrors of their time. They have made the "social scene" of England and France and Germany and Italy another name for universal boredom. When a painter had nothing fresh to express, he solved the problem of maintaining his station in life by copying the costumes and stage settings of his contemporaries. What was originally a virile impulse in Teniers and de Hooch became the deadly photographic sentimentality of Sir Luke Fildes and Meissonier. If one wants to know something important about the social life of Europe between 1875 and 1900, one can find it, written plainly, in Cézanne's and Van Gogh's still lifes, or in Pissarro's and Renoir's landscapes. If one wants to know how many buttons a French soldier had on his uniform, one goes to the painters of genre. If we tolerate the pure genre painter at all, it is because, before the camera was perfected, he presented us with some of the external stuff of history. But no one in his senses would exchange Brady's record of the Civil War for Winslow Homer's.

All this is a preface to saying that there is a fine show of American genre paintings and drawings at the Whitney Museum. Whether you are attracted by Thomas Eakins' sober revelation of Philadelphia life, or even more attracted by Henry Sargent's demonstration that napery was absent from an early-nineteenth-century mahogany dinner table, the show has something to give you. Besides, there is a real find in it. This is David G. Blythe, a wood-carver and itinerant portrait-painter, who was born in Ohio, travelled in western Pennsylvania, and died at the age of fifty in 1865. I had never seen any of Blythe's work before, but these three paintings indicate that he is an important figure in our past. His "Post Office" has a quality of observation that recalls Hogarth, but the figures, in their lively movement and suspense, are his own. Incidentally, this painting solves a problem that has always bothered me—what happened to a wide-bottomed crinoline dress in a crowd. As for "Dry Goods and Notions," both the mule and the lady in this picture are far removed, by their brilliant handling, from the dry woodenness of the lesser realists. Blythe had style.

Up to the present generation, most of the lesser genre painters were more conspicuous for their moral earnestness than for their talents. But note Homer's magnificent illustrations for *Harper's Weekly;* it is high time someone collected all those fine drawings and made them available in a book. That the observation of the daily social routine is by itself a sufficient foundation for art is a superstition. (The most conspicuous successes in the popular mid-nineteenth-century prints were the landscapes.) The overconscientious transcription of daily life may, indeed, undermine the imagination of a good painter, but it cannot release the imagination of a poor one. John G. Brown, the Horatio Alger of American painting, would under any circumstance always be a fifth-rate painter, whereas Morris Kantor, even when he paints a crowd of people at a race track (No. 140), will endow the image with as much subjective vitality as the most Surréaliste conceit. The Whitney show is well selected and pretty full; but I missed the little masterpiece called "The Circus Is Coming," by Charles Caleb Ward.

The retrospective exhibition of the work of the late Bryson Burroughs at the Metropolitan Museum comes under the head of Unfathomable Mysteries. How could a man of such talents have been the curator of paintings at the Metropolitan? Everyone has always known that Burroughs' own paintings were Puvis de Chavannes-and-water mixed with more water; but one has to see his work *en masse* to realize what a jugful of tasteless syrup it was. A curator of painting who did not paint at all would not necessarily be altogether disqualified for his job; but a man who could paint like Burroughs and permit his canvases to remain in existence was devoid of the most elementary capacity for criticism. A few of the drawings are respectable, such as the sketch of Nazimova; but the weak, tepid forms, the feeble color, the dullest clichés of classicism mixed into a sort of ice-cream sundae of adolescent eroticism—these revelations were not pardonable errors of tastes, nor were they mere failures of talent, like Roger Fry's landscapes. They were serious disqualifications. Is it any wonder that under Burroughs the Metropolitan still looked with ill-concealed misgiving on the positive masculine force of Cézanne?

The Metropolitan Museum is a great and valuable institution. It has withstood many attacks, some justified, some pusillanimous. But it will need all its reserve power to live down the fact that it not merely harbored Burroughs but—in a fit of misplaced piety—actually permitted his lifework to go on view. Aesthetically speaking, the whole business is extremely indecent, not to say naïve. It perhaps explains those terrible gaps and flaws in the Metropolitan's representation of modern art up to 1931. On the other hand, the exhibition of Japanese No robes, in a room fragrant with freshly shaved wood, with a fine procession of headless figures moving across a Japanese bridge, is a large advance upon any previous presentation I can remember at the Museum—very fine indeed. The robes themselves, particularly the more geometrical patterns like No. 21, are quite marvellous. The one false touch was the realism of the pink cherry trees; this almost spoiled the effect of the three immense red paper lanterns.

THE THREE BENTONS

Thomas Benton has come to be classified as the leader of the new school of Middle-Western painters. By strutting around and shouting defiantly in the archaic fashion of the Riptail Roarer from Pike County, Missouri, he has done what he could to give color to this notion. He likewise shares with Burchfield and Hopper the somewhat doubtful honor of being the chief painter of Americana, for like them he has elevated a seedy, down-at-the-heels, half-baked, half-ruined America into a national symbol. But Benton is a complex man, and his real talents as a painter begin at the point where his ballyhoo gestures and his sentimental rhetoric leave off.

In the paintings on view at the Ferargil Galleries, one beholds the three main tendencies in Benton's work. The first comes out in his direct sketches from life, usually in ink and wash. Here he is a man with a great appetite for facts who has evolved an effective shorthand for putting them down. His studies of places and characters, particularly in the remoter parts of the Mississippi Valley and in Texas, have a unique value. To find Benton's equal in this department one must go back to Winslow Homer in his best days after the Civil War. A portfolio of Benton's sketches before they are irretrievably scattered would make an important document both graphically and historically.

The second Benton is not the friendly, humorous recorder of raw daily life among the threshers and cotton-pickers and strikers and dancers and crapshooters, the man who swaps stories at the roadside and plays a harmonica in the kitchen after supper. The second Benton is the ambitious fellow who wants to become the Great National Painter by leaving his mark on vast expanses of public wall. The ambition is worthy enough, perhaps, but it has had a depressing effect on Benton's work; for in order to do a big canvas, it is not enough to have big figures. One must also embody significant ideas. Benton's symbols have not usually been equal to his task, because he has deliberately suppressed important aspects of life. Afraid of being highbrow, he takes refuge in puerility. Afraid of being emotional about major issues, he becomes sentimental over minor incidents. Instead of grasping the whole American scene, he uses a small part of our experience and restricts the epithet "American" to that part.

The fact is that much of Benton's larger studies of the American scene, like "Lord Heal the Child" and "Preparing the Bill," belong to the level of journalism. Benton is like a newspaper reporter who spends a week polishing a news story that should have gone into the first edition. The result is not imaginative literature but bad reporting, which has not even the merit of its own kind of quickness and directness. Observe the sketch of "Lord Heal the Child," note the crook of the woman's arm and the swing of the lamp, and compare this preliminary work with the stilted form of the completed picture. The weakness of the idea is proved by the waxen poverty of the painting.

Finally, there is a third Benton—less ambitious, but more human; less assertive, but more profound. This is the Benton who carries over into his smaller oil paintings a sense of the peace and beauty and lonely wistfulness of man facing the earth. He shows us the tired farmer at his plough, or a solitary figure and a water tank and a freight car under the moonlight—"Waiting." Here he is not preaching Americana, in the fashion of the Hearsts; he is being American, and expressing his direct sense of life, sweet and poignant, even if sardonic. There is more living, breathing humanity in Benton's landscape of three horses on a wide prairie, in the current show at the Corcoran Gallery in Washington, than there is in his most crowded external representation of a city crowd. In these smaller paintings, there is no fake hardness, no fake anti-intellectualism, no silly jingoism; they are Benton at his best, observer and poet in unison. After the Riptail Roarer and Peck's Bad Boy have had their fling, there may still be a handful of his paintings that one will not be ashamed to house in the same gallery that holds Ryder.

· · · · ·

Two good exhibitions downtown: an exploration of the contemporary social scene at the A.C.A. Gallery, in which the radicals put their best foot forward; and some handsome gouaches at the Eighth Street Gallery by A. F. Levinson, a man whose work this year far outtops the promising oils he showed at the same gallery a year ago. . . . The Neo-Romantics seem about to crack up on us. A little while ago one of them, Tchelitchew, showed a series of new paintings in which he seemed to cover up a lack of fresh impulse by utilizing the uncorrected distortions of camera perspective. Now, at the Julien Levy Galleries, comes Eugène Berman, suave and accomplished, with a new series of disturbing tricks. He out-rockwells Kent by painting landscapes in which the rocks are full of suggestive resemblances to human heads and torsos. If this is what Neo-Romanticism has come to, I give it only another year. . . . Rudolf Belling's sculptures at the Annot School Gallery were a disappointment. The heads like disembowelled alarm clocks and dentists' dummies one already knew; but they are better than the more realistic forms, just because one expects less of them. Perhaps the most interesting abstractions were the erotic ones—or perhaps spring is here again. . . . Being merely human, I have emerged from the biennial show at the Corcoran Gallery at Washington and the latest exhibition of the Society of Independent Artists with not a single orderly impression in my head. But I recommend both shows—or whichever you happen to be near. . . . You will have to make up your mind about Georges Schreiber's sketches of celebrities at the Fifty-eighth Street Public Library without my blushing aid.

A GROUP OF AMERICANS

According to report, Grant Wood is a modest man. He has a sense of humor and a knowledge of his own limitations—which is almost saying the same thing twice. It is his misfortune at the moment that he has become a National Symbol for the patrioteers. As a symbol he stands for the corn-fed Middle West against the anemic East, starving aesthetically upon warmed-over entrées dished up by Spanish chefs in Paris kitchens. He stands for an independent American art against the colonialism and cosmopolitanism of New York. He also stands for the new regionalism, because he has settled down in Stone City, Iowa, founded an art colony there, and sold some of his paintings to his neighbors. In his innocence of what is vital and original in American painting, Wood, as quoted in the catalogue, sounds a little like the late Vachel Lindsay talking about

Walt Whitman. One would hardly guess from the manifestoes that blow like a dust storm from the prairies that George Fuller and Winslow Homer and Albert Ryder had fifty years ago put the new regionalism on its feet.

But no movement should be judged by its manifestoes. So one turns with interest to the present show of Wood's work at the Ferargil Galleries. Up to 1929, Grant Wood was an impressionist; he painted with a visible brush stroke and a good appetite for color, like a thousand other novices. From impressionism he turned to the careful technique of the fifteenth-century painters, seeking that sober durability which is shown at its best in the portrait, lately at Knoedler's, by the "Maître de Moulins." (This happened, incidentally, at least five years after the German exponents of *die Neue Sachlichkeit* had moved in the same direction.) It is in the portraits produced after 1929 that Wood's real talents have so far been manifested. He has caught the grave, angular faces of the people he knows and loves best; and his "American Gothic" has validity as a symbol that justifies its Flemish overtones. This is his best painting to date. Not all his portraits are as good as this; the background of "Arnold Comes of Age" belongs to the Maxfield Parrish school of picture-book romanticism. As for the famous "Dinner for Threshers," its healthy pink glow cannot conceal the weakness of the design and the vacuity of the portraiture: it looks like a color photograph of a model of Life in Iowa done for a historical museum.

Wood's recent landscapes are almost unmitigatedly bad. The soil is modelled so as to resemble carved plaster, and the trees are made of tissue paper, absorbent cotton, and sponge rubber. If that is what the vegetation of Iowa is like, the farmers ought to be able to sell their corn for chewing gum and automobile tires. Perhaps the most hopeful works in the present exhibition, outside of "American Gothic," are a drawing called "Adolescence," which shows that the sense of humor evident in "Daughters of the Revolution" is still on tap, and "Death on Ridge Road." Except for a certain chaste reserve which he shares with O'Keeffe, Demuth, Sheeler, and Dickinson, there is not a specifically American touch in his painting.

Where does this leave Grant Wood, the great exponent of an indigenous art, the breaker of our slavish ties to Europe, the discoverer of native materials and native methods, the layer of new regional foundations for American painting? In four words, it leaves him nowhere. Wood, the painter, is a colonial of colonials. Wood, the painter, has not yet produced a picture that is not completely derivative in both symbol and technique from the Europe that the Middle West has supposedly thrown off. Wood, the painter, is an honest man still fumbling with his problems—a man who should be given another five years for quiet, untroubled experiment, so that he may find himself, instead of having to live up to an entirely accidental political reputation. Regionalism is a good cause, and art lives by the assimilation and expression of fresh experience which is often personal and local in origin; but one advances neither regionalism nor art by pretending that third-rate art becomes first-rate art merely by the magic of being homegrown.

The painter now on view at An American Place is Arthur Dove. He is not without a certain kinship to Wood, in that he is tempted to transform the visual facts of the landscape into more abstract symbols, but whereas Wood is betrayed into turning trees into lesser objects like rubber balls, Dove goes the whole hog and creates complete abstractions. This gives him a freer range of both color and form, and even at his weakest his paintings have usually had great decorative charm. But at his best they have more than that: "Goat," a painting in browns, olive greens, and sea greens, is a strong, handsome composition, and "Fantasy," a pure abstraction, is likewise very good; the exhibition as a whole is vastly better than last year's. As with Bluemner, one feels about some of Dove's other canvases that his talent would come to fullest fruition in stage design: "Summer" and "Morning Sun" have just the right amount of formalization for the theatre or the opera. As usual, his brief water-color sketches are excellent, though his best oils, like "Goat," go far beyond the original hints in these drawings. Dove is a seriously underrated man. Did not his abstractions stand out as among the best at the recent Whitney Show of Abstract Art?

Among his contemporaries, Borglum, Taft, MacMonnies, French, George Gray Barnard has always been a giant; and if anyone wishes to place his work ahead of Saint-Gaudens', he has my consent. The brilliant young sculptor who did the symbolic statue of "The Two Natures" now so conspicuously shown at the Metropolitan had, to begin with, a very fine technical equipment. His gawky Lincoln is perhaps the best monumental portrait anyone has done in America. And the present show at the Grand Central Galleries confirms Barnard's high seriousness. Unfortunately, there is not a piece of sculpture or a sketch in it that surpasses in any great degree, in either conception or execution, the work he did in his youth. His vigorous, masculine Christ is a victim of misplaced emphasis: its strength is in the naked muscles of the back rather than in the upraised face, which can hardly be seen. Like Rodin, Barnard has felt the need for a more effective unit in sculpture than the isolated statue; so he has imagined temples and monuments on a grand scale. The model for the "Sermon on the Mount" and "Cain's Sin" shows the difficulty of creating architectural sculpture without architecture; lacking a mold in which to set his figures, the allegorical elements occur in the design in the fashion that gems occur in the rocks where they are found: there is no logic of form to bind together the underlying ideas. This lack of articulation in construction leads to a lack of articulateness in expression. The weakness is doubly plain in the Rainbow Arch, which is still on view in the deserted powerhouse at 216th Street east of Broadway. The arch itself does not bind the figures together, as in the portals of a medieval cathedral, where the form emphasizes the hieratic ordering of the figures: dismount the figures and set them on the horizontal plane, and they would have almost the same degree of effectiveness. A man of positive talents, great craftsmanship, generous vitality, and keen aesthetic perceptions—witness, among other things, the Cloisters—Barnard remains a man about whom one feels that a better sculptor has remained locked within the visible one. His work shows the weakness of a purely personal synthesis of art and religion. Lacking collective support, he has not been able to lay new foundations; both in form and idea, he remains an eclectic.

IN CAPITULATION

The season is again wheezing to a standstill. And I haven't managed yet to say anything about the handful of art books that have been deposited on my shelf during the winter. If I wished to discuss half the issues Sheldon Cheney has raised in "Expressionism in Art," I'd be talking the rest of the summer, and the broccoli and wang bok wouldn't get planted. So let's skip it; and you can have the fun of arguing with Mr. Cheney all by yourself. Then, Mrs. Dagny Carter has put five thousand years of Chinese art into two hundred and twenty-five pages, with a bibliography and illustrations. The title is "China Magnificent," and it seems to me a useful outline for the layman. "After Picasso," by James Thrall Soby, is a handsome book that goes into the theories and biographies of the contemporary French Surréaliste and neo-romantic schools. It underrates the influence of Rouault and the German expressionists, overrates Dali and some of the lesser virtuosi, and in general is as provincial in its concentration upon Paris as the prophets of American autarchy are in their concentration upon Kansas. So be it. Perhaps the most fascinating and useful book that has appeared is Professor Max Doerner's "The Materials of the Artist and Their Use in Painting." It is meant primarily for the guidance of artists, but anyone who is seriously interested in painting will find his perceptions enriched by this treatise.

As usual, the graduating classes have been casting up their preferences for various parts of the universe, and I don't see why I shouldn't follow the example of the seniors. Here are my votes on the art season. Best sculpture exhibition: Lachaise at the Museum of Modern Art. Most important retrospective exhibition: Alfred Stieglitz's photographs at An American Place. Greatest surprise: early paintings of Eugene Higgins at the Kleemann Galleries. Most interesting show of proletarian art: Artists' Union's sculpture show. Most belated shows: those on African Art. Best murals: William Gropper's for the Schenley Corporation. Most useful to the historian: Genre Painting Exhibition at the Whitney Museum, and Pennsylvania Folk Art at the headquarters of the National Committee on Folk Arts. Handsomest redecorated gallery: Brummer's. The soundest vintage: the Renoirs at Bignou's and Durand-Ruel's. Most important revaluation: memorial show of Alfred Maurer's paintings. The season's weakest: Burroughs Memorial Exhibition at the Metropolitan Museum. First prize for publicity (a dozen sheets of last year's flypaper and a tin rattle): Señor Dali and Tom Benton. Greatest flop: the Paris neo-romantics. Saddest news: the approaching replacement of the original Barnard Cloisters with an expensive piece of copybook architecture in the manner of the Riverside Church.

There is one item I have held up till the last; namely, the season's most promising young artist. If I am not mistaken, it is Joe Jones, a St. Louis painter, whose work is now on view at the A.C.A. Galleries. Curiously, the three schools that have dominated the scene during the past season— the neo-romantics, the Americanists, and the proletarians—come together in the work of Jones. He has produced a fine hybrid strain of his own—pardon the effect of too many seed catalogues!—which with a little further selection should have some of the suave color of the romantics, some of the rust-resisting qualities of the proletarian artists, plus an immunity from the Parisian beetle which the better American strains, like the Marins, O'Keeffes, and Hoppers, have shown.

To begin with, Joe Jones is a painter. He has either learned a great deal from the early Picasso and his neo-romantic successors, or he has arrived by himself at some of their conclusions. He can use a sombre palette and still keep life in the melancholy blues and blacks: the painting "We Demand" has some of the tonal richness that Berman gets in his better paintings, and the use of the overhead railroad structure to create a counterthrust to the marching figure with outstretched fist in the front rank of the parade is admirable. He is not afraid to paint a girl's body or a bottle of milk and a broken loaf of Vienna bread; and the sober skill he shows here is quickened in the dreadful figures of the garbage-eaters in the right-hand corner of "Demonstration." Incidentally, these figures are better than those in the larger canvas on the same theme; for in the fragment, they are not swallowed up by the dark background, nor is attention diverted by the irrelevant patch of light in the sky.

But Jones is also a Mid-American. He knows the wheatlands at least as well as Curry knows the corn of Kansas, and his landscapes are handsome and confident, quickened by the play of light over the grain as the harvester climbs across the foreground. Perhaps the least convincing of his landscapes are the backgrounds of "The New Deal" and "American Justice." Here both the sky and the land are overpatterned, and the forms are crisp and thin, like paper cutouts. Carried a little further, this would lead Jones into the same sort of weak simplification as Grant Wood's landscapes. There is another kinship between Jones and the Americana school: he has the same healthy ambition to do public art. But in the case of "Roustabouts," the larger canvas lacks the vitality of the preliminary study. In the latter, the various parts are subordinated or emphasized; in the mural, all the masses are dead: the picture has lost in quality, like a photograph that has been over-enlarged and then retouched to recover detail.

There remains the element of social commentary in Jones's work: an earnestness, a fierceness, a powerful reaction to the sombreness of life among the starving and the stunted and the oppressed. This gives a reality to Jones's dour moods that puts his conceptions many degrees above the studied drawing-room melancholia of the neo-romantics. Unfortunately, Jones sometimes works with as narrow a set of political symbols as the painters of Americana. So he weakens one of his best paintings, "Demonstration," by making the central point in the composition a group of signs: "Smash the War Makers," "Don't Starve—Fight." Failing to paint a counter-symbol of hope in contrast to the garbage-eaters, he falls back on words. That is pulseless propaganda.

Stereotyped symbols and brittle two-dimensional painting are the chief dangers that beset Jones, but at twenty-six he has already shown evidence of an aesthetic and social imagination capable of surmounting both these obstacles. Coming at the close of the season, Jones's exhibition brings it to an end not with a whimper but a bang.

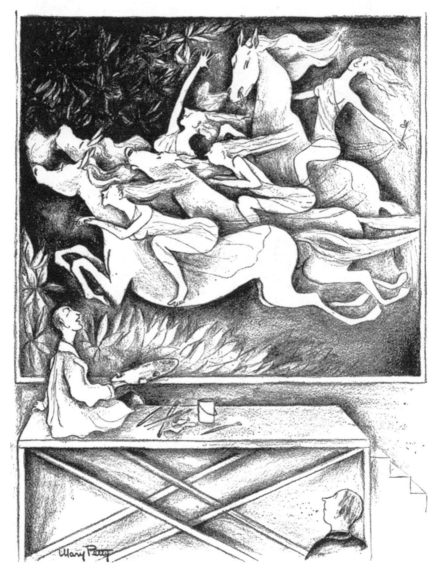

"I've had a few nibbles from the Government."

From the outset of the 1935–36 season, Mumford wrote at somewhat greater length on select exhibitions, probing deeper into the meaning of certain works and the intentions of certain artists. These included Fernand Léger ("Léger and the Machine," October 19, 1935), Albert Pinkham Ryder ("A Synopsis of Ryder," November 2, 1935), and Vincent van Gogh ("The Work of Van Gogh," November 16, 1935). For mounting this last exhibition, Mumford offered rare praise to the Museum of Modern Art's Department of Painting.

Columns in the new year ranged widely. Georgia O'Keeffe was the subject of another lengthy review, in which Mumford gave her work a biographical reading ("Autobiographies in Paint," January 18, 1936), while William Gropper received an unexpected reevaluation ("William Gropper and an Open Letter," February 15, 1936). In a March review of a major Museum of Modern Art exhibition, Mumford discoursed on the often-baffling role of abstraction in modern art and its meaning in modern life ("The Course of Abstraction," March 21, 1936). He concluded the season with an appreciative review of a Frank Duveneck retrospective at the Cincinnati Art Museum ("Looking Backward, Looking Forward," June 6, 1936).

LÉGER AND THE MACHINE

Who shall take the opening bow of the season? Shall it be William Lescaze, the architect who remodelled the entrance hall of the Brooklyn Museum? Certainly, that is a very fine job: mirrored black glass, blue columns, dark-gray composite-stone floor, suave curves, and serene white planes—all these realize to the full the possibilities of honest modern design, in which a sound feeling for form gives the commonest materials the grace of marble and the austerity of the Doric order. Architecturally speaking, all our museums began as mausoleums or Houses of the Dead. One by one they are now being renovated from the inside. Perhaps we may all yet live to see the day when Mr. Clarence Stein's plans for a completely glass building, with a flexible interior, meant for pleasure and study, will take the place of the melancholy monuments that symbolize nothing so much as the disease called "museum fatigue." (Symptoms: a pain in the neck, first stages of blindness, creeping aesthetic paralysis.)

Or shall one salute Fernand Léger at the Museum of Modern Art, even though his exhibition—one had almost said memorial exhibition—leaves one colder than it would have done twenty years ago? Both the architecture and the painting represent similar tendencies, but the growing success of modern architecture somehow begins to overshadow the achievement of the painters who visually helped pave the way for it. By now it is pretty plain that modern painting divides roughly into two great schools. The first symbolizes psychological states; the second derives its attitudes from architecture. Léger belongs to the second school.

Though there is an early figure drawing by Léger in the present show, done with a fluent line, full of vitality, he was one of the first to identify the modern movement in art with the celebration of the machine. Even when Léger's images are not mechanical, they are devitalized. He is tempted to reject life for its soft surfaces and confused textures and impalpable edges: confronted by Lot's wife, his first impulse is to turn her into a pillar of salt. One does not expect Léger's iron leaves to grow or his bloated, cylindrical women to leave their luncheon table and go hastily to a maternity hospital. Although there is movement in his line, it has the click and precision of machinery; even when it is complicated it is expected.

Cézanne's oracular remarks about the cube and the sphere Léger must have taken in all literalness, although he himself shows a fondness rather for discs and for cylinders. He composes his picture of architec-

tural elements, sometimes grouping them in flattened patterns, like abstract sculpture in low relief, sometimes juxtaposing them in such a fashion as to suggest distance and movement. Now the composition strikes
one as pure arabesque; again, as in "The City" Léger suggests enough
three-dimensional space to make one accept the canvas as a structure.
But Léger himself always seems to be outside his forms, as if he develops
them systematically in accordance with a program. His dexterity is that
of a juggler with five balls in the air, not that of an acrobat, who himself
experiences the tensions and pressures of the figure he is creating.

This externalism perhaps accounts for the static quality of Léger's art.
Once in a while he borrows an image from his contemporaries, as in the
Cubist "Village in the Forest" (1914) or the humanoid bones of 1932,
which bear resemblances to Picasso and Miró. Usually he keeps his own
line; neither style nor idea nor feeling has undergone a development. One
looks in vain in Léger's symbols for some hint of the changes that have
taken place in the machine, and in our attitude toward the machine,
these last twenty years.

As paintings, these canvases show an aesthetic poverty. "The City" is
perhaps the best of his larger efforts, while No. 10, "Mechanical Element," and No. 12, "Composition in Blue," are very handsome and effective geometrical patterns. These few pictures are almost sufficient by
themselves to establish his aesthetic contribution. Either his program or
his personality has limited his resources. For not merely does Léger deny
himself texture, one of the elements with which Braque and Picasso made
daring experiments. In contrast to the modern architect, he fails, in addition, to utilize the natural resonance of materials, which gives, as it
were, different tones for metal, for glass, for clay, for stone. All of Léger's
forms might be composed of colored cardboard in the earlier period or
painted metal in his more recent work; and the color is no less monotonous than the material: spots of lilac, red, yellow, repeated in canvas
after canvas. Indeed, Léger loses very little by being reproduced in black
and white.

Are Léger's deliberate restriction and monotony essential, then, to his
interpretation of the machine age? Perhaps; but if that is so, his interpretation of mechanical forms is again an external interest in mere surfaces, and shows no very profound insight. Cylindrical grain elevators,
round phonograph discs, wheels, valves, semaphores are only superficial
symbols. Léger has shown that they have their aesthetic moments. For
that one thanks him. But who would guess from these canvases that the
machine during the last generation had been undergoing a metamor-

phosis, that it was becoming life-sensitive; that, so far from turning men into cogwheels, it was itself becoming "demechanized," more lifelike, more responsive, more organic? As symbols of the machine, Léger's canvases, moreover, lack the refined and exacting craftsmanship of the objects with which he is enamored. In comparison with real mechanical forms in glass, steel, or concrete, any work on canvas, of course, comes to sheer impressionism; but there is a certain sketchiness in Léger's treatment of canvas and paint that compares unfavorably not merely with machines but with the more patient craftsmanship of other painters. This is particularly true of his earlier canvases. A barn by O'Keeffe or an interior by Sheeler has more of the spirit of the machine than many of Léger's more mechanical symbols.

What remains? What remains in Léger's painting is his honest architectural intention. He has sought to give a painting the strength and impersonality of a good communal expression like a building, and if in the end this gives little to the spectator directly, it serves an instrumental purpose—helping the eye of the architect and the ordinary spectator to look upon pure line, volume, and color as the essential ingredients of an architectural composition. For this purpose his geometrical symbols, which serve as the greatest common denominator of our machine culture, are adequate. If they express little that we did not already know, they at least fix our attention on the common elements in our background. Léger's painting does not depend upon modern architecture, nor did that architecture grow in response to his painting; that supposition would be absurd. But they enlighten each other, for they acknowledge a common source.

If Le Corbusier is more of a painter than Léger, it is equally true that the latter is a sounder architect than Le Corbusier. But the weakness of Léger's art is its failure to incorporate the human element. Even in his figure paintings he limits himself to the bare forms of architecture, but forgets that the architect's work is not finished until the living forms of men and women take possession of the building and reorganize it spatially and visually by their movements, their gestures, their life. And because Léger forgets life in the process of creating mechanical symbols, we, the living, have our revenge: when we look at these images, we feel a little bored.

The gala opening show of the Brooklyn Museum—that of Spanish painting—is a little disappointing. For one thing, it is short on Goyas; but, even worse, there is no effort to include any of the original inventive work of the contemporary Spaniards—Picasso, Dali, Miró. This academicism belies the promise of the new architecture of the lower floor.

And it is weak from an educational standpoint, too, for there is a living connection between such pieces of pure abstract art as the El Greco called "Visitation by the Virgin" and Picasso's Cubism, just as there is between Dali and the laborious copies of Flemish painting done by the Spaniards of the fifteenth century. Apart from the incompleteness of the selection, there is deadness of another kind; I am a little doubtful as to whether the handsome new electroliers throw enough light on the canvases. Perhaps lighting tests have been made; perhaps the lighting has been certified as mechanically adequate. But the eye does not confirm the machine; at least my eyes didn't. El Greco's Toledo in this room is simply not the same Toledo that stuns and delights one at the Metropolitan. If that is really so, perhaps some of the rest of the paintings are not quite so dead as I took them to be. But a show that gives us Goya's self-portrait as a young man, his admirable "Don Manuel Osorío," and the dashing "Gossiping Women" is, despite all the qualifications, worth going a few extra subway stations to see.

A SYNOPSIS OF RYDER

Not since the first grand display of Albert Pinkham Ryder's paintings at the Metropolitan Museum in 1918 have we had a better opportunity to see his paintings than this season. The exhibition of twenty-six paintings at the Kleeman Galleries has more variety than the Modern Museum show of 1930, if only because it presents some of his immature work.

Farewell to the notion that Ryder was a painter with a single style or a single fixed technique. Here is pretty much the entire range and development of the man, or at least a synopsis of it: one passes from thin pigment to thick pigment and varnish, from the rapid brush strokes of "Holland" to the sometimes miraculous, even enamel of the final period. And the change of interest and subject matter is equally remarkable.

Sweet adolescent commonplaces, done in soft autumnal coloring, are the marks of Ryder's earliest work. He begins with such feeble paintings as Christ walking with a shepherd's crook in the Garden of Gethsemane, or the "Wayside Forge," a reddish composition, marred by age and fire, that slightly recalls an inferior Blakelock. There is little in these early pictures save a certain delicacy of feeling, a certain timidity that keeps him from making gross and pretentious blunders. Such paintings somewhat excuse the judgment of Ryder's aunt, the good lady who advised the young aspirant to give up any hopes of being a painter. If that advice does not altogether damn her as an art critic, it shows that she was a poor psychologist. She did not know enough about her nephew to appreciate the depth and intensity of his feeling. So she could not guess that he would persevere with his art until his feelings became perfectly articulate, until it reached a pitch of perfection at which every stroke would reflect the quiet harmony and the deepening insight of his own life.

Some of Ryder's early paintings already have merit, even though the style is not yet formed. "Improvisation," a girl at an organ or a spinet, has something fine in it; and "An Idyll" is halfway to the lovely "Perette" at the Northampton gallery. In certain paintings, like the "Landscape with Sheep," there is a real vagueness of form that does not exist in the purposefully obscure figure paintings of his maturity—a vagueness that reminds one of George Fuller. Finally we come to that series of boats under the moon, in which the tone darkens, the greens and blues and blacks supplant the soft autumnal yellows and brownish reds, the technique turns to a lustrous enamelling, in which the design becomes more complex and subtle, and the observation of nature is more intent and exact, as well as more poetic. At this point something terrifying, overpowering, and sweet, like a hopeless love, comes into his painting. This quality is carried over into his great allegories. One of these last paintings, "Macbeth and the Witches," is here.

There were weaknesses in Ryder's original equipment, and if those of technique diminished with time, others, derived from nature, like his festering eyes, which dreaded sunlight, remained. But no painter could have been less handicapped by the frailty of his natural endowments; he used every grain of his talents, and he knew how to harmonize what he was with what he might be. Ryder could not for his life have turned out a popular illustration of bathing or skating for *Harper's Weekly,* as Winslow Homer did, nor could he have engraved a banknote with classic goddesses, like Walter Shirlaw. But he had qualities that more than made up for lack of the superficial brilliance one finds even in the juvenilia of Homer: he had an extraordinary persistence, and a no less extraordinary capacity for growth.

One finds Ryder at the beginning of this series of paintings little more than a child who has aspirations to be a great painter. One finds him at the end, after years of unfaltering discipline and devotion, a painter who, without losing the simplicity of a child, has actually attained maturity and greatness. His paintings belong to the nineteenth century; they belong to it like the tales of Hawthorne or Poe, the music of Wagner, or the poems of Baudelaire; and yet as paintings they are dateless: they are as far from the literalism of the realists, or the externality of the impressionists, as they are from the vapid sermonizings of the Watts and the Böcklins. Originality does not consist in avoiding the influences of history, tradition, and contemporary life, but in completely assimilating them and making them into new flesh and blood; and in this sense Ryder was surely one of the great originals of the nineteenth century.

Of all the paintings in the present show, perhaps the most precious to lovers of Ryder is his self-portrait. It is a small painting, glazed and reglazed without damage to the brilliant colors that glow under the surface, and the finish is remarkably without flaw. Here is Ryder in early middle life: fresh, sweet, even-eyed. Like so many other paintings of his, it has a lesson to teach our generation: the lesson that importance is not measurable in mere space—not in space in the headlines and not space occupied by the canvas on the wall. What counts in a little painting by Ryder is something which I trust I do not make more obscure by giving it a name: spiritual pressure, an unwillingness to be satisfied by the second-best, the half-finished, the unrealized. In the service of an ill-balanced personality, the pressure and grip and intensity one finds in Ryder's work would have made a financial Napoleon or a crazy political dictator; in the case of this harmonious soul, it made a great artist.

Some painters are primitives because they feel that way, and no amount of technical sophistication or fashionable pressure can make them feel any differently. Charles Prendergast, whose paintings are now at the Kraushaar Galleries, is that kind of primitive. As a painter, he is without complications: life, as he shows it and makes one feel it, is full of joy, and his Songs of Innocence will never be tainted by the young harlot's curse of Blake's "Songs of Experience." Charles Prendergast's paintings have the eager directness that one gets in good children's drawings, but they have, in addition, the resources of fine craftsmanship. If the mind is innocent, the hand is cunning, and the gay colors are harmoniously spotted and combined.

Each of these pictures is a fresh glimpse of Heaven, and one can no longer sneer at the notion that Heaven's streets are paved with gold. The fact is one believes in Charles Prendergast's angels, and one knows he uses gold naturally, because gold means sunlight and riches and bliss—which is what the pictures say all over again. Now Heaven is a fabulous bathing beach, as in "Holiday"; now it is "Market Day," with horses cantering in the background and all sorts of delectable fruits piled on the stands; but no matter what the scene, it is inhabited by quite irresistible birds, beasts, flowers, and angels. These paintings are not "mere" decoration; they are far too rich, juicy, and positive to be treated as background. Perhaps the finest picture of the lot is that called "Decoration," but any choice cannot help being a little invidious.

There is an underlying kinship between Charles and his more famous brother, Maurice, but it should not keep one from seeing that, aesthetically, Charles Prendergast is a complete and highly interesting individual who needs to wear no hand-me-downs. If ever I am emerging from a serious illness, I should wish someone could send me one of these paintings by Charles Prendergast; it would be worth a whole shift of pretty nurses and a dozen ultra-violet-ray treatments.

Burchfield's eight recent water colors at the Rehn Gallery are a pleasant surprise. He is one of that group of painters—Wood, Benton, Curry, and Hopper in particular—who are in danger of being undervalued as artists just because some of their admirers overvalue them as political emblems. The present pictures are interesting because they are free from Burchfield's principal weaknesses—an excess of sentimentality in treating the worn-down and battered images of the past, a tendency to substitute bathos for graphic values, and the temptation to reëstablish his aesthetic claim by stylistic prettifications.

During the past year he has even retouched the picture called "Sulphurous Evening," once shown at the Modern Museum, to make the gold in the sky look a little less obviously like a wallpaper background; and the feeling of his buttercups or his red barn owes nothing to bathos; it is clean, straightforward painting. The "Old House and Apple Trees" gives the cold sunlight of an early spring day with a degree of precision which, if it does not by itself make great painting, remains one of the minor pleasures for the eye. "Rain and Wind Through the Trees" has the same sort of cleanness and directness. Burchfield is in danger, when he renounces sentiment and the obvious symbols of the Brown Decades, of falling into competence, matter-of-fact visual statements that have the limitations if not the technical handicaps of color photography; witness "Black Iron." But on the whole this is a satisfactory show; and if I use a lukewarm adjective, it is only to counterbalance the premature and excessive adulation Burchfield has received.

THE WORK OF VAN GOGH

Thanks are due to the Museum of Modern Art for the most thorough, the most exemplary, and the most stimulating exhibition of modern painting it has yet put on—the work of Vincent van Gogh. From Mr. Barr's admirable catalogue, in which the usual introduction gives way to a series of poignant selections from van Gogh's letters, to the reframing of the pictures, not a detail has been slighted.

For those who have not seen the fine collections at Amsterdam and at Wassenaar, this show will have many fresh things; neither the late Mr. Montross's first exhibition in 1920 nor the later selection given by the Modern Museum itself had such a good representation of his early and middle periods. Here you may follow van Gogh's development from his first studies from life, made in 1879 and 1880, while he still had hopes of being a clergyman, through the period of learning from his Dutch contemporaries, Israels and Mauve, up to the burst of flame that marked his culmination as an artist at Arles; you can even mark the swift, black descent at Auvers.

The modern movement in art really stems back to two figures who by temperament and expression stand at opposite poles—Cézanne and van Gogh. In the first, a warm Latin taste for rhetoric, as plain in his painting as in his youthful verses, gave way to an equally Latin passion for clarity of form, architectural form. Van Gogh, by contrast, is a man of the North, as full of vehement, inarticulate passion as Mynheer Peeperkorn in "The Magic Mountain." He is concerned not so much with form as with feelings; his subject is life, whether he chooses as symbols a pair of old shoes, an empty bedroom, or a broken actor. For Cézanne, a human figure is a solid in space; for van Gogh, a solid in space alters its shape and color and texture in response to the pressure and temperature of the human observer.

Note, however, that van Gogh was no bungler in form: he patiently acquired all the primary lessons of craftsmanship. Indeed, during his stay in Paris, his effort to assimilate the technique of Pointillism partly checked his growth, though in the end it perhaps more than repaid him by making him throw away his Dutch palette and preparing him to receive the color of Provence. His development spanned a surprisingly short time: decades rather than a few dozen months seem to separate the sketch of the miners, No. 70, done in 1880, from the crayon drawings of tree roots, No. 78, done in 1882. His draughtsmanship, almost from the first, was strong and competent, sometimes brilliant, even before he developed the characteristic signature of the final period—the dashes, the dots, the waves that contributed their own movement to the underlying form.

Beloved though the paintings of his last five years rightly are, one should not miss or undervalue van Gogh's earliest work. In those studies of the weavers and miners of the Low Countries, pictures as dingy and full of defeat as the life itself, there is already more than a touch of the master. "Potato Eaters," "Weaver," and the heads of peasants lack technical resources; but in these paintings van Gogh strikes a note that comes back at the very end of his life, purified and refined but no less sad, in the blue "Olive Trees and Mountains" (No. 60), in "Ivy" (No. 61), in the portraits of Mademoiselle Ravoux; above all, perhaps, in a painting whose absence one regrets most, the portrait of Dr. Gachet in the peaked cap—Gachet "with the heartbroken expression of our time." But there is an etching of him here that tells much.

By first apprenticing himself to the realists, van Gogh earned the right to use his imagination, and with encouragement from Gauguin—that, at least, is to Gauguin's credit—he began to design freely, using nature only as a basis of form, daring to flatten out his planes, as in the famous portrait of L'Arlésienne, without reference to the camera eye. So he achieved the freedom and the mastery found in the great paintings of the period at Arles and Saint-Rémy: the freedom that gave the self-portraits, the sunflowers, the portraits of Roulin, the postman; and Madame Roulin, and the "Actor" and the "Cypresses" and the brilliant café at night.

Van Gogh's example tells much about the effective expression of social themes in art, for he was as conscious of the blight and corruption around him as were Morris and Tolstoy. He admired the English illustrators, the sentimental realists and the humanitarians, but he knew better than to follow their examples. Their fulsome sentiments, their sweet moralities, their social preaching never went into his canvases. Van Gogh took a harder but more effective route. He painted, for example, "Night Café" in blood red, dark yellow, with yellow lamps and a bilious green table in the middle, a room of clashing colors, sour contrasts. "I have tried," he explained, "to express the idea that the café is a place where one can ruin oneself, run mad, or commit a crime." He fully succeeds in expressing that idea, but how? Not by showing a man brandishing a revolver or sinking mawkishly to the floor, but by the direct medium of paint itself: malachite greens, yellow greens, and reds, juxtaposed in such a fashion as to embody the idea and recreate the mood.

Van Gogh worked. He admired Doré for saying that one needs the patience of an ox. He wrote that "we must work as much and with as few pretensions as a peasant if we want to last." He had none of the willful subjectivism of the dilettante, who tries to create original form out of tepid inanities, who mistakes whim for inspiration, and lazy drawing for an overpowering emotion. Life had battered van Gogh and hurt him. It denied him bread and fellowship and esteem; worse, it denied him the two women he had really loved and gave him the privilege of sharing his few scraps of food and reputation with a prostitute, sluggish and foul beyond even a saint's powers of redemption. His passion, his frustration, as well as his faith, went into his paintings, dictated the colors, modified the subjects, created a veritable dance of brush strokes, like the tattoo of a martyr's feet, dancing on coals. The higher the flames danced about the stake, the more bravely he sang.

Black night, burning sun, gloomy North, radiant South, torment and ecstasy—these are the elements of van Gogh's story. Life as he had found it was terrible and beautiful; that was the sum of it. For him the greatest artist of all worked not in canvas but in living flesh. And in that sense he was perhaps a greater artist than his paintings alone show him to be. The paintings remain, nevertheless, an important manifestation of that greatness.

While you might profitably spend all your time at the van Gogh show, it happens that there are many interesting things in the galleries at the moment. Above all, so far as I am concerned, the year's exhibition of John Marin's water colors and oils. Once one has said of Marin that he is the best water-colorist since Cézanne and the most original painter this country has produced since Ryder, there is little to be added. If the pictures on the north wall of An American Place do not persuade you, no argument of mine will be very convincing. Enough to say that they show Marin still at his peak.

There is a little instruction, perhaps, to be gleaned from comparing Marin with a promising young water-colorist from California, named Millard Sheets, now on view at the Milch Galleries. Sheets, who is still under thirty, has a superb technique: he can match his white skies and gray clouds against nature's without embarrassment, and, if his palette is still a little monotonous, he hits the surface of things with a pleasurable accuracy that recalls Sargent or Hopper. Mr. Sheets' problem is to keep from being overwhelmed by his caressing eye and his knowing hand. A dozen empty technicians can show him the wrong way to favor his talents, but he would do well to go patiently to Marin to find the right track, for Marin has unique powers of rediscovery and self-renewal.

The Utrillos from the Guillaume collection, at the Valentine Gallery, are a very fine lot. Hugo said that the soul of Paris is concentrated in its suburbs, and that is what Utrillo gives us so well—dull buildings with marvellous textures on crumbling wall surfaces, dead vistas of suburban blight, under skies that shimmer and glow with the light of the season. This is the best showing of Utrillo I have seen in New York, and some of the pictures in it—"Le Sacré-Cœur" and the "Rue du Mont-Cenis"—are very distinguished pieces of painting. The paintings with figures have fine passages in the backgrounds; but the figures themselves are pretty discouraging—a man who can paint buildings as well as Canaletto has no right to make kindergarten daubs.

This leaves me with no space to say how fine the Marguerite Zorach embroideries, at the Brummer Gallery, are; or to record why my second impression of Abraham Rattner at the Julien Levy Gallery was more favorable than my first; or yet to say why I liked the paintings of Lonergan, Weston, and Levinson recently at the Dorothy Paris Gallery, but didn't like the current show of Fega Blumbergs. Perhaps it's just as well.

AUTOBIOGRAPHIES IN PAINT

Mid the throng of good shows that have opened the new year, that of Georgia O'Keeffe at An American Place stands out: seventeen new paintings—canvases that are as simple as a polished pebble and as finely wrought, out to the very edges of the picture frame, as the most honest piece of Flemish craftsmanship. This new work glows with poetry and truth; and neither strain nor weariness nor despair is visible.

All art is a sort of hidden autobiography. The problem of the painter is to tell what he knows and feels in such a form that he still, as it were, keeps his secret. He must find a way of obliterating himself at the very moment when he gives himself away most completely. To have nothing to conceal and to have nothing to reveal are pretty much the same thing. So there is a cryptic element in painting that really challenges the beholder, and ultimately every painting is as enigmatic as the Mona Lisa.

Long before Dr. Freud embarked on his career, a British aesthetician, known apparently only to the late Professor George Saintsbury and myself, had written a book which began as a work of genius and rambled off into mediocrity. The author's name was Dallas and the book was called "The Gay Science." In this work, Dallas discussed the "hidden soul" in relation to art, that being nothing more or less than an Early Victorian approximation of the unconscious. Dallas proved very ably, I think, to the discomfiture of all purely rational formulas for aesthetic experience, that the quality which distinguishes a work of art is its pull and hold on the unconscious. What goes before this in design and manner of execution is by way of preparation; it can be analyzed. What follows eludes analysis; it must be directly felt or experienced.

Now, here lie precisely the attraction and the difficulty of dealing with the paintings of Georgia O'Keeffe: every painting is a chapter in her autobiography, and yet the revelation is so cunningly made that it probably eludes her own conscious appraisal. As soon as one realizes that she is neither a botanist who looks at flowers through a magnifying glass nor a comparative anatomist who collects the skulls of the North American desert fauna, one is brought face to face with the real problem. What has she lived through? And what do these turkey feathers and bare hills and bleached bones convey in terms of one's own experience? One grants that her symbols are part of the scenery of New Mexico; but another artist in the same region might find nothing to paint but a railway train or a barroom.

Certain elements in O'Keeffe's biography were plainly visible in the paintings of the previous few years; physical illness cannot be concealed. There was more than conventional symbolism in the dark crosses that stood out against the clear desert sky, and there was a bitter note in the pink rose stuck in the horse's skull. The painting in these pictures was still fine, and there was even technical progress in her modelling of the landscape, but the work lacked the sense of sharp discovery that the earlier paintings had. One felt that the next word might diminish into that silence which is the artist's death.

The present show brings, for O'Keeffe's admirers, a resurgence of life and a resurrection of spirit. The epitome of the whole show is the painting of the ram's head, with its horns acting like wings, lifted up against the gray, wind-swept clouds; at its side is a white hollyhock flower. In conception and execution this is one of the most brilliant paintings O'Keeffe has done. Not only is it a piece of consummate craftsmanship, but it likewise possesses that mysterious force, that hold upon the hidden soul, which distinguishes important communication from the casual reports of the eye. Here one notes the vast difference between those who are able to draw upon the unconscious, because they face life at every level, and the Surréalistes, who have been playing with the unconscious in the same way that a smutty adolescent might play upon a ouija board for the purpose of eliciting an obscene word. O'Keeffe uses themes and juxtapositions no less unexpected than those of the Surréalistes, but she uses them in a fashion that makes them seem inevitable and natural, grave and beautiful.

The ram's-head painting is not alone. The same health and mastery pervade the rest of the show; witness the swirling waters of the "Chama River" and the "Dark Hills," two of the finest landscapes she has ever painted. The series of turkey feathers and horseshoes, and the turkey feathers in a black Indian pot, are very fine, too; even the little pastel of the roses is a delight. Here are serenity, poise, craftsmanlike command; above all, a simple love of beauty. Indeed, beauty, an almost forgotten word, becomes real again in her work.

The John Carroll show at the Rehn Galleries gives me an opportunity to say something that one accident or another has bottled up for a long while, and this is that Carroll is one of the most interesting imaginative painters my particular generation has produced, a man whose work stands much higher than many better-known and more popular painters.

Do not imagine that I have any temperamental affinities for Carroll's favorite young ladies, those anemic, bluish, hollow-eyed creatures with attenuated hands who apparently go through life in frilly nightdresses, who languish in "Sleep" (No. 18) or in "Indolence" (No. 25), who waft themselves at twilight toward lonely young men on horseback (No. 15), or who throw off their nighties altogether and go a-riding with dream-like ease on top of powerful white bulls. Those young ladies are not for me; I would feed them liver and orange juice and milk and eggs and brandy until I got a little color into their cheeks, and I would make them discard their nightgowns for good, bright sports clothes.

But if I had my way, I would ruin Carroll's art. One of his portraits, that of Tina, depicts a little girl who has all the healthy qualities I like, and it is the flattest, dullest picture in the whole exhibition, while that of her brother, Milner, has just the slight touch of pre-adolescent anemia that brings out Carroll's most brilliant qualities. Mind you, though Carroll likes young ladies who look as if they had been buried underground for ripening, he is no Marie Laurencin. He is a man who likes the country and is stirred by the sight of a horse in the field or a pack of hounds gathered for the hunt under the cold sunlight of a leaden morning.

But he sees these objects under the same light as he sees his attenuated girls. The colors for the most part are silver grays and corpselike whites and yellowish greens, occasionally a touch of rose, like that which breaks across the vague sky in the background of the girl on the bull. (It is informingly labelled "The Cowboy's Dream," and Mr. Rehn tells me that Carroll has ridden the range in his day.)

Do not pass the landscapes by, either. "Under the Hill" and "The Pasture" are both very fine, and the picture called "Picnic" is one of the most melting poems about Arcadian love-making I have seen. This silvery dream world of Carroll's takes hold of one, and it is more deeply native than you would perhaps think at first glance. Even the languid maidens represent our old nostalgia for an impossible maiden in an even more impossible Aidenn, whose name is Lenore. These large-eyed and languishing females are, in fact, very lovely. On second thought, maybe I wouldn't feed them liver and orange juice after all.

Alexander Brook, who has a large show at the Downtown Gallery, is one of the few artists who manage to capture the interest of both the conservatives and the moderns. What is the secret of that double power? The interest of the conservatives is perhaps easier to explain than that of the other school, for he draws well and paints well, and he has the same pleasure in textures that made the background and costumes of late Renaissance art so much more important than the figures themselves. In the qualities that give academic people pleasure, he can match his achievement against their best contemporary representatives and win hands down. But there is something more to the paintings than this, and it does not lie in anything I can lay my hands on except his feeling. He reveals, with exquisite delicacy, that sadness, that tenderness, and that irony which are deeply part of the mood of the time. The contents of the picture may be sordid and ugly, as in the automobile graveyard labelled "Approach to Mt. Kisco," or they may be quite neutral, as in the still life that holds the central wall, but the effect is fresh, because the feelings behind it are so genuine. Brook's smallest paintings have the same quality as his larger work. Do not pass too quickly over "Adolescence," "Early Fall," and "Summer Gossip."

Postscript: If you haven't got around to seeing any African art during the last year, I can recommend the comprehensive and many-sided exhibition at the Jacques Seligmann Gallery. It has a handful of quite classic pieces of sculpture, and many examples of a lesser order.

GROUP SHOWS AND SOLOS

The Whitney Museum and the Museum of Modern Art have both blossomed forth with a series of exhibitions. Large group shows, like that of sculpture, drawings, and prints at the Whitney Museum, produce upon me the same effect of bewildered joy I recollect from my childhood experience of auction-rooms at Atlantic City. What the buyers got was never what they bargained for, when viewed in the quiet, sober light of their homes, but the endless array of bargains and the bidding and the wheedling rhythm of the auctioneer more than made up for any lack in the goods themselves.

In this second Biennial Exhibition, the central piece among the sculptures is Gaston Lachaise's "Group." This would be so even if, to our great loss, Lachaise had not recently died. Despite the cold plaster, these intertwined forms of a recumbent man and a woman have a powerful effect. His last work is an appropriate coda in Lachaise's life as sculptor, summing up its great theme, and finally rounding it off. All the more does one feel this symbolism because, though the head of the man is upright, even bent forward, with a sense of effort, the next move, as it were, would be complete relaxation—and sleep. One remembers again that strong, proud group Lachaise modelled fifteen years ago: a young man carrying a girl in his arms. It dissatisfied him, and he destroyed it. But if his interpretation of the threshold of love is now missing, here, at all events, is his vision of its fulfillment.

While there is the usual amount of deft commonplaceness in the rest of the sculpture, there is likewise a handful of outstanding pieces: Martin Craig's abstract composition, Goodelman's "Woman," Marion Walton's "Woman's Head," and Warren Wheelock's very jolly "Paul Revere's Ride." Whether Minna Harkavy's "American Miner's Family" finally comes off I am not sure, for the articulation of the woman's head and neck seems to me a little doubtful, but the conception and composition both challenge one's interest. So far as I could see, there are no surprises among the drawings and prints, but the level is quite high. If I have said nothing, apart from noting the Lachaise sculpture, that quite justifies my enthusiasm for the show at large, the answer is go and see for yourself. It really is pretty fine.

The three-ring circus at the Modern Museum has a different turn on each floor. To begin at the top, the collection of paintings and drawings Mrs. John D. Rockefeller, Jr., has given the Museum is a very fine nucleus indeed. As one should perhaps expect in a personal collection, not originally conceived for the benefit of posterity, the pictures are not numerically well balanced; Burchfield, Demuth, Hart, and Sheeler occupy a disproportionate place, and artists like Munch and Nolde are missing. Still, it is a good collection, and makes a brisk show.

Cassandre's posters are perhaps the very best thing in the line that has been done since Toulouse-Lautrec. In Cassandre's work, the experiments of the Cubists and Surréalistes, which seemed so terribly esoteric twenty-five and fifteen years ago, become the common idiom of expression: easy to read, easy to understand, handsome, brilliant, attention-arresting. All these posters have great carrying power. The symbols are always intelligible and, as in the case of the poster for *Candide,* frequently downright witty. In a word, here is a mural art, far more in the spirit of our time than the cumbrous, nonremovable frescoes that are being perpetrated in so many public places in America, and except for the work of a handful of our painters, it is far more amusing. As for American poster art, there is simply no comparison between Cassandre's dashing advertisements and the sticky, sentimental realism of most American advertisers today. While France has Cassandre, and even England has Kauffer, American advertising is controlled by minds which have rationalized their own lack of aesthetic response by means of statistics and trumpery psychological tests. That sort of business and "science" gets the kind of art it deserves.

The Richardson exhibition, ably put together by Professor Henry Russell Hitchcock, Jr., is a significant performance, and it comes not a moment too soon. Richardson, Gargantuan both as man and architect, was appreciated by his contemporaries as long as he lived, and quickly forgotten when he died; it remained for our generation to perceive that he had laid down the foundations of modern architecture, and had done so from fifteen to thirty years earlier than any of his comparable European rivals. Do not take a hasty glance and conclude that this is just a neo-Victorian revival; it is, rather, the beginning of the first authentically American tradition in architecture. Note particularly what Richardson did with the wooden country house, with his railroad stations, with the Glessner house and the Marshall Field Wholesale Building in Chicago, and with the Pray Building in Boston. These lessons were not lost on Louis Sullivan; and during the eighties and early nineties, before a stupid revivalism and eclecticism became fashionable again, more than one architect learned from Richardson how to build simply and resourcefully in wood. Incidentally, there are some surprises in this exhibition, even to an old lover of Richardson; notably, the façade of the modest little Emmanuel Church in Pittsburgh, a perfect gem. Richardson was a sort of inarticulate American William Morris, but, as an American he had this advantage over Morris: while Morris, in his work, remained bogged in the beauties of the past, Richardson instinctively was in harmony with the forces of his day, and felt that he could both coöperate with them and conquer them. The further we draw away from Richardson, the higher he towers.

In his show at the Dorothy Paris Gallery, Mark Datz has, I think, taken a real step beyond his earlier paintings. As a painter of New York, he belongs to the tradition of Sloan, Glackens, and Luks. Like these artists, he has pleasure in pure color. It is a good tradition, but his personal contribution is, I think, of a different order; Datz's individuality comes forth in paintings like "Anticipation," a pregnant woman, sitting solemnly in the open, attended by a dark and ominous servant. That painting holds one; so does that of the "Girl with Pigeons." At the Guild Art Gallery, one's first impression of Lloyd Ney's paintings is probably one's poorest; one beholds a whole room full of paintings in which the spectrum seems to be repeated in every picture. One's eyes resist the kaleidoscopic reds, yellows, and blues. But as one gets used to the repetition, one discovers that the best paintings are those in lower key, with blues, greens, violets predominating: "Flowers," "Church," "Worthington's Garage."

Ney's imagination, while intoxicated with this world of color, has nevertheless been nibbling at the daily incidents of commonplace life in a Pennsylvania village—New Hope, to be exact. Datz's and Ney's paintings are as much paintings of the American scene as the more stridently native kind. Ney's pictures have even got into circulation in his own community: he has three murals in the village newsstand, and he has decorated the entrance to one of the garages. That seems to me a healthy sign. Americana should show us fireworks on a clear Fourth of July night as well as exploded paper and charred Roman candles and empty bottles of soda pop lying on the grass in the dull drizzle of the next morning.

In reviewing a show of Waldo Peirce's a year or so back, I called the painter healthy, which is almost a dirty crack in a period when people enliven their reputation with their neuroses and surgical scars. But Mr. Henry McBride, in his introduction in the catalogue for Peirce's new paintings (at the Midtown Galleries till January 25th), backs me up when he calls the artist Rabelaisian; for those who know Rabelais other than by hearsay, this is almost saying the same thing. Gusto is written all over these paintings—the gusto of the amateur, who sometimes delivers a painting as well conceived as "Stables at the County Fair," and sometimes manages to be as wholesomely tepid, aesthetically speaking, as in the big canvases of "Haircut by the Sea." But Peirce manages to convey his enjoyment even when he is unsuccessful with his forms. Incidentally, while this painter is a friend of Hemingway, the latter's worst enemy couldn't have hit on a more amusing commentary upon "Death in the Afternoon" than Peirce's painting of Don Ernesto, languishing on a wounded bull's back, and delicately dipping his pen in the gore. I have the impression that the paintings which Peirce showed in New York before were more soberly painted, and were perhaps better in their formal qualities. The present work is done with a sort of exuberant carelessness, as though someone were trying to frame a sentence and hum a tune at the same time. The tune is there. Perhaps the sentence doesn't matter.

GOYA, HOMER, AND JONES

You had better take a few untarnished adjectives with you when you go to see the new Goya exhibition at the Metropolitan Museum. While most of the paintings, drawings, and etchings have been drawn from their own collections, they have never been put on full-dress parade before.

As with Delacroix, one may look upon Goya as either the last of the princely line of Renaissance painters or the first of the new republican succession that otherwise began with Manet. In any case, he was a giant. How many painters after Goya had so many important things to say and so many effective ways of saying them? Daumier and van Gogh are perhaps his nearest rivals, yet neither of them quite had his immense technical span. That fact is impressive to begin with. The rich, easy coloring of the cartoons for the tapestries, such as the woman's dress in "Confidences in a Park," passes into the brilliant, sombre textures of "Don Sebastian Martinez" or "Doña Teresa Sureda." Again, the firm, sensuous clarity of "Doña Narcisa" gives way to the grave shadow-modelling of "Don Ignacio" (No. 13). And at the very end of his life, the rapid movement of "The Bullfight" anticipates the utmost achievement of Manet before Manet (who studied him well) had arrived on the scene.

In a sense, there is no Goya style; but there is Goya in all his styles; no other artist knew better how to adapt his method and his point of view to the subject. The result is that ultimate style in which the painter's individuality is so completely blended with the subject that it can not be extracted as a separate mark. There are, of course, great painters whose style is easy to identify, like the villainy of a Squeers or a Bill Sikes, as soon as they appear on the scene; but there is a handful of even more consummate stylists whose individuality is too finely disciplined to leave such a coarse trail on the canvas: Tintoretto and Giovanni Bellini, for example. Goya belongs with the second group. One does not recognize his tricks first and then enjoy the painting; one enjoys the painting and then recognizes that only Goya could have painted it.

Marvellous as Goya's paintings are in range of expression, his drawings and prints are no less remarkable. The sepia washes, represented here by specimens from the Metropolitan's recently acquired album, are worthy to rank near Rembrandt's drawings. As for the etchings, in particular the "Disasters of the War" series, the quality that made them odious to nineteenth-century collectors only brings him closer to sound contemporary taste. Goya respected the reproductive process, and maintained the same even level in his first impression as in his last. He did not achieve a few good prints by way of a series of messy approximations. His combination of aquatint and etching gave him the same range in prints as an original pen-and-brush drawing; and when lithography was invented, he quickly applied himself to it and demonstrated its serious possibilities. If only a few drawings, such as a "Crowd in a Park" or "Foul Night," were left, one would still be assured of his power and reach.

The change in taste that has taken place during the last generation has given us a new insight into Goya's aesthetic achievements, but the revival of Goya's fame is also due to the fact that our knowledge of the human personality and our experience of the series of catastrophes and mass brutalities that began with the World War have given us a new insight into his message. Brutality is no longer for us, as it was for the Victorians, something that exists on the edge of the jungle; it is something that may break at any moment into the parlor, in the form of a Fascist squad or an aërial torpedo. What is peculiarly "modern" in Goya is his combination of an intense realism and a high regard for fact on one hand, with an imagination that stops at nothing, and understands that nightmares can be realities and realities can be nightmares.

The Goya who drew the "Caprices" and the "Disparates" did not have much to learn about the murkier sides of the personality from Dr. Freud; he understood the character of our present psychoses—the fears, hatred, obsessions that keep men from being sane and magnanimous and human. Only the most courageous of spirits could have faced both the terrors he found in his own consciousness and the brutalities he found in the world outside. "God Spare Us Such Bitter Fortune" is the title of his drawing of a man showing a dagger to his wife and child. What the alternative was Goya shows in the print called "You Can't Look"—a group of victims shrinking before the points of massed bayonets, driven toward them by unseen soldiers. "The man," wrote Goya, "who shuts his eyes to the unsteadiness of fortune sleeps soundly amid danger. He can neither dodge impending harm nor make ready for calamity." Goya sought to open the eyes.

Love of life, love of women, love of the day's drama, all plainly vibrate through the work of this stormy, passionate, and tremendously intelligent man. During the latter part of his life the catastrophes of war turned this love into an equally passionate hatred for all manner of frustration and cruelty and evil; instead of the Duchess of Alba, he shows us the butchered naked bodies of women, sprawling not in wantonness but in a last spasm of agony. One can say of Goya, as one can say of few painters, *he told the whole story.* And his horror and hatred are all the more terrible because none knew better than he how deliriously good life could be.

Have Winslow Homer's water colors been overpraised? I asked myself that question at Knoedler's the other day and, a little guilty about my own moments of praise, I am still asking it. In mastery of his medium, Homer undoubtedly stands high; he explored pretty much all the possibilities, from thin, suggestive washes to masses as solidly built up as oils—as in "Fishing, Adirondacks," No. 16. But even more than his oils, his water colors are a little bleak; this is as true of his tropical studies as those of the Maine woods. One must admit that he knew the value of intense color in small amounts, and half the life of "Nassau" (No. 24) is perhaps due to the tiny spots of red in the climbing figure and the palm-tree fronds; the same is true in the flag and water line of "Stowing Sail." But alas! he repeats the trick too often—and always with red. If his gamut of color was narrow, his command over textures was remarkable—witness the fragments of the stern of the boat in "After the Tornado"; and at times he could recapture some of the dash of his original woodcuts in *Harper's Weekly,* as in the beautiful easy lope of the Negro in No. 33, in which he was not afraid to distort the perspective.

While Homer's gun was beautifully oiled and the sights were accurate and the hand was steady, he somehow had a way of aiming, pictorially speaking, at clay birds, and though his marksmanship was exquisite, he now leaves one hungry at supper. Is it heresy to say that this man who loved action rarely achieved it in the one way that it is possible to achieve it in a painting—in the design itself? Possibly it is significant that only one painting in this very complete show depicts a boat under sail. I think the best of his designs is the rapid and relatively uncharacteristic "Coming Storm," in which the impending clouds and bending palms convey the excitement of the beholder. For me, Homer's water colors as a whole seem more important than Sargent's; but I would not put him on the level of either Maurice Prendergast or Marin.

The sudden success of a young painter always makes one a little old-hennish as to what may happen to his ego and his work, but Joe Jones's recent show at the Walker Gallery was reassuring. The painting, at all events, is unspoiled; indeed, the various manners which showed signs of increasing divergence in the paintings he exhibited at the A.C.A. Gallery last spring now seem to be coming together in a coherent style. The outstanding painting in the latest show was, I think, "Wheat with Farmers," which is mainly wheat, ready for mowing, rippling in the wind, done with a swift assurance that recalls van Gogh at the height of his powers: the vague flocculence of the nearer clouds is in fine contrast to the sharp stab of the dry stalks of grain. The calm spaciousness of "Grain Elevator" puts it on the same level with the three small wheat-field canvases, and if the foreground of "Straw Stacks" had been as dexterously painted as the stacks themselves, it would perhaps have been among the top paintings of the show. Neither of the two big figure paintings is quite as good as those in last spring's collection. In that of the miners, the puzzled face of the seated miner is the essence of the picture, but there is lack of realization in the other faces, and parts of the background are so far forgotten as to merit their removal with a shears. But Jones can draw, and he has a sense of land and crop and cloud that is full of feeling expressed in the surest and tenderest touches, particularly in the sky. He has been called a proletarian painter and a propagandist painter. Perhaps he is. But he is closer to Whitman than to Marx.

WILLIAM GROPPER AND AN OPEN LETTER

One of the fine things about American art at the moment is that William Gropper is painting. When his mural for the Schenley Corporation appeared in the mural painters' show last year, one could say simply, "This is a painter," in the same fashion that Lincoln, when he saw Walt Whitman pass the White House once, could say, "That is a man." Gropper's show at the A.C.A. (through February 22nd) establishes him definitely, I think, as one of the most significant painters of our generation. I have weighed those words. If you like, I will repeat them.

Do not fancy that my admiration for Gropper's radical political satires has colored my judgment here. That side of him completes the man, brings his imagination into contact with the everyday world, gives him bottom and substance; but Gropper's virtues would be obvious, if more limited, if he confined himself to painting such an entrancing *Schlaraffenland* as "Picnic," which shows a lover embracing his girl while a pig is being chased through the foreground. Gropper can paint a tree, or a landscape with figures, as few people now painting landscape can do; he ranges from the condensation and simplicity of a cartoon, almost in monochrome, to subtle canvass like the CCC workers felling a dead tree. In "The Senate," his political windbag with waving arms is the condensation of a hundred *Congressional Records,* but the canvas is painted, painted with decision.

There are, happily, no labels for Gropper's art. He is a realist and a Surréaliste and a fantasist and an objectivist and a satirist and an idyllist—which comes pretty near to saying something much more definitive and comprehensive: he is a man. His paintings have a quality that is often missing in so-called proletarian art—a gay courage, a sense that the battle is worth fighting and that no mere bad luck can snatch the victory away. Even in one of Gropper's most dour paintings—the crumpled figure hurtling through space in "Suicide"—he somehow gives this effect; the meaning is horrible, but the *substance* of the picture is not.

This show of Gropper's has left me with a desire to write him an open letter. It would go like this:

Dear William Gropper: Where have you been keeping this talent of yours all these years, and why have you not shown it more freely? When I put that question to you the other night, you said something about your skepticism about the value of painting under the present capitalistic order of society. I understand that feeling. For a while William Morris could be the idle singer of an empty day, but toward the end of his life his gorge rose. Today art is neither the honest day's work it was during the Renaissance nor the elegant, self-disciplined play that it might be in a society that knew how to extract leisure from the slavery of machines. Almost the only people who look upon painting as more important than a bathing-beauty contest or a cocktail party are those who would exterminate it altogether because they do not find the American flag in the right-hand corner of every canvas. So far, your skepticism and your scorn are both understandable.

"But if you mean that you can't take painting seriously so long as the state of the world is rotten, I think you are wrong. The world would long ago have become depopulated if lovers had acted on that premise. And Brueghel the Elder might well have stopped painting had he realized that the century he lived in was ushering in that first development of large-scale finance capitalism, mechanized warfare, and militarized industry which was to sound the doom of the ways of life he depicted with so much spirit. No. The fact is that painting is as natural to man as the more primitive biological acts that preserve his existence. It began in the Aurignacian caves, and it will outlast the subway and the bomb shelter. Yes, the machine age itself.

"To create images, to play with images, to contemplate images, to share images are part of what it means to be human. Painting today, by reason of what it stands for, is both an act of protest and an affirmation. A protest against fear, routine, dullness, meaningless restriction—in short, the defeat of life—and an affirmation of what it means to be truly alive. Your own paintings have this quality of affirmation in a very high degree, the more because you have not kept your eyes off the vindictive realities that surround us. People cannot rebuild a rotten world unless they have a sounder and richer one inside themselves. Whatever exemplifies life assists in this process of growth and renewal. And those who have your gifts must have the confidence to use them."

Vlaminck, whose fine show at the Lilienfeld Galleries includes both oils and gouaches, is one of the strong, healthy influences of his generation. He has that sane touch of the earth which so often distinguishes the men of the Low Countries, whether they are as mad as Jongkind or as sane as Rubens. And though Vlaminck is a Frenchman by birth, his aesthetic and physical ancestry are both in the North; witness his flower pictures. His realism is realism under the stress of emotion, for, as he says in the quotation that prefaces the catalogue, he paints with his heart and kidneys, without bothering about style. He communicates that stubborn exhilaration one gets when the wind is whipping the clouds over the gray buildings of a suburban street or a ploughed field. The very pigment conveys the confidence of tingling limbs and panting breath; there is movement in the quick stroke of the brush, in the passage from the foreground to the background, an urgency, a restlessness, as of the wind, hammering against shutters and making the timbers creak. While one of his paintings, "Cornfield," recalls Derain, with whom he lived as a young man, no contemporary has a more distinguished personal touch.

The Soutine show at the Valentine Gallery is the first big exhibition of this painter that has taken place in New York. Without Vlaminck's solid peasant sense of reality, Soutine gives one a world ripe with the colors of decay. One looks at it eagerly, but at the same time one feels that one should not, perhaps, breathe too deeply, lest the taint mingle with the blood. Except for the fact that his color is richer, Soutine bears a resemblance to our own Franklin Watkins—or should I put it the other way round? In Soutine, one sees a sort of descent by progressive deformation from van Gogh: the figures bulge, the houses writhe, the faces become pinched and distorted. No. 19, a lady in red, might be a Gainsborough tortured in a mirror at Steeplechase Park. Sometimes the pressure on the brain lifts, as it were, and Soutine can paint an image that is clear without being commonplace: "L'Arbre à Vence." Otherwise, one follows him through a private hell in which a chicken with feathers partly plucked becomes a diabolic bird, hatched in some Stygian cave, obscene, malignant, foul. Psychologically speaking, these paintings seem to take up the story at the point where van Gogh left it during the last months at Auvers.

The remaining painters, though I have no space to come to grips with them, are all worth your attention: Jacques Zucker, at the Guild Art Gallery, because of his sensitive touch. Whatever can be felt and touched, the textures of the foreground, the nuances of the sky, he can do justice to. What requires spatial penetration or intellectual analysis has only just begun to appear in a few of his later canvases. But the feeling is fresh, sincere, personal—rare enough qualities. A. F. Levinson, at the Dorothy Paris Gallery, merits your interest because he is an exceptionally well-balanced painter. He has learnt much, and he carries his knowledge easily. Note particularly the figures, likewise "Boat on Beach" and "Mysterious Hour" among the gouaches. In all, genuine strength and equally genuine charm. Then there is Virginia Berresford at the Walker Galleries. Despite a dangerous tendency toward brittle stylization, she has done some distinguished landscapes, like that of "Chilmark," and some fine, highly dexterous water colors. Finally, there is Campigli, at the Julien Levy Gallery, one of the few moderns this side of Derain who paint portraits without going back completely to the realistic tradition. If I say nothing about the other openings during the past fortnight or so, it is either because I have not seen them—Kandinsky at Neumann's and Allen Tucker at Rehn's and Homer Martin at Macbeth's—or because I am not well enough acquainted with the work of Schwieder or Azzi Aldrich to risk even a snap judgment.

THE COURSE OF ABSTRACTION

Often it is not till one is halfway through writing a book that one discovers what the opening chapter should contain. Something like this
seems to be true of the development of the Modern Museum of Art. The
present monumental show, tracing the movement of Cubist and abstract
art, belongs logically, perhaps, to the Museum's first year's exhibitions.
But there is this compensation for its belatedness: the resources, the organizing talent, and the insight that produced this exhibition were not
available half a dozen years ago. Perhaps the great weakness of today's
show is that—was it out of deference to the Whitney Museum, which
had an abstract show last year?—American art is not adequately represented.

Before going over the ground, we might clear our minds if we faced
the fact that the abstractions of the present generation of painters offer
no essentially new elements in art. To begin with, all painting and sculpture is abstract; even at its most realistic, it is a displacement of something that exists in life with a symbol that has only a limited number of
points of resemblance. A sculptured head can smile, but it cannot wink;
it can also live without the aid of a body and the usual apparatus for
breathing and for digesting food. Every work of art is an abstraction
from time; it denies the reality of change and decay and death. Only on
a Grecian urn can a lover console himself over his inability to catch his
mistress with the reflection that beauty and love will remain permanent.

Visual art, again, demands an abstraction from the four other senses.
It belongs to a world where taste and smell and sound are absent, where
touch exists by means of a visual counterfeit, and where (at least in painting) the movement of the observer and the many-sidedness of things are
lost in a static image. The truth is that almost all that we call culture is
based upon a system of abstractions; the signs of language and the symbols of art and religion are mere shorthand curlicues for the reality they
indicate or express. The most fulsomely realistic genre picture of a country grocer's store in Kansas is closer to a geometrical form by Ozenfant
than it is to the patch of life it seeks to imitate. The man in the street has
been looking at abstract art all his life without realizing it. What he
falsely calls realism is only a more familiar series of abstractions.

By nature, any single work of art is a thinning down of concrete experience. If this were its only characteristic, one would have to reject art
as a weak surrogate for life, as the Philistine does—a tepid beverage, for
people who are not strong enough to take life neat. But art makes up

for its limitations by a series of special advantages. By means of abstractions, certain qualities of experience can be intensified. Divorced from immediate practical necessities, art can respond to experiences our daily duties usually shut away from us, and it can rearrange our perceptions and feelings in new patterns, more significant for us than life as we have actually lived it. In a period of social development, art can make us anticipate new experiences, and put us in a frame of mind to welcome them, as the sharp eye of a good hunter will pick out a bird in a faint stir of leaves, before it takes wing. It was in this fashion that the Renaissance painters, who invented deep-space perspective, and built it up on a strict mathematical basis, prepared us for the visual background for our new conquest of space through maps and ships and rapid means of locomotion.

How does this apply to the development of abstract art during the last thirty years? As Mr. Alfred Barr has well shown in arranging the exhibition, that movement had many aspects, and the new abstractions pointed to many different modes of experience. But surely one of its main expressions was an attempt to symbolize in new forms the world in which we actually live, to call attention to those particular experiences that alter our spatial relations and feelings, and to represent, by means of the image, the same attitudes and perceptions that were being expressed in the physical sciences, in psychology, in literature, and finally in all the mechanical arts. So, far from being divorced from the currents of life, the abstract artists were closer to the vital experiences of their period than were the painters who kept to more traditional forms. The meaning of any particular painting was not always clear, nor were the efforts at expression always successful. But the connection between the image and contemporary reality was close.

The facts about abstract art have been obscure partly for the reason that artists, and the few critics who understand their aims, were more concerned with the formal and technical problems raised by these new abstractions than with their underlying content. In fact, in a revolt against banal illustration, the abstractionists even claimed that their art had no contents, except lines, surfaces, and volumes, duly organized; they attributed to paintings and sculptures the characteristics of architecture, without being able to supply either the rational uses of a building or the symbolic uses of a monument to justify their new organizations of form. They deceived themselves, these critics and artists. Their forms were sometimes undecipherable, but our initial inability to read their unknown language was no proof that it would remain meaningless once we had a clue to its word forms and vocabulary.

Take the derivation of the early Cubist forms from African sculptures. Is it not absurd here to overemphasize the form and forget the social milieu? This drawing upon Negro art for a fresh impulse was a sign of a new respect for primitive races and cultures that came in with the twentieth century. People began to realize that although the primitive African had not invented the steam engine, he had successfully expressed in his art certain primal feelings evoked by fear and death; likewise, he knew a great deal of essential lore about the erotic life, which the "civilized" white had emptied out of himself, as Havelock Ellis's contemporary treatises on the psychology of sex were demonstrating. Remember, too, the impending fear of war that ran in successive spasms through the peoples of Europe. In his admirable essay on Strauss's "Elektra," Mr. Paul Rosenfeld has pointed out how these terrorized mass feelings expressed themselves in Strauss's music, prophecy of the catastrophe to come. So with the rigid shapes, the barbarous heads, the deformed fragmentary images in the early Cubist paintings—the human body exploded on the canvas. Half a dozen years later, the war came, and those shattered forms were "realized" on the battlefield.

I do not say that this is the whole story, for one may look at the Cubist's analytic dismemberment of form in still another way. The disappearance of the realistic image and the building up of a picture from a series of separate points of view have a scientific reference. This side of abstract art connects closely with Einstein's first theory of relativity, published in 1905: an announcement of a fresh way of looking at the world, in which the fixed station of the observer was no longer, as in Renaissance painting, taken as one of the main elements that determine all the lines in the picture. Do not misunderstand. Einstein did not produce Cubism any more than Cubism produced Einstein. They were, rather, both contemporary formulations of the same common facts of modern experience. Looking at it in this fashion, one may better appreciate Marcel Duchamp's beautiful painting, "Nude Descending a Staircase." Plainly, it was an attempt to incorporate time and movement in a single structure. That picture is one of the masterpieces of the Cubist movement, although originally it was one of the chief targets for mockery. Patently, such symbolism often failed to come off. Witness the comically feeble and pathetic painting "Dog on a Leash" by the Italian Futurist, Giacomo Balla.

· · · · ·

The next great contribution of the abstract painters was to prepare the eye more acutely for the new rhythms and the new spatial arrangements and the new tactile qualities of an environment that had been radically transformed by the machine. The engineer, in the course of the previous century, had often dealt with aesthetic problems accidentally; occasionally he would even make aesthetic decisions. But in the paintings of Léger, the sculptures of Brancusi, Lipchitz, Duchamp-Villon, and Gabo, there was a recognition of the fact that the machine had by itself profoundly altered our feeling for form. We liked hard things, finished things, accurate things, required less assurance of solidity, of static balance, and of symmetry, and found a fresh use for glass to symbolize that new world in which electric waves and light rays could pass through "solid" bodies. The language of these new symbols has scarcely been worked out even now, but one cannot doubt its importance in projecting the new facts of our experience.

This aspect of abstract art led directly into the new machine arts and crafts, and one of the best features of the present exhibition is its demonstration of the effects of these new symbols upon typography, poster art, stage design, architecture, and furniture. Sometimes the suggested relationship is too tenuous, as in the composition of "Danse Russe" by Doesburg and the plan of a building by van der Rohe in 1922, but in the construction of the penguin pond for the London Zoo by Lubetkin in 1935, the connection between the new pure forms and their practical application in the other arts is clear and undeniable. True, the lead taken by painting during the nineteen-twenties in ordering new architectural forms often worked as perniciously as a very similar influence did in the Renaissance, but this proves, if it proves anything, the extraordinary *practical* effectiveness of abstract art.

I have no space to deal with that other great wing of abstract art, which began with van Gogh and developed through the various phases of Expressionism up to the orderly nightmares of the Surréalistes. But these subjective explorations parallel and re-express a whole series of psychological interpretations which are as characteristic of our modern period as our achievements in the machine. At all events, these two broad schools of abstract art, the objective and the subjective, the school of form and the school of feeling, the technological and the personal, have done much to clarify our sense of the modern world. What was achieved during this period of experiment, achieved sometimes under extravagant risks and not without losses and derangements, remains one of the permanent contributions to the tradition of Western art. Only those who have been through these major experiences have earned the privilege of going beyond them. And no one has the right to ignore them.

DRAWINGS AND ILLUSTRATIONS—PICTURES FOR THE PUBLIC

Most art dealers agree that there is no market in America for original drawings, that people will pay fabulous sums for prints, of which there may be fifty or even a hundred in a series, but they will not look a second time at an original drawing. If this is so, it merely means that we are still a nation of aesthetic illiterates. Postage-stamp collecting, with its concern for rarity, watermarks, series, cancellations, and shades, fully represents the quality of our general aesthetic interest. The result is that important drawings go begging. Prints issued by fashionable etchers, on the other hand, become costly commodities as soon as they leave the studio, whereas they should be disposed of in gross lots to interior decorators who prefer not to buy their wallpaper in rolls.

All this is merely a preface to the announcement that Maurice Sterne's drawings at the Milch Galleries are at the same high level of excellence as the Bali paintings he showed a year ago. Where shall one begin in one's praise? With the beautiful balance of weights in the Indian woman in No. 2? With the dark, decisive strokes of the child resting in No. 3? With the austere simplicity of the group sitting in No. 4? The fact is that there is scarcely a drawing in the exhibition that does not, for one precious reason or another, evoke one's admiration. In these drawings, Sterne is not tempted to sacrifice immediate feeling to knowledge; the vice of academic overelaboration, which vitiates some of his oils, simply does not exist in these swift, spontaneous flashes of the pencil. The stroke is tense, the concentration complete; the result gives the clean satisfaction of a perfect smash at the net in tennis. And, incidentally, only a sculptor could show himself such a master of the silhouette.

Eugène Berman's drawings, lately at the Julien Levy Gallery, have a different order of interest. They bear the same relation to his paintings that the sweet disorder of the dressing-table does to the properly gowned and painted woman who emerges from the boudoir. These drawings are not, as in the case of Sterne's, the aesthetic equal of the paintings; they represent, rather, a more inchoate state of thought and feeling. Perhaps the most interesting examples in the present show are the water-color drawings for stage designs; these often have a fine architectural sense, and they are far less subdued than the oils.

It is a long jump from either of these shows to the opposite extreme in art—the etchings of Ferdinand Schmutzer at the Kleemann Galleries. Schmutzer is a sort of John Taylor Arms of portraiture—a man whose patient etchings of Einstein and Freud and Richard Strauss and Pablo Casals have a permanent documentary interest because of the firm and faithful craftsmanship that has gone into their making. (The tortured, somewhat sinister head of Freud is quite good.) When Schmutzer turns to subjects that require more than the seeing eye or the faithful hand to keep one from boredom, as in his landscapes and his genre subjects, the result is just plain dull. One suspects as much, indeed, in some of his portrait studies. Here he sometimes works on enormous plates which count not as art but as a feat in weight-lifting.

"Modern Painters and Sculptors as Illustrators" is the title of the exhibition that Mr. Monroe Wheeler has brought together for the Museum of Modern Art. This comes as a sort of complement to and continuation of the Abstract Show, for it demonstrates the capacity of much the same group of artists to deal with traditional subjects and permanent human interests. Most of the illustrations are for books put out in limited editions, in which the text is treated as an illustration of the drawing rather than the opposite. No one need be surprised to find that Picasso is not content with a vegetable or a geometrical love, but has illustrated, with his usual devilish skill, Aristophanes' "Lysistrata" and Ovid's "Metamorphoses"; but what should perhaps be stressed is that in these illustrations he recovered some of the more genial human qualities he possessed during the so-called Blue Period—qualities which were later often lost in colossal but sterile experiments. More than half of the illustrations in this exhibition, I should guess, are chiefly variations on the charms of naked women—proof that the spirit that had awakened in Renoir and Rodin has not been completely diverted during the past generation in the artist's difficult encounter with Chaos and the Machine.

The American artists represented in this exhibition, painters like Grant Wood and Thomas Benton and Boardman Robinson (whose illustrations of "The Brothers Karamazov" should be better known), have explored the more difficult field of illustrating the books put out in relatively cheap editions, sometimes for the regular trade. But very properly Mr. Wheeler has included four original water colors by the late Charles Demuth for Henry James's story "The Turn of the Screw." Those illustrations are among the very best things that Demuth ever painted, and it is a great pity that they were not reproduced during his lifetime. Incidentally, why has no American publisher had the imagination to employ Thomas Benton to illustrate "Huckleberry Finn" or "Life on the Mississippi"? No closer match could be found between artist and material.

The Derain show at the Bignou Gallery presents a very unfamiliar Derain indeed—the young man who went to London in 1907, when the great man of the progressive ateliers was Matisse. This is usually dubbed Derain's *fauve* period; but in what, precisely, did his wildness consist? What shocks us about these pictures is not their slashing style, or their lack of naturalistic reference. Nor are we shocked by the *fauve* color— the pink that verges on red—which gives a sort of young raspberry-sherbet touch to the whole performance. What shocks us about these pictures is their banality and thinness; in other words, their extreme youth, so different from the grave, masterly Derain landscapes, weighted with learning and sadness, that we are so familiar with today.

These London paintings of Derain's are in direct succession to those of Monet; some of them, indeed, are attached to the same stretches of the Thames. But instead of employing tiny points of color, like Monet and Seurat, Derain used spots of pure color for the sake of giving a certain rough mosaic texture to his otherwise bald surfaces. This was not post-Impressionism but poster-Impressionism. (Ten years later Derain might have been commissioned to do posters of London scenes for the London Underground.) All this does not mean that these pictures are without interest. While "Sunset Near Greenwich" is merely a vulgarized version of Monet, "The Embankment," which probably owes a debt to Matisse, and "Hyde Park," which owes a more palpable debt to Gauguin, both have solid charm. Superficial but daring, limited but confident—that is the impression one carries away. But the Derain who could paint the pink trees and the green roadway of the swerving vista of the Thames Embankment already had distinction.

To say that I have not done my duty this season by either the Municipal Art Shows or the WPA Federal Art Project Galleries is to put my sins very mildly. But if I have been silent, it is not because these enterprises have been unworthy; on the contrary, the work done in both galleries seemed to me more important than anything one could say about individual contributions, which in some cases were fine, and in others were pretty awful. The recent show of prints and photographs at the Federal Gallery was a very well assorted exhibition, with enough good things in it to stand comparison with any print show that has been on this winter. Politics aside, such an exhibition gives an answer to a question that might be asked about our artists as well as our children: Why keep them alive?

As for the Municipal Art Gallery, all the current shows are worth looking at, and that of the group lately associated with the Dorothy Paris Gallery is distinctly above par, as one might expect. In arranging these group exhibitions, one for each floor, the Gallery has hit upon a very happy means of getting a little coherence, as well as a varied representation which will be just to as large a number of artists as possible. But instead of being a single gallery on Fifty-third Street, competing hopelessly with all the fashionable exhibitions nearby, such a municipal enterprise should, I think, be decentralized: there should be at least a dozen such galleries in various parts of the city, acting as the centres for a system of picture-loaning for a small fee. This would help reimburse the artist and eventually increase the number of purchasers. In art, as in everything else in our metropolitan life, the old French gibe about centralization holds true: apoplexy at the centre and paralysis at the extremities. To build new libraries with adequate art galleries attached, supported by municipal funds, would perhaps change the whole aspect of the relation between the New York artist and his potential public. Am I dreaming too fast—or do you follow me?

LOOKING BACKWARD, LOOKING FORWARD

In art, there has been scarcely a surprise during the past season—except, as you have guessed, the fact that there have been no surprises. The frenzied popular approval of Van Gogh, which had begun in a best-selling novel, ended up on Fifth Avenue in a series of dress ensembles: the resurrection was the prelude to a second crucifixion. Our old friends the Surréalistes, by furnishing copy for the newspapers, lost their chief claim to attention—the belief that they were so terribly esoteric they could not even understand themselves. Now almost everyone is aware that a bad dream does not necessarily make a good picture, and that an academic figure with a gimlet instead of a leg may be as tiresome as any other kind of academic figure.

The Americana boys have been less vocal and vociferous, too. The Artists' Congress last February may have made them a little sheepish lest they be taken for Fascists—if, indeed, an exhibition of their all-too-uniform symbols of American life did not also make them queasy over the possibility that they might be mistaken for sheep. As for the so-called proletarians, the best of them, William Gropper, fully justified one's expectations, while the most promising of them, Joe Jones, caused one to suspend judgment and wait for further seasoning. Perhaps one of the signs of the times, too quietly assertive to be called a movement, is the reëstablishment of abstract painting and sculpture. The retrospective show at the Modern Museum probably had a hand in this; this massive demonstration gave confidence to those who still wished to use non-representative symbols.

Meanwhile, though the schools strive and struggle and stampede, now in this direction, now in that, an occasional individual, quietly picking his way across No Man's Land and humming to himself, can still be heard. Even the Dark Ages could not demolish the Latin lyric, and what is true in poetry is also true in painting; witness the continued strength of lyrical souls like O'Keeffe and Dove and Hartl and Prendergast and Kuniyoshi and Carroll—to name only the first that come to mind. While murals are ramping through the corridors of every new community building for the edification of a conscientious but walleyed generation, some of the most important paintings of our time might be rolled up in a weekend bag.

The curious show of American art at the International Building in Rockefeller Center rounds out the season in a very inconclusive way. The show is arranged regionally, and the number of artists corresponds roughly to the population of the places represented, but these are not the chief handicaps. Its worst burden is simply that it is a big show, and a big show is an arrangement for handy shopping, like a big department store. Unfortunately, as an aesthetic spectacle, any first-class department store is infinitely more amusing, and serves the purposes of art quite as well. Another handicap is a background of pressed sea-grass blocks, which some officious wretch unfortunately painted in the worst imaginable shades of gray. (How long will it take exhibition directors to realize that, beneath dull artificial lighting, there is no substitute for white?)

Furthermore, this exhibition is under a special political handicap, for the three or four hundred American artists who have decided not to show their work at group exhibitions without being paid a rental fee have not taken part. So the representation is pretty spotty, especially for the more thickly inhabited and class-conscious parts of the world of art, like New York. On the whole, the Middle Western group seems to hold the most interesting lot of unknowns, but I am sure that a score or so of pictures would have been much more impressive than these hundreds, many of which are not worth the cost of transportation by slow freight.

· · · · ·

It happens that I have lately come back from a much more important kind of regional art exhibition at Cincinnati—the large retrospective show of the work of Frank Duveneck, who died in 1919. Duveneck was a man of real talents but erratic growth. If we know too little of his work in the East, however, it is for the happiest of reasons: his paintings were eagerly purchased by local patrons. Born at Covington, Kentucky, he found employment as a boy doing church paintings, waxen altarpieces that remind one of the work of the German painters who preceded the English Pre-Raphaelites in method and exceeded them in piety.

Like a good son of his region, with its large German population and its still-excellent beer, Duveneck, at the age of twenty-two, went to Munich, where, under the influence of Leibl, he developed into a bold, forthright realist, a remote heir of Frans Hals. Some of his best paintings were done during the next dozen or so years; they include "He Lives by His Wits," a portrait of a young gamin smoking a fag; a fine landscape of Venice; the unfinished "Cholera Girl"; and a stunning portrait of Amy Folsom, done in a blander manner. His most famous painting, the "Turkish Page," has not weathered well in any sense; both the subject and the physical materials have deteriorated.

Returning to Cincinnati in the late eighties, after his wife's death, Duveneck became a great local figure, the chief teacher in its art school, a helpful patron of its museum, the arbiter of taste as well as the glass of fashion. Had there been a dozen Duvenecks in the region during this period, the relation might have been stimulating for both the man and his community. One suspects that he missed the friendly competition of the best artists of his time, which he had met in Munich and Florence; the fact is that the work of his later years fell off, though he sought to meet later changes of taste by working in the high-keyed palette of the Impressionists. In all that matters, Duveneck was easily the superior of Bastien-Lepage; at his worst, he never, I believe, descended to the inane color photography of Bouguereau. We will not have any secure bottom to our art in America until minor masters like Duveneck are respected and studied and appreciated. To neglect their best work is an even more serious error than to overvalue their shallower paintings.

All in all, the relation between the artist and his community, in the case of Duveneck and Cincinnati, was a happy, perhaps even an exemplary, one. The fact that Cincinnati now has two of the most important smaller collections in the country—well worth breaking a Western trip to see—is an indirect tribute to the fact that the community once had an artist in its midst and cherished him.

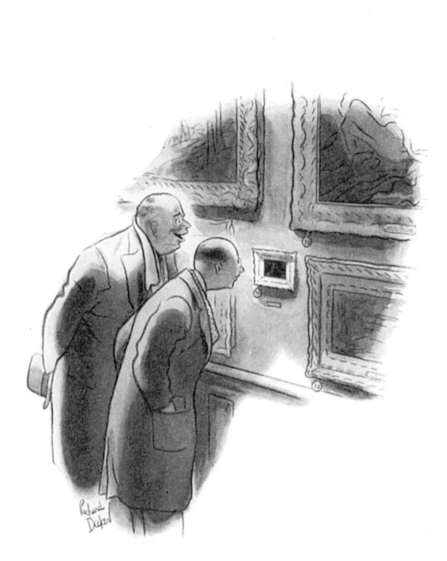

"Sort of hits you in the eye, doesn't it?"

Mumford, early in his final season as the *New Yorker*'s art critic, gave a prominent position to works produced under the auspices of the Public Works of Art Project (PWAP) and its successor, the Works Progress Administration (WPA). Exhibitions at the Museum of Modern Art and the Whitney Museum of American Art ("East and West," September 26, 1936; "The Treasury's Murals," October 17, 1936) provided an opportunity for Mumford to speculate on the role of mural painting in contemporary public architecture. He continued the previous season's trend toward more in-depth analysis in commendatory columns on John Marin, Pablo Picasso, and Winslow Homer ("John Marin," October 31, 1936; "Pablo Picasso," November 14, 1936; "Winslow Homer," December 26, 1936). As the holiday season approached, Mumford delivered an amusing discourse on the nature of fine arts reproductions ("On Reproductions," December 12, 1936). A major surrealism exhibition at the Museum of Modern Art caused Mumford to reflect in elegiac tones on the deteriorating state of modern civilization ("Surrealism and Civilization," December 19, 1936).

In the new year, Mumford reviewed an exhibition of the Ash Can realists at the Whitney Museum of American Art and a photography retrospective at the Museum of Modern Art ("The Life of the City," February 27, 1937; "Prints and Paints," April 3, 1937). His last review considered the exhibition of Pierre-Auguste Renoir's works at the Metropolitan Museum of Art ("Pierre-Auguste Renoir," June 5, 1937). Mumford saw in the artist's fervent embrace of humanity a potent shield against the growing totalitarian menace.

EAST AND WEST

About all you have to do to keep me away from an exhibition is to call it "New Horizons in American Art." I have lived through too many suburban renaissances, and have bunked my shins against too many broad horizons upon which the sun almost rose. An old dog knows that if he wants to pick up the scent, he must keep his nose to the ground and let the horizons take care of themselves. But don't let this keep you away from the opening show at the Museum of Modern Art. For once, the title means something.

No one could have imagined in 1933 that the first attempts to keep a few amiable souls from starving would broaden into a movement as solid in achievement and as encouraging to the younger painters and sculptors as the Federal Art Project has now become. In the early days—if your memory for initials is good, it was under the PWAP—even the artists had a tendency to look upon the provision of public funds for their support as a mere windfall, and the work they turned in was almost a face-saving device—like leaving behind a few sketches when you move out without paying the landlord. But the government has done something more than provide makeshift jobs. It has set up schools, it has created museums and art galleries, it has exposed, for the artist's exercise and the public's delight, whole acres of hitherto desolate walls in schoolhouses and post offices and libraries and prisons. And the artists have admirably risen to the challenge. Gone are their art-dealer blues and their barren monkeyshines.

It is all very sudden and unexpected and fabulous—enough to set one singing "The Star-Spangled Banner" aloud while walking down Fifty-third Street. Most of the talk so far has been about the murals, but I am not sure that the emphasis is right. While there are some fairly promising murals, like that of Hester Miller Murray and Mitchell Siporin in Illinois, and Arshile Gorky in the Newark Airport, most of them tend to fall into heavy-footed platitude—even Gorky's abstractions are by now something of a platitude—while for really fresh talent one must turn to the easel paintings. Here are some fine things: Jack Levine's "Conference" and Loren MacIver's "Dune Landscape" and Louis Guglielmi's "Wedding on South Street," to say nothing of Rainey Bennett's two water colors, and the freshly conceived "Houses on the River"—in green, edged unexpectedly with red—by Karl Zerbe of Massachusetts. There is not a touch of officialism or nationalistic bumptiousness or academic timidity in the whole show; that in itself indicates what an able piece of work Mr. Holger Cahill and his assistants have done.

Children's art, created under the Art Teaching Project, is not the least vital part of the show. But if one person stands out as a capital discovery, it is the New Mexican sculptor, Patrocino Barela, who worked as a day laborer until the Art Project singled him out. He is a young man of imagination, drawing upon some childhood memory of saintly figures from old churches, but refashioning his fantasies in terms of solid blocks of wood till they are as strong, if not as highly finished, as a Congo idol. His "Heavy Thinker," with a weight crushing down the figure's head, telescoping his legs into his trunk, whilst two angelic figures hold him up, is as accurate as it is funny; and "Hope, or the Four Stages of Man," is another fine piece of carving, full of meanings, too, about being born and dying. No cultivated primitivism here; this is the real thing. I have a special curse ready for the first cameraman or newspaper interviewer who tries to get hold of Barela. So far he has been in good hands.

Exciting as all this original work is, there is still another section: the Index of American Design, which is making a documentary record of old American furniture, pottery, textiles, painting; and for the first time an adequate folio of materials toward a cultural history of the country will be in existence. This exhibition gives one a queer shock; but it is hard to say whether one is more happily surprised by the aesthetic competence or by the administrative intelligence that has brought it into existence. If Mr. Roosevelt chooses to confine his platform to art, he may consider himself elected as far as I am concerned—and I'll give him either Mr. Harry Hopkins or Mr. Holger Cahill for Postmaster General.

Back in the late seventies, a young professor of politics and economics went forth from New England to teach at the Imperial University in Tokyo. And this, if you see the connection, is the reason you will probably want to take the first train to Boston to look at the exhibition of Japanese Art that will be on view at the Art Museum there through October. The young professor's name was Fenollosa, and when he got to Japan he had enough sense to forget what he was there for and devote himself not to Ricardo and Mill but to Japanese art. His hosts at the moment were in the midst of a sort of mining-town boom in Western Civilization, and they were emptying their houses of precious heirlooms in order to replace them with meek copies of Western trash.

Fenollosa, aesthetically speaking, brought the Japanese back to their senses, and they have never ceased to be grateful; hence the peculiar eminence that the Boston Museum has had in the collection of Oriental art. A variety of public and private sources have contributed their treasures to the present show, so you will probably see things in Boston that you wouldn't ordinarily run across even in Japan. There are Gigaku masks from the seventh century, more interesting to a modern, perhaps, than the more familiar Buddhist statuary of the following centuries; there is a splendid collection of paintings from the Ashikaga period, that of Japan's "renaissance"; there is even, in Buson, an eighteenth-century painter who carried the pointillist technique further than Monet or Seurat, for he used a different brush stroke for each type of foliage. (Try that some time—if you can find the right brush!) But above all, there is Sesshū.

Precisely forty years ago, Anderson, one of the first Occidental writers on Japanese art, could say, "Although Sesshū was one of the giants . . . his work will rarely appeal at once to the imagination of the European critic." But a lot can happen in forty years. Japanese painting and Japanese domestic architecture have helped reëducate the Western eye, and a host of artists, from van Gogh and Redon to Frank Lloyd Wright and Le Corbusier, have made us ready for Japanese art. No longer does our generation regard "bare" as another name for ugly, nor do we consider factual realism the indispensable foundation garment of beauty. So by now Sesshū should be easy. If he isn't, you had better console yourself with Jakuchū's "Fowls and Hydrangeas."

Most Japanese regard Sesshū as their greatest artist; and it was a mighty handsome gesture to send so many examples of his work across the Pacific. So far as my poor knowledge of Oriental art goes, I would agree with their judgment. Sesshū was what we should call a Romantic; he believed in the freshness and fluidity of life, hated ritual and merely outward form, and if he could say a thing in three lines, he did not bother to put down twenty others, just to prove that he was a hard worker. In general, this is true of Japanese painting as a whole, even of the more realistic order. But Sesshū was a master of suggestion; the actual painting of "Rocks and Waves" is even more economical than one of Rembrandt's sketches. Like Rembrandt, he had his "Night Guard" side, represented in the present show by "Flowers and Birds." But in general he carried on the great Chinese tradition of seizing the essence and suppressing everything else; indeed, he was so good in this mode that he made a conquest of the Chinese court. His successors, like Sesson, his pupil, and Tannyu, were also masters of the swift line and the delicately bounded void.

There is another side to Japanese art, a formal and architectural side, that is equally entrancing. Most of the portraits show this side—note Nos. 28, 45, and 46—but for me the high point is reached in the painting of the Imperial Palace, attributed to a twelfth-century master: a clean spacing of rectangles on the diagonal, harmonized in extremely subtle greens and browns. If Sesshū has the sensibility of an exposed nerve, this painting, done in the same frail medium, has the massive impact of granite; like the Uji bridge screen, it is built with a formidable craftsmanship.

To call either of these great types of expression "decorative" is to apply the sorriest of all misleading labels to them; they are just the opposite of decoration, in so far as this means embellishment or superfluity or meaningless arabesque. Look at the vertical trail of the brush in Niten's "Pigeon on a Plum Branch." That represents a feat of will and sensibility and physical control which is easily the equivalent of an acrobat's leap from a high trapeze, a concentration of life into a single but ineffaceable moment which means either disaster or triumph. There are a few paintings in this Japanese show that I don't profess to understand, but painting like Sesson's landscape or Sesshū's "Dialogue Between a Fisherman and a Woodcutter" should leave any critic breathless with delight. That means silent, too.

THE TREASURY'S MURALS

Almost all the buildings put up by the federal government are under the control of the Treasury Department. Aesthetically speaking, most of them are additions to the public debt; and whatever can be done to hide, diminish, or defeat the official architecture of the country, as embodied in the new buildings of the Triangle in Washington or the new Supreme Court Building, ranks as a public service. If I had my way, I'd commission murals to cover the outside walls as camouflage and paintings for the roofs to amuse passing aviators; anything would be good that distracted the eye from the superannuated classicism of these great monuments.

Fortunately, the Treasury Department got mixed up with contemporary art in a large way when Mr. Edward Bruce was put in charge of the first Public Works of Art Project, back in 1933, and since that time, with the help of many local committees, it has been busily fostering the arts of the mural painter and the monumental sculptor. Since the more money is spent on painting and sculpture, the less there will be for regiments of corpselike columns, there is a lot to be said for this kind of patronage; mural painting is perhaps the most obvious way of ploughing the architecture under. And the most drastic criticism I can make of the present show is that some of the painters have not succeeded.

The models and cartoons of federal art that are now on view at the Whitney Museum are a pretty fair cross-section of the work. While any detailed criticism of the painting must await actual inspection on the site, there is enough work halfway to its final stage to enable one to detect the general drift of things. As for the painters, the committees and supervisors seem to have made a very fair selection; a group that includes Biddle, Fiske Boyd, Fiene, Gropper, Lozowick, Mangravite, Robinson, and half a dozen equally distinguished artists will not fail because of the hacks and mediocrities that have been taken in, too. Twenty years ago, when Kenyon Cox's influence could still be felt and Blashfield was our preëminent mural painter, no one could have hoped for such catholicism and such positive taste in a federal project.

The sculptors—does one feel the heavy hand of the academic architect here?—are not so representative and not so good. Some of the better sculptors, indeed, seem paralyzed by the opportunity. William Zorach's Franklin is just another Franklin—it certainly is not another Zorach; and except, perhaps, for Berta Margoulies's and Chaim Gross's statues, the series of postmen that have been done look like magnified figures from a Rogers Group. Sculpture, I am afraid, can never rise above the level of its architecture. It is perhaps no accident that the best sculpture in the show is not for a marble-colonnaded monstrosity. It is Heinz Warneke's groups for the Harlem River Housing Project, built under the PWA in New York.

In general, then, the paintings show up better than the sculpture, for there is often a certain element of opposition and conflict between a painting itself and what lies on its periphery; sometimes the contrast even helps a little. Some of the painters have risen quite masterfully to their opportunity. George Picken's panels seem a long advance upon anything he had painted before, and Harold Weston's mural, if not better than his lyrical nudes, shows at least his capacity to conquer an entirely new set of problems. George Biddle's symbolism of Justice, in his contrast between a sweatshop slum and a decent family dwelling in a pleasant environment, takes the first prize for pith and economy. There's not a bandage or a scale in the whole mural.

But compared to the work done by the WPA artists, a certain staleness hangs over the present exhibition. Partly this is due to the fact that the Treasury Department has been dealing with well-established and gilt-edged reputations, reputations which it hopes will be redeemable at par thirty years hence, with interest at two per cent. It has taken no chances and has brought out no dazzling unknowns to compare, say, with Jack Levine in the Museum of Modern Art's show. The Treasury Department

Art Projects are also a little mediocre in that the symbols are pretty dead, which means that no one has yet seriously asked what a modern mural is for, or where and how and when it should be used.

Our whole contemporary interest in mural paintings is, in fact, pretty confused. It has arisen in America largely out of three things: an interest on the part of the painter himself in technique, provoked by a desire to recapture the clarity and brilliance of painting on wet plaster; a desire to escape from the patronage of individual buyers and art dealers, to have an everyday public instead of a precious one; and, finally, an honorable wish to achieve some of the élan and social purpose that the Mexican mural painters had as the result of the Revolution in Mexico. All these reasons are perfectly good ones, perhaps, but it happens that they labor under a series of handicaps.

The most important of these handicaps is that very few painters in America have anything to say that requires the spacious and complex representation of a great mural design; hence they tend either to create a series of small pictures, unified only by juxtaposition, or to crowd their walls with surging and writhing and squirming figures, terrifying in posture but meaningless in design, filling the space with weak aesthetic Samsons whose hair has, unfortunately, been shorn since Michelangelo first conceived them. For one artist, like Gropper, who knows what placing and spacing count for, there are a dozen who blister the walls with incomprehensible dynamics, or who, in honest dullness, arrange a series of puppet figures, which are too like Alexander, Blashfield, and Cox to be funny.

One knows what all these empty gestures mean. They mean one thing: an absence of need and pressure, created by a common emotion and a common purpose. The mural paintings of the past were icons; that is, they were sacred images, reminding the worshipper in a church or the courtier in attendance at court of the magnificence and majesty of the powers that he was serving. Now, modern painting has forfeited these public icons, just as it forfeited "the beautiful subject" about the time that Sir Lawrence Alma-Tadema treated beauty with embalming fluid; if a modern painter wanted to introduce one of Michelangelo's naked figures, it would have to be in a panel on the Significance of Hygiene or on the Advantages of a Regular Medical Examination. The chief symbols in the present exhibition are the Pioneer and the Machine, and by now they have been worn blank by repetition. In short, contemporary mural painting lacks just the touch of freshness and originality that we now find so indispensable in a picture, new qualities that a less standardized but more traditional age easily forewent without any sense of deprivation.

Painting today, in other words, is something to which we give both less and more attention than people did in the seventeenth century. We expect to see it less often, but to make up for that, we give to it a certain intensity and concentration that are lacking in the corridors or offices of a public building. The major justification for a mural painting today is that occasionally an artist arises who needs a wall of vast dimensions. Since neither the private home nor the art gallery will satisfy this demand, a public building, which may be opened like a museum outside the hours of daily work, is probably the most suitable place for such paintings. But it is preposterous to think that such murals should have some specific relation to the function of the building, to fancy that one needs pictures of people sorting or transporting mail to feel at home in a post office or to understand that stamps may be purchased there. There is plenty of room for another type of mural in such buildings: local maps, graphic statistics about industry and agriculture, panels which could be filled up from time to time with posters, such as those used by the London Underground. All these things are properly within the province of the artist. Such art would be the major mural art of our generation. It would be ephemeral, it would serve a practical purpose, it would be lively, and above all it would *not* be a pretentious fake.

We shall never realize the possibilities of the mural in our time until we also realize that modern architecture differs from all the modes of the past in that it can aim legitimately at neither monumentality nor permanence. We need a type of painting that is as flexible and as renewable as a glass-partition wall; we need a painting which, instead of being embedded in plaster "forever" (that is, until the building is torn down to make way for a garage or a skyscraper), will be capable of renewal every month, or as often as a Japanese changes a *kakemono*. When we have hit upon the proper way to incorporate such murals in buildings—which means providing accessible storage space, too—there will be work, not for a single lucky artist, but for a whole succession of artists. But before we can do this, both painter and architect must banish from their minds the stale examples of the medieval church and the Renaissance palace. Those examples account for the continued misapplication of our energies.

JOHN MARIN

A few years ago I came upon John Marin in the Metropolitan Museum. He was looking intently at some fifteenth-century Flemish primitive. When he turned to me, he said, "Sometimes, when I am walking down

Fifth Avenue, I say to myself, 'Marin, you are a mighty fine fellow, but do you know your job as well as those old boys did, and will your stuff last as long?'"

The answer to one part of this question is now spread over the walls of the Museum of Modern Art: a superb exhibition, beautifully ordered and arranged. Here, for the first time, one can see Marin's work as a whole, from the sweet, youthful beginnings of his pencil sketches to the masterly, graphic condensations of his mature work. Here it is, in all its complicated inwardness, its subtle feeling, its audacious decisions. The creator of these paintings is now sixty-six years old, and no one who has been painting during the last generation in America has a greater claim on our attention. To say that he is the best of our water-colorists today is at best grudging praise. The truth is that he is, without reference to the medium, one of the few American painters whom one dares place confidently in the first rank, with Constable, Bonington, Cézanne.

Marin belongs to that lonely aristocratic band which includes Thoreau and Ryder and Frost—men who are not afraid to withdraw, to see what they see and to feel what they feel, though the world look somewhere else and think differently. Artists with large, copious social talents often show their best traits as readily at twenty as at sixty: the Raphaels in one age and the Sargents in another are more apt to spread themselves thin with maturity than to develop beyond their first intuitions. It is different with the lonelier type of artist. There is often a long period of conventional effort, of fumbling, of trying to "be like the rest," before the artist discovers his real sphere of interest and his appropriate method of attack. John Marin was thirty-five before he finally started on the road that led to the creation of the completely individualized paintings of his maturity—those paintings which are more like the work of the Chinese masters of the Sung dynasty than that of his European contemporaries.

The path of Marin's growth led through Whistler, but fortunately it went beyond the point to which Whistler, or even his Japanese exemplars, had carried it. And at the beginning, as shown in the present collection, there was a tiny germ that was Marin, awaiting the right moment for fertilization and development. In the very first etching, of a few barges on the Seine, there is the hint of those breathless abridgments, short-circuiting and sharpening the ordinary apprehension of the eye, which one finds in his latest etchings. Marin, indeed, was to learn at an early stage the general truth expressed by the Chinese philosopher of landscape painting, Kuo Hsi: "If you wish to paint a big mountain, you must not paint every part of it, or it will not seem high." Similarly, in the earliest water color shown here, that of a London omnibus, done in 1908, one observes the most typical of Marin signatures: the use of rectangular shapes—here timid and scarcely visible—to serve as a sort of dynamic internal frame for the central motif of the picture.

Up to 1910, if one may judge by Marin's etchings, he was at home in cities—the great culture cities of Paris, Amsterdam, Venice. At this point a break came in his work. It is marked by the effulgent rainbow lyricism of the scenes in the Austrian Tirol, radiant and gay, with a rich blue which was to return in more than one later picture; observe the water in No. 153. Then the return to America and the discovery of another kind of city, more uproarious in energy, but also more disturbing to the soul. From then on Marin became rooted in the land of his birth, and the roots sank deep. New York became for him not simply another city to paint, a shattering place, filled with movement, visual disturbances, broken rhythms, exaltations, irritations; New York became a sort of radioactive substance, transforming itself, bombarding and decomposing the spirit.

No other contemporary has better caught the beat and tempo of the great city: its crazy exaltation and its restless surge, the disordered march of slow beats and fast beats, the dead spots that seem an eternity spent on a stalled subway train, and the live spots, so packed with unmanageable vitality that the juice overloads the circuit and causes a blowout. The two Movements Related to Downtown New York (Nos. 72 and 73), the "Lower Manhattans" (Nos. 37 and 39), the paintings of the black sun over the dishevelled geometrical shapes and the red sun smoldering between the cables of the Brooklyn Bridge—all these are splendid. Like Alfred Stieglitz, Marin has faced the city, has utilized its violent contrasts and its intense stimulations.

Some of this quick, urban sensitiveness never departs from Marin's fingers. While weak spirits seek a refuge in nature because they wish to escape the tortured hours of contact with their fellow-men, the stronger ones do not refuse to carry the lesson of those moments into their solitude. Before new patterns can form, old ones must be broken; and it was New York that perhaps made the Maine and New Mexico landscapes "ready" for Marin. Marin is an inquisitive and persistent questioner of nature. He delights in the moods of the sky, the varying qualities of the surface of the sea; and the play of light over distant water, framed by a cove or a group of islands, quickened into movement by a sailing ship, is often triumphantly achieved. But the relation between Marin and nature is one of give-and-take; there is more when he has finished with it than originally met the eye. And what appears in Marin's painting is there in a double sense, *by design.* Hence his remoteness from the sentimental realists; hence his ability to give body to those essences that escape the realists.

In its freedom from sentimentality, Marin's attitude toward nature is as healthy as that of a trapper, a hunter, or a fisherman. He angles for his picture as a fisherman angles for his trout, conscious of the light, the ripple of water, the dart of the dark body under the stone, conscious of the beauties that arrest smoother artists, but always waiting for the moment when his interest in all these accessories will coincide with the lift of the rod or the pull of the trigger which will give him his game. Nautical nature, geological nature, meteorological nature, all have a share in these paintings, but instead of provoking further thoughts about the sea or about the formations of the land, they bring the spectator to the point of rest where further thoughts are impertinent. Marin has no need to justify his pleasure by relating it to something else. These paintings are as American as an old coverlet or bed quilt of the forties, and I think an American Indian artist might understand them better than a painter of Americana.

I have singled out for special praise a few of Marin's urban water colors, but it is almost impossible to choose this or that landscape without emphasizing one type of achievement at the expense of another, equally precious. The grave moment of blank serenity of "Popham Beach" (No. 107), the dark brooding of the coming storm seen through a windshield (No. 102), the sharp accuracy of the forms in Deer Isle Harbor (No. 93) are all extraordinarily fine; but no less characteristic, no less important, are "The Little Boat," the complicated composition of No. 84, the lacelike tree at Cape Split, the serenity of "Tree Forms" (No. 22 and No. 28), or the marvellous purity of No. 30. The endless invention of these pictures, the range of resources, the achievement of textural depth without the use of body color and without muddiness, the deftness of the sudden strokes and quick washes—all these things are beyond praise. No less masterly is his color—a narrow palette whose combinations seem inexhaustible. It needs a rich spirit to evoke such craftsmanship; the very existence of these technical resources points to an inner demand.

But perhaps the greatest surprise of the show is that Marin's oils, far from being dwarfed by his water colors, easily establish their own right to existence; some of them, like "Pertaining to Fifth Avenue and Fortysecond Street," have won the right to be considered among his major works.

· · · · ·

It is not easy to sum up the works of such a spirit as Marin or to estimate his final significance; much remains to be discovered, even after one has looked long and patiently at his work. Marin grew up in our brittle American world, and his art has both expressed and transcended the environment in which he was placed. His brush, marching to a quick tempo, has recorded a civilization in which the swift and the unexpected become the traditional, in which stability consists in a gift for improvisation, in which the frame has disappeared into the picture and the picture spread out into the frame, and in which, at all events, the old boundaries and guiding lines have disappeared. Seeing that world in Marin, one greets it with a sudden sense of exhilaration and astonishment; it was not what we thought, but far different. And by means of art such perceptions, even when most strange, most lonely, most isolated, lead back into society.

PABLO PICASSO

When the great Picasso show was assembled at the Galeries Georges Petit in Paris in 1932, one naturally supposed that New York would see it soon thereafter. But the next opening was in Zurich, where Dr. Jung beheld it and wrote a learned and amiable paper on its psychological significance: typical schizophrenic symptoms. After that Picasso came to Hartford, probably in search of the ghost of Mark Twain—who was also pretty schizophrenic—or the no less elusive corporeal self of the lawyer who wrote "Le Monocle de Mon Oncle." At all events, New York was treated like a tank town. It is only now, with two handsome and fairly exhaustive exhibitions on view, at the new Valentine Gallery and at the Jacques Seligmann Gallery, that Picasso and New York are on even terms once more.

Sooner or later, everyone will have to make a reckoning with Pablo Picasso, which means, in fact, that everyone will have to figure out for himself what the meaning of modern civilization was between 1900 and 1935. The man has not merely been a great artist; he has been a barometer, sensitively recording in advance the state of the cosmic weather. The symbols he used were not, perhaps, quite as clear as those on the dial, but even scientific barometers require a lot of interpretation before they tell anything.

From moment to moment, Picasso has recorded the go of things: sentiment, humanitarianism, primitivism, constructivist architecture, mechanization, the nightmare of war, the unreality of peace and sanity, above all the racked and divided minds of all sensitive men. These things occur successively in Picasso's paintings. Part of his paintings will survive as art, great art; the rest will survive as history. Rarely does one find an artist of Picasso's dimensions who is so much both the victim and the master of fashion. His invention has been copious, wild, outrageous, and yet somehow inevitable. He has all the characteristics of a major artist except the capacity for consecutive growth. He has had many clever imitators and loyal followers, but the only person of talent in his generation in Paris who refused to be drawn into the Picasso circle was Pablo Picasso, his most envious rival, his most treasonable disciple. Most of his life has been spent escaping from his latest self.

It is customary to associate the experiments of the post-impressionists with the constructive theories of Cézanne—attempts to reconstruct order on a more logical basis. But this element played a small part in Picasso's early development. Picasso's first paintings, at the Seligmann exhibition, show something strikingly different; he began, as a serious artist, at the point where van Gogh left off, when darkness gathered about him, and the black crows flew over the dark-blue cornfields at Auvers. The Blue Period was a period of deep emotional response to the blues of life: poverty, wretchedness, chills and weariness and starvation. The "Woman Seated with Fichu," the "Old Guitar Player," and the "Woman Crouching" are paintings to be hung in the same gallery with van Gogh's "Potato Eaters."

A terrible sincerity, a deep sympathy, characterize most of the paintings of the Blue Period. This sympathy united him not only with the miserable waifs and wastrels he portrayed but with those other painters of the meek and the humble—Daumier and Goya, painters who were to be restored, at this very moment in history, partly because their images had at last bitten, like an acid, through the solid armor of the proud and the righteous. In this group of paintings, the "Woman with a Crow," done in 1904, strikes me as one of the supreme examples; the drawing of the elongated hand here is quite unsurpassable. In 1905, this note of despair, which could have led only to suicide, lifted. Picasso's palette changed, as browns and roses succeeded the blues, and his mastery of line disclosed itself in a series of nudes and harlequins whose beauty equals and sometimes, possibly, surpasses Degas. For a moment, Picasso was in poise. Note the "Woman with the Loaves," in which the bread she carries on her head rhythmically balances her breasts. Picasso's humanity was perhaps succored by gaiety and love—the charms of the body, the tender forms of children, the dream world of Harlequin and Columbine and the acrobats. Such nudes as "The Toilette" (No. 29) and "The Coiffure" (No. 33) are infinitely better than the ponderous vacuity of the columnar neoclassic matrons that ushered in Picasso's postwar phase.

After 1905 came the period of experiment, and here one turns to the Valentine Gallery for the examples. The "Corsage Jaune," begun in 1907, presents a new palette for Picasso, a palette composed of ashen grays and acidulous yellows and unrelenting blacks; and for the world it presents a new type of imagery. Art from the time of the Renaissance had rested on two important assumptions. If you knew enough about the appearance of an object, you would finally be able to embody its reality; hence measurement, hence perspective, hence natural color scales, and finally the movement from the studio to the open air. Likewise, if you knew enough about the physical reality, about the anatomical or constructive form, you would eventually arrive at a true order of appearances. Picasso renounced these assumptions. The inner and the outer world had for him no such connections as the classic painters assumed; to deform the image, to decompose the human body, to suppress external shapes—these were other paths to reality, a reality more akin to the physicist's or engineer's world than to that of naïve humanity.

After 1910 Picasso became a byword, among collectors, for the audacious and the original and, above all, the incomprehensible; and perhaps Picasso was tempted to justify his reputation, or at least to live up to it—all the more because it may perhaps have touched his mordant Spanish sense of humor. At all events, Picasso became an international performer, a man whose gestures became fashions. His infinite variety of technical resources served only to set off the emptiness of his later development; there is a close parallel here between the development of Picasso and that of James Joyce. The further he went away from the Blue Period, the more fashionable his tricks became, the more obvious it was that—as Hawthorne once said of another—he had cut himself off from the magnetic chain of humanity.

In some ways, there was genuine development—mastery of fresh realms of color. But among the audacious and amusing paintings of the last few years—the "Nature Morte" and the "Dame Ecrivante," and vital, luscious paintings they are—there is nothing that I would place beside the "Blue Boy" in the Seligmann show or the "Femme au Peigne" at Valentine's. At the top, sheer genius; at the bottom, emptiness, sterility, a failure to find material sufficient to justify that genius. If that is a true picture of the man, it should be obvious why his paintings are, in their good and bad qualities, a portrait of our civilization. Another case of poverty in the midst of potential abundance.

Reminder List: Walter Pach's water colors at the Kleemann Galleries challenge the dogma that the technique of one art is irrelevant to another. They are built up with enormous technical resource, and they have the body of an oil painting, without a smudge of muddy color. A remarkable feat in itself; all the more remarkable because the paintings glow with vitality of color and design. The portraits are particularly good, not least the self-portrait, but the painter of "Yellow Lilies," "Friday Lunch," the "Blond Model," and "Beethoven, Opus III" is obviously a man with a wide range as well as sure mastery. For those who have been stumped by a certain overconscientiousness in Pach's oils, this exhibition should be a happy revelation. . . . The individuality of Maril's paintings, lately at the Marie Sterner Galleries, is unmistakable, but the note is thin and a little monotonous, a disappointment after the glimpse of his work at the first PWA show two years ago. . . . On the other hand, Tromka, at the A.C.A. Gallery, has gained rapidly during the last couple of years; the color is more vigorous, the design more dynamic, the play of light much more subtle. Two of the paintings, "Deserted Brickyards" and "Winter in Greenwich Village," are very good indeed. . . . The new arrangement of the Downtown Gallery, with a backlog of veterans, such as O'Keeffe, Marin, and Karfiol, and with a lot of kindling wood to make the fire in the front rooms, is admirable. For the latter, Mrs. Halpert has picked the best young painters the WPA has unearthed.

MODERNS: ASSORTED

When the exhibition of contemporary Soviet Russian art was opened at the Squibb Building, with the Russian Ambassador and all sorts of other worthies present, Mr. Lee Simonson departed from the usual routine of complimentary speeches. He told the company assembled for the occasion, I understand, that the gallery looked pretty much like a Munich Secession exhibition of 1920, and that the artists were plainly under the influence of bourgeois tendencies and ideals. A little clear talking like this probably will go farther toward establishing friendly relations between any two countries than the usual official blather, so I must honor Mr. Simonson's example. Whether he was being nasty or flattering, harsh or complimentary, he was, on the whole, right. The early paintings and sculptures of the Russian revolution might have been terrible, but at least the artists conveyed the notion that something unique and incredible had happened, and even if they could not cope with it plastically or graphically, they showed, in their constructivist stages, and in monuments that were like shaky scaffolding, that something big, consequential, and decisive had taken place.

That spirit is absent from this exhibition; only the faintest remnant of it seems to linger in the choice of vivid scarlets for a handful of the paintings. Instead, one has a symbol, not of a country in upheaval, but of an academy in the act of settling down, an academy trained on the French moderns, but never getting too personal or too emphatically out of hand, an academy friendly to the neo-Romantic personal note, welcoming tender and lyrical expressions; in short, an array of painters who are often pleasant but hardly ever deep. What this means about life in Russia I don't know, although one might be a little disturbed at the parallel that holds between Soviet Russian art and the Italian Fascist show that was here last year. Does it mean that the same stultifying influence that has made itself felt in the last few years in Russian architecture applies to all the other arts? Again, one cannot say; it might take a whole year in Soviet Russia before one would really have a clue. So the conclusion is a negative one; no powerful collective vision, no intense and dominating personality, is yet visible in this work. Whatever virtues or defects these paintings may have, they are very traditional ones.

Having emerged from a week's reflection over the third biennial show of contemporary American painting at the Whitney Museum, I should at least be able to tell you what American art has been up to these last two years. There are one hundred and twenty-three artists in this exhibition, and thirty-nine of them were not represented in the second Whitney show. As one might expect, the collection is safe and sound and representative—enough good painting to atone for the mediocrities and enough mediocrities to make one wish there were more good painting. But American art is as large and various and unpredictable as the country itself, and since the threatened Americana landslide of a year or two back hasn't taken place—Grant Wood isn't even in the show—there is no Dreadful New Tendency to talk about.

For the fun of it, I have been checking the marks in my catalogue to see if the painters who seem good to me fall into any sort of grouping. Of course they do; or at least I can make them, if I try hard enough, and slip the exceptions behind my chair. One group, perhaps that most favored by the museum directors, is the Excellent Craftsmen. In this group one sometimes finds an artist, like Brook, with a highly sensitive and personal style, but their view of the painter's job is essentially the traditional one, and most of these artists do not have to depart from their studios in order to find something worth painting. Some of the handsomest paintings in the Whitney show are done by this group: Eugene Speicher, with the usual young lady in costume; Isabel Bishop, with the head of a girl, done with rare knowledge and exquisite touch; Henry McFee, with a still life of glass; and Louis Bouché, with the figure of an almost naked young Jewish girl—a querulous and mystified look upon her face which says plainly "What the hell?"

In the next group, divided not so much by technical method as by their attitude toward their subjects, are the Poets of the Actual. These painters are often equally good craftsmen, but they have a special fondness for the tough, the grim, the sordid, the bawdy: they can take life on the chin, and they feel jaded if they remain too long with the *mise en scène* of the traditional studio. In the present show, the best of this group are Schnakenberg, with his "Subway Entrance"; Hopper, with his old movie theatre; and Reginald Marsh. Though this group looks to contemporary life to save them from the shopworn and hackneyed themes of studio art, some of them have by now made contemporary life pretty hackneyed, too. Branching out from these painters is another group, more penetrating, more human, less given to elevating accessories into matters of prime importance. Raphael Soyer and Nikolai Cikovsky are perhaps the best representatives: Cikovsky's "Problems"—a social worker and her pathetic case—is very fine indeed.

These poets of the actual shade into another group: the Tender Romantics. Henry Mattson, with his spray of quinces, is one of the most distinguished members of this group, but there are likewise Higgins, with his "Indian Shepherd"; Nathaniel Dirk, with his figure mourning over a corpse; Mommer, with his sombre landscape; and one might even add Arnold Friedman, with his fruitstand in April. When one is attempting to decipher the visage of America, one must remember not merely the hardboiled and brassy painting of the realists; one must also recall this other mood, delicate, brooding, yearning, but none the less real.

As for the fifth group, it is not really a group at all, but a collection of artists who have found their own centre and created a "world." I would include among these, from the Whitney show, Marin, Prendergast, Carroll, Kuniyoshi, Gropper, and Weber—and I defy the most scholastic mind to find a common denominator for them. Art, of course, has nothing to do with schools or groups or tendencies. Art individualizes: it finally concentrates into a symbol the life experience of one individual so as to make it become the unique reality and possession of another individual. So specific is this that the touch of a brush, the quality of a color, will reveal the work of a particular mind on even a fragmentary or half-obliterated work. Once that essence is achieved, tags and classifications become irrelevant. In the end, one asks for a man.

One's attention at the Rehn Gallery is pretty evenly split up between the Burchfield show and the Peggy Bacon show: both are unusually good. In his dozen new water colors, Burchfield has surpassed himself; that is to say, he has pretty well conquered the tendency to sentimentalize and overdramatize his subjects, and he has come to rely instead upon the sheer virtuosity—more than that, the strength—of his painting. The still life called "Pussy Willows" is very fine: its main motif is an overcoat hanging from a rack in the bleak, wintry light of a nearby window; the frost actually bites into the color. His technique varies from the calm organization of such a picture to the eager strokes of "Wire Fence in Snow," but both are painter-like and neither owes much pictorially to sentimental associations. Burchfield is a man whose reputation was achieved quite early, on the basis of paintings whose weakness was overlooked because of the fact that he had struck a fresh note. Today, in his early forties, he seems to me not merely a more accomplished painter than he was ten years ago; he is also, paradoxically, a more promising one.

As for the delicate feline trail that Peggy Bacon has left over the surface of American life, I hope I don't have to say in so many words how good that is. Miss Bacon catches everyone, as it were, in undress, making grimaces and gawky gestures before a mirror, a real looking glass or the mirror of other people's eyes; and in her prints she spares no one—not even herself. From a graphic point of view, I think, her best prints are those in which she has concentrated on a few figures: the draughtsmanship is decisive and the observation more concentrated. "Pleading for the Oppressed" and "Al Fresco" are two of my favorites, and the only ones I don't fall for are the few in which the literary conceit is essential to the graphic expression.

ON REPRODUCTIONS

With Christmas almost here, I am tempted to turn aside from the galleries for a moment to deliver a sermon on the Art of Graphic Reproduction, or how to keep a blessing from turning into a curse. It may ease your problems a little if you decide to go in for prints or color reproductions for Christmas gifts, and at all events it will ease my conscience.

During the last few years the late-lamented example of Currier & Ives, so long neglected, has come back again—with a difference. At least three new series have been started by American artists, one of them offering a variety of original prints done from steel plates, another a group of color reproductions of paintings by contemporary Americans, and the third a number of reproductions of American paintings from Copley to people like Homer and Prendergast. In addition, hundreds of other reproductions and facsimiles of the work of old and new masters are available, at prices ranging from a dollar for a small print to twenty dollars for one of the larger and more faithful copies.

If so far I have kept silent about all these developments, it is not because I have any qualms about the machine process or about mass production; most of the reproductive processes were, in fact, developed by artists themselves, who sought to escape the limitations of a small circulation and a narrow circle of admirers. What has kept me a little uneasy over this new development is that those who are promoting it have fallen in too lightly with the notion that the main purpose of a picture is to serve as an ornament, part of the permanent furnishing of a room. Until that notion is demolished, and until our current domestic habits are radically altered, no one need attempt to convert me to the idea of bringing art into the American home.

Most middle-class persons over thirty-five can remember the time when the American home, in parlor and back parlor and bedroom, swarmed with reproductions of the great classics in contemporary art— Gérôme and Sir Luke Fildes and Millet. Every room in the house was a veritable Louvre, gold frames, confusion, and all; indeed, the pictures themselves were almost as fixed as those in a traditional museum, for one could not move them around till one was ready to replace the wallpaper, lest dark patches show where the light had not faded it. When prints were used as permanent wall decorations, certain pictures were ruined forever by their excessive familiarity, ruined as Julius Caesar used to be ruined in the public schools of New York by being analyzed, parsed, and declaimed in both grammar and high school.

Many of the popular pictures of the nineties were, of course, dead even before they were hung, but these domestic exhibitions completed the work. Irrespective of the merit of the reproductions, they jaded the eye, and their life was as brief as a popular song; but unfortunately, unlike the song, they would remain long after the last drop of pleasure had been drained from them. The best that could be said of these appalling works of art was that they sometimes played an important part in the secret imaginative life of little boys and little girls. Herman Melville as a child was deeply stirred by a certain print of the Bay of Naples, and I know at least one lady whose course in life was embellished, if not wrecked, by a teasing image of Cleopatra and her handmaidens that she had communed with on the chaste walls of her mother's boundoir. Wherever one went, one saw the same pictures and lapsed into the same state of boredom.

In the nineteen-hundreds, two influences seeped into the American home, and altered the attitude toward pictures. One of them was that of William Morris, who had observed that no one should ever possess anything he did not know to be useful or believe to be beautiful, a principle that obviously left most reproductions in limbo on both scores. The other crept in subtly at the very moment that the Kaiser was shouting about the Yellow Peril: the Japanese influence, brought to these shores by La Farge, Whistler, Fenollosa, and the French Impressionists. It may also be, as a writer in *Camera Work* once suggested, that the photograph, with its austere mountings, set an example for the style of decoration in other departments. One by one, reproductions left the walls of the American home, sometimes to be replaced by original paintings, sometimes leaving behind a blank spot.

The same quality of mind that made the Japanese house anticipate in its method of design almost all that is best in modern architecture enabled the Japanese to develop a fine ritual for showing and enjoying pictures. Both Japanese precedents are, by some accident, closer to the practical needs and psychological insight of the modern man than anything the Occident can show by way of precedent. One may sum up the Japanese practice in three simple injuctions: Do not use pictures as permanent wall decorations. Look at one picture at a time. (If it won't stand up under this scrutiny, throw it out!) Change your pictures frequently. If these principles were generally observed, the presses of America might turn out millions of reproductions without hurting anyone; and until they do become popular, even original pictures should be kept in museums, if only to keep their owners from becoming weary of them.

Up to the present, the Japanese influence has been chiefly a negative one; we have scraped the late-Victorian pictorial litter off the walls, but neither the architect nor the furniture manufacturer nor the ordinary owner has thought of supplying the necessary physical means of storing and showing pictures. While, during the last generation, every well-to-do American increased the number of bathrooms in his dwelling and lavished imagination on their equipment, the special aesthetic services were neglected. Maybe Marcel Duchamp was a social diagnostician rather than a mischievous playboy when he offered a toilet bowl for exhibition at the Independent Artist's Show in 1917. In any event, the result was that most people who made no pretence to being collectors did not own more pictures than they had space for on their walls. If someone gave a man a picture, the recipient was up a tree. If he didn't hang it, he felt guilty, and if he did, he sometimes felt even worse.

Now, the first step toward making prints *permanently* popular is to further their correct use. The American house must have special print racks and picture closets and print boxes; there must be special facilities for storage, and special facilities for exhibition, instead of foolish attempts to make the wall itself serve both purposes. To begin with the smallest unit, you must have a portfolio, and as soon as your collection grows, a box for holding prints. So far as I have been able to find, there is no box on the market. If you want one, you can get one made in the usual black linen binding—or, of course, in any suitable cloth or leather you may select—by a bookbinder. Spink & Gabore, 26 East Thirteen Street, make these boxes for museums and art galleries. As an alternative, you might have them made in plywood, to be waxed or painted to fit your scheme of decoration, by any moderately competent cabinetmaker.

You will still have to devise a place to keep such boxes, particularly when you have more than one; Grand Rapids has not thought of combining a print rack with a bookcase. A group of such boxes could be designed a little above the usual table height for the living room, and the top could be used as the base of a rack to hold a picture. For the special showing of prints, you can get hints from the practices of museums and art galleries. Raymond & Raymond and the F.A.R. Gallery both have fairly ingenious devices for showing facsimile prints that are too large to be held in the hand, like the usual etching or lithograph. For hanging prints on the wall, there is an adjustable holder called Braquette, which does its job very well; you can get it at department stores and photo-supply stores as well as through your print dealer. As for the background, if your room permits it, you might have wallboard, plain or covered with burlap, or even a Celotex panel. Best of all, perhaps, would be a movable rack or screen—either a less clumsy sort of artist's easel or something like the movable blackboard used in college lecture halls—so that a picture may be shown in the best light, by night or day. A good modern achitect could have a lot of fun finding the right solution for this particular function of display, but though some designers have been very zealous in considering the problem of the museum, very few of them have taken art in the home seriously.

In the matter of choosing color reproductions, there are three things to be guided by: your taste, your purpose, and the adequacy of the process itself. Almost every lover of art delights in reproductions of significant pictures, as memoranda or as souvenirs; often a black-and-white photograph or postcard will please him, recalling—rather better than a tram ticket or a theatre progam—the happy original experience. Speaking with a touch of Ruskin's dogmatism, I would say that no reproduction of an oil painting or a fresco can, in the nature of things, be anything but a memory-tickler of the original; it is in no sense an equivalent, no matter how laboriously and lovingly it may be reproduced. Indeed, I find Jacques Villon's reproductions of van Gogh's paintings, which are pretty frankly interpretations rather than facsimiles, more satisfactory than those which aim more closely to simulate the originals.

On the other hand, reproductions of drawings in pencil, crayon, charcoal, pen-and-ink, pastel, and water color may be so close to the original that the artist himself cannot distinguish the difference. Among reproductions, these wear the best; they are practically on the level today of prints made specially for reproduction, such as wood engravings, etchings, and lithographs.

To sum it all up, there is no limit to your enjoyment and profit in collecting reproductions once you have adequate means of storage and display. Everyone might have ten to a hundred times his present collection of such pictures, provided he kept them mobile and did not waste his substance, and make the paintings themselves a universal bore by putting them in frames and placing them on permanent display. But mind! Reproductions are not an *alternative* to patronizing original art; they are an accessory. Their use, after all, is to whet the appetite and extend the capacity for appreciation, so that one is ready to recognize a good thing when one sees it—even if it is the single product of an unknown artist. So in making up your Christmas list, don't forget that, even on the score of price, a contemporary sketch or a water color may, despite the triumph of machinery, prove to be more available, as well as more desirable, than a copy of an important classic.

SURREALISM AND CIVILIZATION

At the moment, the town is practically crawling with surrealist exhibitions. There is Joan Miró at the Matisse Gallery, and Salvador Dali at the Julien Levy Gallery, and Man Ray at the Valentine Gallery; and, for good measure, Bedlam and Bloomingdale and Cloud-Cuckoo-Land and Cockaigne have broken loose at the Museum of Modern Art. If you don't know yet what surrealism is, you will never have a better chance of finding out for yourself—or increasing your present confusion. Is it a passing fashion or a new sphere of painting? Is it a variety of art or a metaphysical theory of the universe or a subversive political weapon or a series of practical jokes? Is it a meaningless revolt or a revolt against meaning? Or merely paranoia become playful? All these are weighty questions. One or two of them, incidentally, have something to do with art.

Usually, one of the easiest ways to place a movement is to ask where it began and who started it. Some say surrealism began with a group of young European exiles who sat in a café in Zurich in 1916, concocting a revolution in art called Dada (the art to end all art) at the very moment that Nikolai Lenin, a lover of the classics, was planning a revolution in politics. The two revolutions split at that point, but both were deeply in revolt against the heavy platitudes, the unctuous moralities, and the drab acceptances of the world of "reality," and they came together again in 1925, when everything fashionable had suddenly to prove its right to exist by showing that it was connected with Marxism. Most of the books and manifestoes that have been written on surrealism confine themselves to these Continental origins. They therefore neglect the wild surrealist element that has been present in American art and in American humor from the very beginning.

One of the great merits of the Modern Museum show is that it presents the immediate origins and achievements of surrealism against a broad background of fantastic and irrational art that goes back to the Middle Ages. Scarcely anything that has conceivably paralleled the present movement or contributed anything to it has been neglected by Mr. Alfred Barr: now a painting by Hieronymus Bosch, now a photomontage from the New York *Evening Graphic*. The final result of such inclusiveness and exhaustiveness is that one begins to find surrealist images sticking out of every hole and cranny, and one loses sight of two or three of the great landmarks in painting that lead up to surrealism. These landmarks, though included in the show, are swamped in the weltering, dreamlike confusion of it. If I single them out, it may make the going a little easier.

The main divisions of surrealist art are distinct, but have a common foundation in the mind: the pathologically irrational, the comic, and the unconscious. Each of these sides is in opposition to the conceptions and practical needs of everyday life; each of them stresses the private and the subjective and the whimsical, and belittles the public and the objective and the dutiful. The first, and at the moment the most engrossing, side of surrealist art begins with Goya. He etched a whole series of prints, called "Caprices," which for more than a century seemed only a perverse mystery to most lovers of art, prints with strange demonic figures leering savagely or obscenely at the spectator, or with natural figures in crazy attitudes, committing obscure follies. These prints seem to rise, like a miasma, from the murder and torture Goya depicted in the plates on the horrors of war. Today, Goya's images recur too frequently in the photographic sections of the newspapers to be dismissed as "unreal," and it is perhaps no accident that a country that has known brutal irrationality in so many forms should have contributed so many leaders to the surrealist movement today—Picasso, Dali, Miró. If this were all there is to surrealism, one might justify Mr. David Gascoyne's beginning his "Brief Survey" with Gilles de Retz and the Marquis de Sade.

The comic side of surrealism is familiar to the English-speaking world from "Mother Goose" onward. "Hey-diddle-diddle, the cat and the fiddle," the Jabberwocky, the Yonghy-Bonghy-Bò, and the folk tales of Munchausen and Paul Bunyan have had their counterparts in an equally crazy folk art, like the china cat decorated with flowers in the present show. This part of surrealist art flourishes on the incongruous and the unexpected. It is at its best, in painting, in Dali's picture of the wilted watches, in those curious collections of objects that Roy assembles in his canvases, or in those marvellous montages of old woodcuts that Max Ernst has put together with such loving patience. One does not have to read Bergson's disquisition on the significance of laughter to enjoy this part of surrealism. Surely, the very worst compliment one can pay it, even when it is savage or sinister, is to greet it with a respectfully solemn face. If Goya contributed the sadistic nightmare, Edward Lear discovered the magical release of nonsense. (But surrealism has its practical side, too. It was a surrealist experimenter who had the courage to put sugar into a concrete mix to make it stronger.)

The last ingredient in surrealism is the unconscious. Ever since the Renaissance, painters have conscientiously been painting only what they could see with their eyes. "I don't paint angels," said Courbet, "because I have never seen one." But images of all sorts are perpetually welling up out of the unconscious: modern man, concentrated upon conquering Nature and piling up riches, penalizes daydreaming and forces these "irrelevant" images back or keeps them from germinating; he has invented a score of contraceptives for the imagination, and then is surprised to find his life has become a sterile one. At night, however, the repressed images spring up again. These products of the unconscious are not necessarily sinister or macabre. In a more benign form, they took shape in the paintings and prints of Odilon Redon, as they had done in those of William Blake before him, and though Redon has had very little influence over the French, German, or Catalonian surrealists, the benigner unconscious activity he exhibited can be seen in the works of modern Americans like O'Keeffe and Dove.

If one judges surrealism by the aesthetic and human values that lie outside it, a good part of it is rubbish; its value lies not in what it so far has found but in the fact that it has opened up the gallery of a mine which may, with more adequate tools, be exploited for more precious ore than that which has so far been brought to the surface. One of the most powerful and inventive of the European surrealists, Max Ernst, is only a moderately good painter; and if the earlier surrealist paintings of Chirico, spacious and noble in composition, still remain very fine, if Roy is always an admirable craftsman, and if Masson and Miró both have a graceful and deft touch, the quality of the paintings remains an incidental if not a negligible part of the whole movement. To judge the art fairly, one must realize that it is a symptom—a symptom of the disorder and brutality and chaos of the "real" world; an attempt through disintegration—as in a Freudian analysis—to dig down to a point solid enough to serve as a fresh foundation. With all its praise of the irrational, there is method in the surrealist madness.

Until a generation ago, only soothsayers and ignorant folk believed in dreams. It took the genius of Freud to combine the ordinary consciousness of the neurotic with the ordinary dreams of the normal man, and to see that there was an underlying identity; *dreams meant something,* and in a sense, the more irrational they were, the more they meant. We can no longer go around pretending that the world is the same world it was before Freud gave us this clue. What we can see and measure and count is only a part of the picture. The complete picture is not so clear and not so orderly as the mind, for practical purposes, would like to have it.

This is one of the great commonplaces of our generation; and the proof is that it has made its way into literature so thoroughly that no one bothers there to call it surrealist. In Virginia Woolf's "Mrs. Dalloway" the returned soldier, Septimus, is suffering from a psychoneurosis, and this is the way she describes his feelings: "He lay very high, on the back of the world. The earth thrilled beneath him. Red flowers grew through his flesh; their stiff leaves rustled by his head. Music began clanging against the rocks up here. . . . It cannoned from rock to rock, divided, met in shocks of sound which rose in smooth columns (that music should be visible was a discovery) and became an anthem, an anthem twined round now by a shepherd piping." Need I point out that one has only to transfer these images onto canvas to have a complete surrealist painting?

Anything that can be imagined is real, and nothing is so real as an obsession. In those words one might sum up the present attitude of the surrealists. Like every new school, they have wilfully lost sight of the partial reality which they wish to supplement or replace; they deny the orderly, the rational, the coherent, the visible. But what they are doing, in fact, is to increase the scope of reality. They are exploring foul underground caverns where one hears only the whir and whistle of invisible bats; they are holding the manacled hands of prisoners in moldy dungeons; they are making their way, by touch rather than by sight, through slimy passageways that may bring them up to the surface of "normal" life with a better comprehension of what lies beneath. Like the modern psychoanalysts, the surrealists have approached the normal by way of the pathological. That follows inevitably from the fact that the willing, wishing, urging, passionate part of man's life has been slighted, stifled, and even banished altogether in favor of practical routines. Distrusting the imagination, we let it sneak back into life only in the guise of fancy dress or an even fancier disease—just as many of us never get a real opportunity for pleasurable idleness until we find ourselves on our backs in a hospital, recovering from the birth of a baby or an operation for appendicitis.

But it would be absurd to dismiss surrealism as crazy. Maybe it is our civilization that is crazy. Has it not used all the powers of the rational intellect, all the hard discipline of the practical will, to universalize the empire of meaningless war and to turn whole states into Fascist madhouses? There is more here than meets the eye. Demons, for the modern man, are no less real than electrons; we see the shadow of both flitting across the screen of visible reality. Surrealism makes us conscious of this fact; it arranges the necessary apparatus. Before we can become sane again, we must remove the greatest of hallucinations—the belief that we are sane now. Here surrealism, with its encouraging infantile gestures, its deliberately humiliating antics, helps break down our insulating and self-defeating pride. Even in perverse or sinister or silly forms, the surrealists are restoring the autonomy of the imagination.

WINSLOW HOMER

After a fortnight of poking around the surrealist exhibitions, it is a relief to come up to the surface for a little fresh air. That is what makes the two Winslow Homer shows so timely. Homer has the bite of the northeast wind and the rejuvenating effect of the sunlight after a long, wet blow; what was vague and slippery and unformed was outside his province. Devil take the underworld, with its murky vaporings, its sadistic jokes, and its carefully arranged posturings. Here, in the keen-eyed American Homer who painted, is the eternal surface pattern of things that one finds in the blind Greek who sang. The wind, the waves, the forest, the agile bodies of tough men and shapely women—these are Homer's realities.

These two shows celebrate the centenary of Winslow Homer's birth. They give the most rounded view of his work in all its phases and aspects that has yet been disclosed; we can see Homer, indeed, as he could never have seen himself. The show at the Macbeth Gallery, which long handled this artist's canvases, is a sort of preliminary exploration; it deals mainly with the products of his early manhood. No one can follow the later details of Homer's development who is not familiar with these first vigorous buds of his talent, a talent so positive and self-assured that he was never unduly inflated by the ingratiating applause that was his almost from the beginning. Even some of the minor revelations of this Macbeth show are charming. In the little oil of the sharpshooter firing from a tree, for example, one discovers, in the button of the soldier's cap, that small, fierce spot of red that was to appear with dramatic effect, again and again, in his later water colors.

As for the Whitney Museum exhibition, it is all that a memorial show should be. The putting together and the hanging of this show were plainly a labor of love, and Mr. Lloyd Goodrich, who has also written an admirable introduction for the catalogue, deserves to be given everyone's thanks. With the Whitney Museum presentation of Homer before us we can at length take the full measure of the man.

Looking back over my own earlier estimates of Homer, I find that, if I have little to retract, I have a great deal to add. During the last ten years

I have had occasion repeatedly to call attention to the value of Homer's journalistic drawing for *Harper's Weekly;* and Homer's many dashing successes in this department are now being more generally recognized at their full value. But I myself have now to recognize that Homer's achievements as an illustrator were carried over successfully into the oils he painted about the same time.

His career really divides into three phases, quite irrespective of the medium in which he worked. In the first period, he drew upon the commonplaces of the life around him, the happy commonplaces like skating and fishing and sailing boats, or the dreary, unheroic commonplaces of the camp and the bivouac during the Civil War. At times the painting of this period is dry and factual, very close, indeed, to Eakins. The palette itself is warm and rich and full-bodied, and the compositions, which often involve the nice balance of human figures in action, are the work of a man who wields a free hand. If one is sometimes inclined to dismiss some of Homer's late canvases as mere illustrations, one must pay the opposite compliment to the illustrations themselves. They are not lucky snapshots. Indeed, not only are Homer's illustrations worthy of the oils he made after them, but in a few cases—"Snap the Whip" is one—the black-and-white seems to me the stronger picture.

The first phase of Homer's art has up to now been pretty generally underrated. There is a very close parallel here between Homer and Corot, and the very qualities in contemporary appreciation which make us go back so eagerly to Corot's Roman days bring us close, likewise, to the early Homer. Homer's second phase is associated with a growing tendency to isolate himself physically from the rest of the world. From the age of forty, he developed into what Melville called an Isolato—a testy old curmudgeon who had perhaps swallowed some bitter personal disappointment in his private life and who was resolved that the world should never have a hint of it. His sojourn at Tynemouth in England, in the early eighties, brought about a definite change in his art. His palette becomes narrower in range, if more subtle in its tones; he paints with a broad, flat brush stroke, very emphatic, very dashing, conspicuously "virile"; he concentrates his aesthetic effect in some focal spot of intense light, the reflection of the moon in the water or of white spume rising over the edge of the beach. And for a time he seems to need the extra excitement of bold external drama—a storm, a rescue, a hard fishing haul—to key him up to his work. He still uses the human figure, still draws it superbly, but his invention is rather commonplace. Rarely does it rise to the level of his early "illustrations."

This is the popular Homer. One recognizes his signature at a glance; indeed, it has become too familiar to us, and his subjects themselves have been made banal by the endless near-Homers that followed in his wake at Gloucester and Ogunquit during the last generation. There are passages in this middle Homer that are a little monotonous. For him the northeaster seemed to brew a storm merely to create a heroic scene, just as the mists seemed to gather around Père Corot's cottony trees in his later years merely in order to provoke a twilight pastoral. But although few of these middle paintings are great, one cannot dismiss this Homer any more than one could the earlier one. "Coast in Winter," for example, is a mighty canvas; Courbet himself could have done no better.

Finally, the third phase of Homer appears again and again in his water colors, and it comes to a climax for me in two of his oils: "The Fox Hunt," done in 1893, and "Right and Left," done in 1909. This is the Homer who has overcome his conscientious dependence upon the eye, and who, indeed, is ready to choose a subject in which his invention, in the nature of things, must be independent of any mere photographic verisimilitude. Ruskin always insisted that design could not be taught. In Homer's case, his theoretic belief in naturalism, in painting only what he saw, destroyed some of his native capacity for design; he might eliminate, but he did not usually feel free to create. The fox over whom the crows are brooding shadows, and the crumpled ducks brought down by both barrels of the gun—these "uncharacteristic" canvases are among Homer's best in the later period. I would put them alongside the noble pastoral called "The Brush Harrow," dated 1865, and that other fine bucolic scene, "Weaning the Calf," painted in 1875. None of these pictures depend upon dramatic props; they represent, rather, that deep and affectionate contemplation of life through which "vision" becomes "design." What one calls a painter's style is often the marring, through habit or through a mere narrowing of interest, of gifts that were originally more varied and abundant; style in this sense implies a partial denial of the artist's birthright. In Homer's case, this denial was overcome by the unflexing of his talents in his later years through his return to water colors—if one can speak of return to an art which had such auspicious beginnings as the little gem called "Waiting for the Boats" (No. 39). Also, perhaps, the change of scene, his winter journeys to the Bahamas, helped effect his release. His craftsmanship, his willingness to take pains, like a good ship's carpenter waiting for his wood to season, stood constant. Rarely, even at his most commonplace, does he completely let one down. Always he could see clearly and record plainly. But there was a volcano in the heart of this ice-capped New Englander, a volcano that, when the pressure was high enough, would break through the crust and steam over the landscape. Then he justified the long years of patient workmanship. In a few brilliant flashes, he could put down "The Coming Storm"—perhaps his greatest water color.

None of the generalizations about Homer has been inclusive enough. People have said he was a naturalist and an illustrator; he turns out to be a bold designer and a tender poet, one of those awkward seabirds that must run long on the ground before they take to the air, but seem to fly the more gracefully once they are on firm wing. People have said Homer was a simple, healthy extrovert, but it is given to few extroverts to have such a capacity for living silently and within themselves, absorbing so fully, brooding so deeply, giving out again so richly. I would not say that Homer is a bigger artist than Ryder or Eakins. But his eye was as steady and keen as Eakins' and his insight was as calm and unfaltering as Ryder's; and in his best work, if not in his still most popular work, he is well on their level.

WOOD AND STONE

The attitude of most contemporaries toward sculpture is one of the great puzzles of an art critic's life. And the sculptors are puzzled, too, if one may use such a word to describe their sense of being baffled and choked by the fog of indifference that surrounds their work. Art dealers say that when they have a sculpture show in their galleries, people poke their heads through the door, look around, and remark frigidly, as they back out again, "Oh, I thought there was an *art* show here." Apparently, when sculpture vanished from the tops of mantel-shelf clocks, it ceased to keep time with the modern world. I have even heard of a patron of painting who wanted a sculptor to cut the price of a small work in half because, she remarked plaintively, she only wanted it for a doorstop.

One ought to be able to fake a theory to account for this neglect and indifference and contumely, but I can't pretend that I have any. Historically, one might say that sculpture has always been closely associated with building. Sometimes it dominates the conception of structure, as in the time of the Egyptian monument builders; sometimes it comes as a final touch of grace and spirit, enriching and deepening the meaning of the structure, becoming part of its drama and ritual, as in the great figures of the Bamberg Cathedral. Perhaps the fact that stone and wood are no longer essential building materials has robbed the sculptor of his natural foundations and his workaday relations as a craftsman. His art, instead of being an integral part of a building, is something that can be added or taken away at the discretion of the architect—who himself, through his bookish education, has often lost a feeling for the materials.

One might pad this notion out a little by adding that if sculpture has been losing ground in relation to painting since the time of Michelangelo, it is partly because the detached easel painting was more adapted to the needs and fashions of modern life than the monumental statue. Even the biggest canvases can be rolled up and carted away easily; they occupy little space in storage, and they can be passed from one place of exhibition to another without any great effort. Sculpture, however, is not so detachable; even to move it from one side of the room to another may require the combined services of a couple of flunkies. Sculpture demands fixity and stability; it symbolizes durability. When sculpture cut itself off from the temple, the tomb, and the cemetery, it lost, paradoxically, one of its most important sources of life.

Still, this accounts only for the unpopularity of the more bulky, monumental sort of sculpture; it does not take into consideration the fact that figurines have always filled a considerable place in the art, from the earliest Stone Age figures of fertility, through the charming statuettes of Tanagra, down to the Meissen ware of the eighteenth century. If the room for living were all that troubled the sculptor, the answer has been furnished by some of the best masters during the past century: many of Barye's animals were meant for the desk top and the table, because in the first half of the nineteenth century there was still a demand for such objects. Obviously, this question of size and bulk is important—all the more so when the possibility of making cheap reproductions is taken into account; but if the public once eagerly demanded, even the vainest of sculptors would change the scale of his figures. Maillol has shown that size is not necessarily an attribute of spacious design.

This jumble of explanations would be more plausible if the lack of popular demand had led to the extinction of the race of sculptors, but the facts are just the contrary. Ever since Rodin, the star of sculpture has been well over the horizon, and the best sculptors of the past generation are fully the equals, if not sometimes the superiors, of the best painters. Fresh thoughts and feelings have been embodied in plastic form by sculptors like Brancusi, Gaudier-Brzeska, Duchamps-Villon, and Lipchitz; while old thoughts, as self-renewing as mankind, have been reëxpressed by Lehmbruck, Maillol, Epstein, Lachaise, and Despiau. Even in America, with its meagre traditions, the circle of good sculptors has grown. As if to sharpen all these dilemmas, there has been a flurry of sculpture exhibitions during the last fortnight.

The two best shows are those of Ernst Barlach at Westermann's and Ossip Zadkine at Brummer's. At this late date, Barlach should need no introduction. He towers above every other German contemporary both as an interpreter of humanity and as a supreme carver in wood, and the drawings and woodcuts that form the greater part of the present exhibition would make his name memorable even if he had not left a chisel mark on a single block. The best place to see Barlach is Lübeck, where his monumental figures in the old medieval church that now serves as a special museum are like the blooming of a fresh bud on a withered stalk. But the spirit of Barlach is a universal one, and such figures as the "Peasant Woman" or the "Avenger" in the present show would dominate any background. Working in wood, habitually simplifying his planes and endowing even his most grotesque figures with a classic breadth, Barlach never gives the impression of being cramped by the original block; the form is always extricated, as it were, without a birth scar. In his ability to make the individual a type, and to give the type the vital touch of the individual, now sad, now hopeful, now terror-stricken, now joyous, Barlach shows himself a master of his art. The firmly tooled texture of his surfaces, the clean envelope of his form, his ability to suggest the organic movement of a frightened man or a drooping beggar, without external agitation—all these qualities are at the service of Barlach's tender and passionate feeling for life, the visible symbols of a noble mind as well as a great artist. Barlach's figures help solve the old problem of how the artist is to do his duty toward society without sacrificing his aesthetic discipline.

Zadkine's art is superficially more sophisticated than Barlach's, and its technical achievements cover a far wider range. Barlach effectually renews a tradition that goes back to the wood-carvers of the fifteenth and sixteenth centuries; Zadkine has been affected by the world of the machine, and even though he works in hard, natural materials—unyielding stone, like diorite, or tough, metallic wood—he is governed by the necessity to experiment in the dynamics of form. Now he takes a branching tree trunk and, with as little deviation from the original wood as possible, composes a figure of Niobe; now he conceptualizes his form and creates a figure drawn neither from man's world nor nature's. Zadkine has carried much farther than Archipenko the experiment of modelling in concave surfaces that reverse the ordinary rondures of the body; the process heightens the dramatic contrasts of light and shade, breaking up old associations and checking pat responses. Sometimes, too, the heads are suddenly cut in cross section, with the eye and the nose incised on the flat plane. But what distinguishes Zadkine's sculpture from that of his nearest contemporaries, like Lipchitz, is the fact that he is at his best in billowy forms and curved lines. He has, as it were, taken the baroque masters' swirl and movement and dashed them against the static abstract forms of the Cubists; it is not by accident, perhaps, that the form of the baroque violin, and even the scalloped-shell motif, became essential parts of many of his compositions. Zadkine, in fact, is at his best in the figures that express movement; above all, I feel, in the little group playing with a ball. There is sometimes violence, sometimes an arbitrary desire for originality in these forms, but there are also the strength and fortitude of good sculpture.

The mixed sculpture show at the Milch Galleries ranges all the way from Manship and Epstein to Lachaise and Sterne. But the figures that took most of my attention were two little stone statues by Flannagan, and, above all, two animals by Heinz Warneke. One of the latter, a large calf, looks as if it had been hacked out of the wood with an axe (as, indeed, it actually was). The modelling is as rough and awkward as the creature itself—joy expressed with a shout and a hug, rather than in a polished gesture. But the jolliest piece in the show is Warneke's "Orangutan Thinking"—the creature recumbent, huddled in thought; one arm over the head, the other wrapped across his chest. It is an exquisite piece of carving—all the planes beautifully proportioned and related, without a superfluous stroke. If there were more of that sort of thing in sculpture, and fewer solemn, imbecile Atlases, sculpture might make a little head-way as a popular art, even if we *are* a hurried and time-minded generation, too impatient to enjoy the slow, tactile forms of intimacy that sculpture, like love, demands.

THE LIFE OF THE CITY

The other day, while I was prowling through the exhibition of the New York realists at the Whitney Museum—it was not the critics' preview—I became suddenly conscious of the other visitors. They were the sort of people you might expect to find at a fire but never at an art gallery. There were groups of crisp, black-haired men, with cheeks like Westphalian hams, whom you might see dining at Cavanagh's, or at Joe's in Brooklyn; there were shrewd, horsy-faced fellows you'd more likely meet in the paddocks or the prize ring, judging limbs and shoulders, than in the midst of a collection of paintings. Politicians, real-estate brokers, contractors, lawyers—what were they doing here? My guess is that they were New Yorkers, pulled into the gallery by that dark, secret love for the city that New Yorkers hide from the world even when they brag about the city's wonders. And they had come to the right place, for the nine artists who are represented in this show, through the work they did between 1900 and 1914, loved the city too; not less, perhaps, because five of them came from the dingy, unexciting, provincial streets of Philadelphia as it was at the beginning of the century.

The greater part of the painting of all these men—Henri, Luks, Sloan, Glackens, Bellows, Coleman, Lawson, Shinn, and du Bois—was a mirroring of the life of the city around them. They did this without romantic evasion or prettification, although never without a buoyant reaction to whatever was aesthetically alive; this is their title to the now almost meaningless label Realist. It was not for nothing that they were contemporaries of Stephen Crane and O. Henry and Mrs. Wharton and Theodore Dreiser. Their attempt to get away from the sweetened formalities of the studio picture was like the writers' effort to get away from the inevitable happy ending, the well-groomed hero, the well-coiffured girl, the ritual of mere middle-class manners.

These manners hung heavily over the painter's studio. Helen Appleton Read, in her admirable introduction to the catalogue, reminds us how Chase, the leading teacher of the day, made a fetish of empty technique and glorified brushwork as a sort of end in itself. The realists, in revolt against this doctrine, sought the vulgar, the commonplace, the sordid aspects of New York for the same reason that Huckleberry Finn left the Widder: they couldn't stand the cussed tidiness. And they were right. New York had never turned out to be so beautiful as when people stopped cultivating beauty at polite teas and asked for a chunk of life, hot, red, and dripping. There are paintings in the present show—like the view of New York roofs in Sloan's "Pigeons"—that will declare more, a century hence, about the beauty men experienced in New York than the well-preserved corpse of, say, the Public Library.

To their contemporaries, these artists were tough babies. Four of them had got their training after art school doing sketches for the Philadelphia *Press*, and they all had the journalist's eye for news and human interest, and they weren't afraid of going off the old beats to find them. There had been genre painters of New York life before: men like J. G. Brown, who had painted bootblacks and gamins. But these figures had no more aesthetic importance than a Horatio Alger hero, whose precise counterpart they, in fact, were. When Luks caught two little urchins dancing wildly, he didn't bother to change their clothes or wash their faces; he slashed their figures onto the canvas with a vigor begotten of his own delight. When, in the "Wake of the Ferry," Sloan shows a lonely figure of a woman, standing partly exposed to the rain, looking out over the gray waters, he symbolizes forever the intense loneliness, as final as that of a deserted hermit on a Himalayan peak, almost everyone has known in the midst of crowded Manhattan.

These new men felt the city through and through; their images range from the slums of Doyers Street (Coleman) to the windy escarpments that bring the Westchester Hills into Manhattan (Lawson). Their feeling comes out in their sensitive tactile qualities and their atmospheric effects, as well as in their formal modifications of their subjects. Note Bellows' sombre portrait of Prosper Invernizzi, entirely free from the self-conscious mannerisms of his later work, or examine the movement of the horses in his "Steaming Streets," a painting that surpasses most of his more artful efforts. Robert Henri's "Evening, North River" and his "New York Street in Winter" show the sad, wistful side of the city; Glackens' "Green Car" and "Parade, Washington Square" show its heady gaiety. Such moods were deeply felt and sensitively expressed, for these painters were a thoroughly human lot, and their art was best when it was not practiced for art's sake.

As to the relative merits of this group, I think one may say that they began with fairly even endowments but showed varied capacities for growth. Glackens, lured on by Renoir and the Impressionists, essayed the most difficult feats, but his most successful paintings are not those, like the pretentious family group, on which he tried hardest. Bellows sought to add a cubit to his height by finding a mathematical formula for beauty—sheer delusion, which was as fatal to his later work as the annoying mannerisms he developed. Shinn wore thin quickly; du Bois, who could do the deadly, vulturelike politicians in one of his smaller canvases in this show, remained fixed in a trivial mold. Lawson perhaps showed the firmest texture over the longest period. But the earlier canvases of Luks and Sloan and Henri were, it seems to me, the most central contributions of this group; they expressed its pervasive, understanding humanity. Their paintings are not "pure"; they are full of overtones and sentimental associations, full of observation and history, but they wear well because these men had found fresh images for the experience of living—with a smile, with a wry grin, with a throttled tear—amid the Four Million. The realists of one generation are the poets of the next, provided that, beneath their realism, they were poets to begin with.

The contemporary artists who have contributed to the "Waterfront Art Show" that is now on at the New School for Social Research are in effect continuing the work of the earlier New York realists, although they are perhaps more self-conscious about their mission and more bewildered by the problem of technique as it has been modified by all the influences that have played on the painter since Cubism, Post-Impressionism, and Surrealism arose to vex the mind and qualify the artist's perceptions. The earlier revolt against the smugness of refined painting was only half-consciously a revolt against bourgeois society, though it is true that Sloan, Bellows, and Coleman were doughty contributors to the radical *Masses* after 1912. Many of these newer painters, on the other hand, paint in more or less intentional alliance with the workers' group which is sponsoring the "Waterfront" show. But I doubt if the present-day public is as bewildered and outraged by this fact as the public of the nineteen-hundreds was upset by the "Ashcan School." The range of experience and form in the present show is very wide, and the show has value quite independent of the political questions it evokes or settles. Even the politicians and the horsy gentlemen will find something to their taste. Some of the paintings are by people whose work is little known, and unless my first impression, based on a show that was only partly hung, is incorrect, some of these unknowns will be worth uncovering further.

One splendid, breath-taking canvas dominates the new exhibition of Henry Mattson's paintings at the Rehn Galleries, a seascape called "Wings of the Morning." It is a painting of rock and sea and sky: gaunt, dark rocks, such as Mattson must have seen in the Orkneys as a boy; a great lift of blue water dashing into fine spray in the middle distance; and a curving bank of clouds, catching the sun as the sea gulls' white wings sometimes catch it in soaring, hovers above. The whole painting is in movement, but the movement has the sort of serenity that might settle on one's soul after one had risen and fallen with the waves, and floated between hard rock and a yielding, timeless sky, for a thousand years. Two great seascapes in a single winter is probably more than we deserve, but this painting of Mattson's must be put alongside one by Marin that I commented on a little while ago. As for Mattson's other canvases in the same show, they are of diminished stature only by comparison with "Wings of the Morning." "Fan Rock," with its feathery, green foreground, is very fine, and "House by the Dam," in the eerie moonlight, embodies that mood of tremulous wonder that Mattson captures so well. But "Wings of the Morning" has a new brilliance and firmness.

Chaim Gross's exhibition of sculpture at the Boyer Galleries came a week too late for me to include it in my comments on other sculpture shows, but it would be unfair to overlook work that has as much positive merit and indicates as much further promise as this has. Gross carves in an assortment of hard woods, and his chunky figures of acrobats, bicycle riders, and dancers are conceived in squat poses that tie them closely to the block, often with a deliberate touch of caricature. These figures have an unmistakable individuality, but I am half-conscious of wanting to stretch their bunchy muscles and disentangle their huddled limbs. Gross's carvings do not translate well into bronze, and the reason for this, I think, is that in simplifying his form for the wood, he also softens it. Barlach, for example, simplifies quite as drastically, but his planes remain sharp and his edges crisp. Hence such wood carvings of his as have been cast in bronze lose little of their original vigor. The best piece of "soft" carving in this show is the little humorous figure called "Madam," because the curves and sleek surfaces are essential to the expression, but the blocks I like most, on final judgment, are the less characteristic ones: "Two Torsos," embracing; the ebony carving called "Adolescent"; and the even more abstract composition called "The Black Figure." I am sure the last carving would keep most of its qualities in metal.

PRINTS AND PAINTS

About fifteen years ago a hot battle took place in that long-lamented weekly, the *Freeman*, as to whether or not photography should be taken seriously as an art. It is doubtful if the present exhibition of photography at the Museum of Modern Art will raise a flicker in any of those dead embers of controversy. The museums have quietly been collecting photographs during the last twenty years, and though private collectors have not been quite so avid for prints as they might be, that is probably because the illustrated newspapers and magazines have made good photographs commonplace. While the dividing line between photography and the other graphic arts is perhaps more firmly defined now than it was a generation ago, scarcely anyone doubts that the best work has aesthetic validity. Fine photography remains scarce, just as first-rate painting is scarce. More than half the prints in the present show have greater significance as historical landmarks than as aesthetic achievements. A David Hill, an Atget, or a Stieglitz is a rare bird.

The present exhibition covers the entire history of the art on both its technical and its aesthetic sides; it begins with Porta's device, the camera obscura, and it ends with the microphotograph and the infra-red exposure. After Daguerre's demonstration of his perfected process in Paris in 1839, the world went mad about the new invention, for it made every amateur into a potential painter—to about the degree that the newly invented revolver turned every coward into a hero. The painters were not immune from this excitement. Delacroix was a charter member of the French Society of Photography, and it was David Octavius Hill, a mediocre portrait painter of Edinburgh, who made the finest calotype portraits, within a few years after Talbot had perfected the process of printing on paper.

Despite photography's slow development into an independent art, there has been a steady flow of interest back and forth between the darkroom and the painter's studio. Where, indeed, would photography have been originally, without painting? Accuracy, objectivity, factualism, concentration on the external world, the fixed angle of vision, the translation of line and color into form modelled solely through light and shade—all these aims were pursued by painters from two to four centuries before the mechanical method of achieving the same results was perfected. The abuse of photography by "artistic" photographers, beginning with Salomon, came not through its intercourse with painting but through the attempt to dress and pose and light the subject so that the photograph speciously resembled an old-fashioned painting, which grew out of a different culture and a different consciousness of the world.

The long period of visual preparation for photography perhaps had something like the same effect that manuscript printing had on the invention of movable type. It may account for the fact that both arts achieved a high pitch of aesthetic perfection within a relatively few years after their invention. Later improvements in photography, which have made all its instruments more speedy, more sensitive, more wide-ranging, have done little to alter the *nature* of the image. David Hill's portraits, Charles Marville's studies of Parisian alleyways, and Matthew Brady's solid documents of the Civil War set a high level for their respective fields; these primitives have a sincerity and a forthrightness that their more facile successors, despite extreme technical adroitness, often miss. Not that stunning examples are absent from the prints shown by contemporaries. A landscape by Paul Strand or Edward Weston, a building by Steiner or Sheeler, a torso by Steichen, a portrait of Sinclair Lewis by Man Ray, a street scene by Berenice Abbott or Walker Evans are all significant contributions to the art. But to single out these American names from a much longer list is a little invidious, especially because the most important modern photographer, Alfred Stieglitz, is not represented in this show by any of the work he has done during the last twenty-five years. An amazing omission that at least called for explanation in the catalogue.

Mr. Beaumont Newhall, who assembled the photographs and instruments for the Museum, did an admirable job in ransacking the important collections for historic examples; his catalogue, too, is a very comprehensive and able piece of exposition—one of the best short critical histories I know in any language. So perhaps it is a little ungrateful of me to suggest that the Museum of Modern Art has begun to overreach itself in the matter of documentation: the precedent of the Surrealist show seems to be hardening into a permanent vice. For what is lacking in the present exhibition is a weighing and assessment of photography in terms of pure aesthetic merit—such an evaluation as should distinguish a show in an art museum from one that might be held, say, in the Museum of Science and Industry. In shifting this function of selection onto the spectator, the Museum seems to me to be unfairly adding to his burden, and to be reducing its proper sphere of influence.

Eugène Berman, whose neo-romantic landscapes were haunted by a tender, melancholy fantasy that the original romantics of the nineteenth century did not always achieve, has been for the last two years in America. The sea change has brought an alteration in his work; but to judge from the examples now on view at the Julien Levy Gallery, the change is not a happy one. The sign of exhaustion in any art comes when the artist begins to feed on the debris of past symbols and dead aesthetic forms; witness the Pre-Raphaelites. In Berman, this apparent exhaustion has taken the form of copying the lame mockeries and practical jokes on the eye that the architects and painters of the seventeenth century sometimes practiced. One of Berman's paintings in this show consists of a frame painted to look like marble, surrounding a smeared brick-red panel on which fragments of spattered paintings are hung by illusory nails. Pierre Roy uses this sort of illusionism with a humor that remains fresh for at least the first view of his paintings, but with Berman the trick seems tedious, all the more because the painting, however trivial, never lacks his refined and sensitive touch. Once upon a time, Berman's spacious landscapes might have been peopled by princes; now the foregrounds are occupied by beggars in rags, crawling about under festoons of wretched cloths that droop like deflated balloons. What are these paintings, with their uneasy figures and their sense of being infested by some lower order of life, but the wreck of a nostalgic faery world that no longer believes in its own make-believe? Emptiness and the mockery of emptiness are the sum of Berman's present symbols; a sordid derision of the beauty he had once had the impulse to make manifest. This deflation of neo-romanticism makes one doubly conscious of a weakness one had always suspected in the movement—its imaginative self-indulgence, and its failure to touch the vital core of contemporary experience.

No one has yet successfully defined what modern art is or where it began, but one might make a good case for beginning it with Goya, and if one rejects such an early lineage, one might easily start with the Frenchman who studied him to such good purpose—Edouard Manet. The show now on at the Wildenstein Galleries is the best opportunity one has had to view his work since the comprehensive retrospective exhibition held by the French government in Paris in 1932.

Perhaps the easiest way to describe the profound change made by Manet would be to say that it rests upon the perception that much that had hitherto seemed indispensable in painting after the sixteenth century could be taken for granted, and that much that had hitherto been suppressed or subordinated could be emphasized. The word "impressionism" describes Manet's method far more accurately than it does Monet's; it was a method whereby the nervous sweep of the brush adds to the quivering vitality of the scene itself, as in No. 14, the crowd of people on a quay under a holiday sky. Manet himself, despite his many audacities in conceiving and interpreting his subject ("Olympia" and "Déjeuner sur l'Herbe"), did not arrive at his bolder formal departures without painting a great many pictures in the older tradition. Just as he had two palettes, one French, one Spanish, so he had two styles, a classic style that linked him with Velásquez and the more courtly Goya, and a "romantic" style that broke the shell of the old art.

In the present show, the "Guitar Player" is probably the strongest and handsomest example of the first style, while the portrait studies No. 10 and No. 28 are the most startling examples of the second. The first portrait, "Angelina," leads straight to Picasso and Derain, while the other, through its amazing background, jumps across the years to Matisse. Manet had a fine psychological flair, such as the good Parisian gets in his cafés, sipping his cognac quietly and making a private drama of the faces around him. The girl in pink (No. 24) painted with scarcely the trace of a shadow, but remarkably modelled for all that—with her ice before her on the table and her unlit cigarette—is the very essence of plaintive solitude.

If Manet's more classic studies rarely are as good as those of Degas or Renoir or Courbet, in his more personal manner he seizes one by his intellectual vivacity. "This is something," he seems to say, "that you have never felt sharply before. Look quickly—from here—now—or it will vanish!" And he puts it on his canvas in a dozen strokes before the moment has gone. It was precisely when he was breathless, agitated, impetuous that Manet was most himself. To have achieved these fresh forms in the tradition of European oil painting, with its complicated technique and its insistence upon palpability, was a feat. By now, his successors have gathered most of Manet's laurels; Degas, Toulouse-Lautrec, Matisse, Derain have surpassed him in their special departments. But he had this unforgettable distinction of the pioneer—he got there first.

Other Galleries: A number of shows going off on April 3rd are worth a last-moment reminder. If you did not see the brilliant water colors of a young Southern artist, Hardie Gramatky, at the Ferargil Galleries recently, you will want to make up for it by inspecting landscapes of Millard Sheets at the Milch Galleries. The horses and birds in Sheets' foregrounds are a little weak, but the skies are excellent. Note especially Nos. 10, 13, and 15. Ary Stillman's paintings of New York at the Guild Art Gallery, particularly two which he did for the Federal Art Project, "Sleety Night" and "Outdoor Theatre," show a sensitive and well-individualized hand; and if you missed the recent group show at this gallery, as I did, you had better seize the opportunity to catch up on the recent work of Joseph de Martini, whose landscapes now have a complexity and depth that put him very near the first rank.

ACADEMICIANS AND OTHERS

Every year when spring comes I try to think charitable thoughts about the National Academy of Design. If it was good enough for Ryder, Homer, Shirlaw, Eakins, surely it ought to be good enough for the rest of us. Why be put off by the fact that academies tend in the nature of things to be filled by people who look upon social punctilio as the essential underpinning of the arts—the people who keep on attending official dinners, and who never forget to attend official funerals, with just that touch of jauntiness which enables the spectator to distinguish them from the undertakers and the deceased?

Why should not a Bohemian shirker of both dinners and funerals feel grateful to the people who vicariously perform all these duties for him? If only I could keep away from Academy exhibitions, I could perhaps hold onto this benign frame of mind. But sooner or later one must look at the pictures that this body sponsors; and though the Academy has made efforts to refurbish its membership during the last few years, one has to confess that it remains on the whole—obviously with honorable exceptions—a group of nondescript mediocrities, who no more represent the living art of the country than the man who paints billboards on Longacre Square.

Almost half the exhibits of painting and sculpture this year are by non-members, but unfortunately like has a way of calling to like, so even this means of lifting the level has no appreciable effect upon the general standard. The award of the Isidor Medal to a painting like Gerald Leake's "Into the Night" might well take the savor out of any other award that a prize jury could make. It is only in the black-and-white room that any of the stir and excitement that American art has exhibited during the last generation is recorded.

Recently the Academy has become busier. It has been forming groups in various cities and has been endeavoring to "exercise," as the catalogue says, "a really nationwide influence in the interest and advancement of American art." These annual exhibitions prove, however, that the Academy cannot really claim to be a central institution in American art. Its success might improve the cooking or the minor amenities of art in other regions, but it would be a disaster to painting and sculpture.

By a sort of parallel sense of duty, I try every year to think uncharitable thoughts about the Society of Independent Artists. Has it not lived long enough? Has not the original gesture of protest become a stale one? Isn't it just as futile for such a society to extend a welcoming hand to John Taylor Arms as it is for the Academy to invite Reginald Marsh to exhibit? What, if any, purpose is fulfilled by this grand free-for-all at the Grand Central Palace? Who has been helped by such a show to find himself or to find his public? Would anybody, except the newspaper reporters, regret the passing of this show—and haven't even they begun to complain that the Independents have become tame and respectable? In short, hasn't this society turned into a National Academy of Designlessness, with not even the excuse that it can supply a polite gentleman, on short notice, to a Park Avenue or East Hampton dinner table?

But each year I am forced to take back these thoughts by the fact that the Independents' show is always, somehow, as full of defiant mass vitality as Coney Island on the first warm Sunday in May. One has to walk further to find the good pictures than at the Academy, but there are more of them, while those that fail do so, as often as not, with a loud, eloquent noise which is almost as much in the spirit of art as the genuine achievements. Someone has figured out that the directors of the Louvre, if they had bought their paintings by mathematical chance every year, instead of buying on the strength of the artists' current academic reputation, would at the end of a century have acquired a great collection more cheaply than by their method of exercising their intelligence and taste.

One may say much the same thing in comparing the Academy show and that of the Independents. Even if one momentarily includes pictures so bad that they would not get by an Academy jury, the average of the hit-or-miss system would be higher than that achieved by academic good judgment. For the standard of any academic body is almost inevitably the standard of some past life, some past success. If it could understand the excellence that exists only in embryo, it would no longer be an academy. The real standards of any generation are formed by a small body of creative people who first impose upon themselves a new discipline, and first create for themselves alone a new pattern of organization. The authority that such artists exercise does not need the backing or prestige of an Academy; indeed, as soon as such sanction comes, it is a sure sign that the initiative has passed over to some other group. It is this invisible élite, sometimes invisible even to themselves, who erect the new standards from generation to generation. They may not appear even at an Independent Show, but they are far more likely to be found in such a place than in the more rigorous galleries of the National Academy.

Now that abstract art is becoming vocal and visible again—a young group of abstract artists have banded together to put on a show at the Squibb Building—it is time to say a word about the curious neglect that Arthur Dove has suffered, a fact that comes home with special force after one has seen his brilliant new show at An American Place. Dove is one of the least derivative painters of abstractions now working in America; instead of hanging on the coattails of Picasso, Kandinsky, or Arp, he has established an idiom of his own, and he has become, after a long and not by any means even development, a painter whose force, decision, and originality give his latest work the full stamp of maturity. Some of his earlier fantasies seemed to me, I confess, a little thin, a little willful; and though I liked his humor, I was not, a decade ago, a very hearty admirer of his more serious paintings. But Dove's art during the past few years, which culminates in the present show, has removed my earlier doubts. Oils such as "Me and the Moon," "The Moon Was Laughing," "Golden Sun," and "Water Swirl" are vigorous, well-rounded works of art, in which an original vision has been recomposed into an equally original structure. People who think that wholly native American art must portray Iowa farmers or New Jersey filling stations should look long and prayerfully at Dove's paintings.

Ever since Paul Cadmus scandalized the dry-land admirals by exhibiting a painting which showed bluejackets flirting with the gay girls of the Nineties on Riverside Drive—without the aid of the Bluejacket's Manual—he has been more or less in the public eye. His present show at the Midtown Galleries is, however, the first one-man exhibition he has had. By interest and conscious intention, Cadmus is a satirist who wishes to touch off the vulgarities and weaknesses of the present-day American scene; by actual achievement, he is a caricaturist who utilizes the technique of academic painting to deface the nobilities and the ideal forms that academic painters delight in. Cadmus studies the slack cheeks of suburban businessmen at the golf links, captures the levelheaded fiend who takes a prompt snapshot of a polo-game accident, portrays the leering buttocks of the young ladies parading on a suburban main street or the Coney Island beach. He paints these phenomena with an extra touch of fleshliness, an extra shriek of mawkish color, that make his subjects completely repulsive. The result is not so much satire as inverted sentimentalism; his hand lingers too lovingly on the flesh he would chastise. Instead of hating the subject the painter holds up to scorn, one comes pretty near to hating the artist himself for giving one such an unpalatable mouthful. Aesthetically, Cadmus's compositions are still extremely conventional, even academic; his figures are usually arranged within the old triangular field. But his touch has improved during the last few years and his most recent paintings are not as sleekly wooden as his earlier ones. None of the paintings in the present show seem to me fully to live up to Cadmus's declared intentions; but he is young enough to overcome his academic bondage and his ambivalent attitude toward his subjects.

If you are interested in the relatively younger people, as you ought to be, you will find a number of other contemporary shows that are rewarding. Emlen Etting's paintings, at the Boyer Galleries, are the work of a lyrical talent, melodious, a little thin and plaintive, but very attractive. Hermine Loughney, at the Artists' Gallery, has a gay palette, and though in most of her paintings her forms are subordinate to the surface pattern, her "Nude" and her "Italian Family" lead away from her textile-like surfaces into maturer, richer compositions. As for the three Pintos, at the Valentine Gallery, the show is interesting for introducing a less well-known member, Biagio, whose sombre "Fruit" (No. 17) provides an admirable foil to the gayer, higher keys of Salvatore and Angelo.

PIERRE-AUGUSTE RENOIR

The Renoir exhibition at the Metropolitan Museum was fitly prefaced this spring by the Manet show at Wildenstein and the quite ravishing Degas show at Durand-Ruel. It is the last big show of the season, and fortunately for lovers of Renoir—perhaps I should say fortunately for all lovers—it will remain on through the summer.

Pierre-Auguste Renoir was born in 1841 at Limoges. This makes him a close contemporary of Rodin and Claude Monet, and a little younger than Manet and Degas, who were born in the early eighteen-thirties. His birthplace, where the famous enamels were made in the Middle Ages, is the great pottery centre, and in 1854 he went to work as a china-painter in a porcelain factory. By honest origin, then, Renoir was one of those creatures who are so often talked about nowadays—a proletarian painter; and I think he disposes of the patronizing middle-class superstition that a proletarian painter would naturally spend all his life depicting the grandeurs and miseries of proletarians.

Not merely did Renoir originally have to seek a living as a factory worker; he lost his job because the fashionable machine processes that were being introduced in the fifties did away temporarily with the need for china-painters—an early victim of technological unemployment. At seventeen, he entered the studio of Gleyre, where he met Monet and Sisley. So Renoir rose into the new aristocracy of the unemployed—the painters and sculptors who were in revolt against the tastes and standards of the bourgeoisie; people who created art, as the aristocracy flirted and danced and went to the hunt, because it was, despite the meagreness of the artists' subsistence, a profoundly satisfactory mode of life.

Renoir's first salon picture was shown in 1863, but he destroyed a good part of his early work, and the present show opens with a portrait of Mme. Darras, done in 1871—a grave piece, carefully modelled, in beautiful repose, the work of a man who was already well within sight of maturity. Meanwhile the Franco-Prussian War had taken place, followed by the tense, exalted period of the Commune and the savage horror of its suppression. Frenchmen were humiliated by the disasters that had overtaken them, but not exhausted, and a gathering and tightening of energies took place among the élite. One marks that sombre intensity in much of Renoir's early work. It achieved its fullest expression toward the end of the seventies; note "La Fillette Attentive," "Two Little Circus Girls," "L'Ingénue," and "La Petite Margot Bérard."

Even in his early maturity Renoir was perhaps more open to the influences around him than any of his peers. He made sorties now in one direction, now in another. "Le Pont Neuf à Paris," one of the new sunlight paintings of the Impressionists, was done as early as 1872. Many of these pictures, even as late as "The Duck Pond," are executed with the fine pointillist stroke of Monet. On the other hand, in "Child with a Hoop," of about 1875, the lace of the collar is put on with a heavy touch that his friend Cézanne applied to his early pictures; only a certain tenderness of contour in the child's face marks it as especially Renoir's.

Through this early period, Renoir's palette was as undecided as his technique. Those who think of Renoir chiefly in terms of those streams of scarlet and carmine that issue out of Rubens and Fragonard and suffuse so many of the paintings of Renoir's old age must bow to the cooler charms of the olive greens and dull oranges and gray blues of Renoir's "Melon and a Vase of Roses," painted in the middle seventies. Some of Renoir's greatest paintings, indeed, are built out of these cool colors and sombre tones. One of the most marvellous of these is the full-length portrait of Mlle. Durand-Ruel, now in the Barnes Foundation Collection and not in the present show, but No. 19 and No. 23 are close runners-up to that picture. There was a moment, marked by "La Pensée," when Renoir's delicacy of touch created forms that were almost emanations, rather than solid bodies, figures that remind one of the feminine wraiths that our own George Fuller evoked during the same period. Yet Renoir's diaphanous girls are composed with an underlying firmness that saves them from dissolution, and even in his most ethereal moments he never lost touch with solid earth. For during this period, Renoir did the study of Anna that is now in Moscow, I believe—one of the first of his lush, round-bellied, almost-pregnant girls.

I cannot leave the Renoirs of the seventies without dwelling for a moment on the portrait of Mlle. Legrand, "La Fillette Attentive" (No. 11), and that of "La Petite Margot Bérard" (No. 26). Neither of these portraits owes any direct debt to the new experiments in light and color that Renoir was making, even though the pinafore of "La Fillette" is slashed in with some of Manet's easy freedom. Their incomparable beauty is due to Renoir's tenderness in dealing with his subject; they are the visible outcome of his exquisite sensitiveness and fineness of feeling. The artist's brush, Renoir once remarked to M. Vollard, should caress the canvas, and it is in this fashion that he treated the wide-eyed and wistful children who sat for him. The pallid delicacy of Margot's skin, the even more transparent touch of shadow, the soft aura of her hair, are done with a craftsmanship a Roger van der Weyden might have striven to surpass. In his later years Renoir showed, no doubt, a deeper individualization of style, and even when he was crippled by arthritis he could paint such a richly textured portrait as that of Mme. Tilla Durieux. But he never surpassed, in sheer adequacy of means to an end, the best work he did in the seventies. A Harvard sociologist has recently suggested that what we hitherto conceived as development, evolution, progress should be regarded as mere fluctuations. That is a true figure, at least, for Renoir's life curve.

There was, indeed, a period of extreme fluctuations, more rapid and violent than in the years just before, that lasted from about 1879 to 1888—changes that perhaps seem especially decisive because the artist himself had become conscious of them. This period was marked by a series of foreign journeys beginning with a trip to Algiers in 1879, by his marriage in 1880, and by his fatherhood in 1885. It was perhaps that *crise à quarante ans* that so often overtakes men of ability in middle life; the period when they desert their wives, run away to the South Seas, change their occupations, take to drink, or commit suicide, a period when they write over the doors of their private chambers an urgent "Now or Never!" or a regretful "Too Late!" During this decade Renoir was in a state of uneasy turmoil; some of his best and some of his worst paintings belong to this second adolescence. Not merely did Renoir find himself fed up with Impressionism and openly renounce it; he had moments of intense disgust when he felt that he knew nothing about paint-

ing and had accomplished nothing. Such revulsions are usually as un-
sound as they are subjective, but they save the creator from a smug con-
tentment with minor successes and they often lead to a more disciplined
hold over his weaknesses and a more enlightened exploitation of his
strength.

So with Renoir. It was during this very period of self-criticism that
he reached a new level in, among other pictures, "Le Déjeuner des Ca-
notiers." In this painting, the somewhat diffuse composition is brought
into focus by sheer mastery of the color relations, and the faces and the
bodies become part of a double field of interest in which the still life of
wine, fruit, and tablecloth plays a major part. The feeble spot in this
composition—for there are occasionally feeble spots in Renoir's painting, like the man's hand in No. 39—is the body of the white-shirted man
standing on the left. Here Renoir failed to create the slightest illusion of
distance from the girl in front, and the white surface itself remains paper-
thin. But the painting, nonetheless, is a superb work, a celebration of the
joys of youth, a sort of repainting of the grand picnic that Victor Hugo
described in the early pages of "Les Misérables" without the possibility
of Hugo's sordid aftermath.

What separated Renoir from his fellow-Impressionists was chiefly his
sense that the artist was more important than his palette; he recognized
that Velásquez's noblemen were dignified because the painter had en-
dowed them with his own dignity. Though Renoir loved to paint nature,
he disdained to paint her *au naturel*. Under the influence of Cennino
Cennini, he even sought, by a crisp draughtsmanship, to emancipate
himself from the mere transcription of nature, not realizing, perhaps,
that he had always done so unconsciously.

But after 1888 the new Renoir definitely emerges; he is really the old
one, strengthened, clarified, reunited. Both his palette and his form from
this time on tend toward the typical. By a curious irony, he is hardly less
the Impressionist than before, but now he is an Impressionist who seeks
a conscious dignity of form, a painter whose Impressionism is a tool and
a method, not an end. Lack of interest kept him from experimenting with
those spatial compositions in which both Degas and Cézanne were to
excel; distance lent no enchantment to Renoir's view. The foreground for
him was so nearly all-important that, as often as not, the background is
silent or is reduced to a lazy hum of color.

The "new" painter was already in existence in 1879. Mark the formal use of red, blue, lilac, and lavender in the "Lady Sewing," No. 25.
Nevertheless, in Renoir's later work there was a marked settling down

into type; he even tended to give all his figures certain generic features: slanting, half-closed eyes, wide mouths, broad cheekbones, and ample bosoms, while his palette, now rich and sensuous, rarely returned to the cool end of the spectrum. Of the paintings of the later years, there is perhaps a less adequate showing in the present exhibition, but that of "Gabrielle with Jean and a Little Girl" is very fine, while "After the Bath" is a representative sample of those nude figures to which he so often reverted. "Claude at the Easel," done around 1906, is one of the most happy of his later studies of children, and if the face here is less completely realized than that of Margot—if perhaps something precious has indeed been lost—the painting as a whole is more completely individualized. Every inch of it is "signed."

So much for Renoir's paintings *as* painting. But what of his symbols? Is Renoir an example of the proletarian artist gone wrong? Is this an old story of youthful integrity turned into bourgeois compromise and middle-aged escapism? Or is Renoir a proper subject for a medical biography which would show how his arthritis produced a special love for tender flesh and flexible joints and healthy bodies whose very limbs seem tumescent with ecstasy? None of these things is true. Renoir, like his great predecessor Rubens, is one of those artists whose harmonious relations with life were too deep to be disrupted by war, disease, pain, and social frustration; artists whose only form of rebellion or criticism is a renewed gusto in creation. Such people encounter tragic defeat like the pair of birds that Ernst Toller describes in his autobiography. When their nest is broken, they build it again, and when it is broken a second and a third time, they return, with insistent vitality, to the task of rebuilding it. The period in which Renoir painted was blighted at both ends by a catastrophic war and was sharp with economic and political crises, but one searches Renoir's canvases in vain for an expression of these facts. Or, rather, one does not search in vain. He has an answer. He opposes to misery, cruelty, and barbarism the rejuvenating images of life.

Roger Fry, who conquered with difficulty a temperamental aversion to Renoir's art, referred in his "Vision and Design" to the commonplaceness of Renoir's vision. In one's first approach to Renoir, he explained, one was reminded of pictures that would be the "delight of servants' halls." Renoir would not have been embarrassed by that snobbish allusion. He enjoyed the servants around him and said that a woman's hands were not worth painting unless they had been molded by housework. It was natural that his symbols should be commonplace enough and vital enough to break through the factitious standards of caste. In a realistic sense far different from the warped mysticism of the Nazis, Renoir was the artist of blood and soil, the veritable commonplaces of life. He painted glowing landscapes and animated flowers. He painted men and women in acts of simple enjoyment, dancing in the country or the city, picnicking, boating, bathing, eating, conversing, flirting. He was the painter of all those relaxed, sunlit moments whose immediate reward is grace, laughter, ecstasy, and animal health. He makes one feel it is good to be a lover and taste the appeasing sanity of a lover's body; good to be a parent, watching a child's miraculous passages of growth. Renoir brought to these elemental biological states all the force of his imagination. In a civilization impoverished by abstractions—progress, the machine, the State, financial power, imperialist exploitation—Renoir renewed the natural appetites; he turned men's eyes toward bread and wine and sunlight and sex, the sources and symbols of life. So he extracts from lovers their rapture and gives it back in double measure. And today, no matter how the world wobbles at its poles, Renoir remains close to the hub of human reality, perhaps closer than any other artist in his century.

Frontispiece: George Platt Lynes, *Lewis Mumford*, c. 1934. © Estate of George Platt Lynes.

Plate prior to "Introduction": Helen E. Hokinson, *New Yorker* cartoon. © The New Yorker Collection, 1935, Helen E. Hokinson; from cartoonbank.com. All Rights Reserved.

Plate prior to "The Metropolitan Milieu": Alan Dunn, *New Yorker* cartoon. © The New Yorker Collection, 1933, Alan Dunn; from cartoonbank.com. All Rights Reserved.

Plate prior to "1932–1933": Alain, *New Yorker* cartoon. © The New Yorker Collection, 1932, Alain; from cartoonbank.com. All Rights Reserved.

Plate prior to "1933–1934": Whitney Darrow Jr., *New Yorker* cartoon. © The New Yorker Collection, 1934, Whitney Darrow Jr.; from cartoonbank.com. All Rights Reserved.

Plate prior to "1934–1935": William Steig, *New Yorker* cartoon. © The New Yorker Collection, 1935, William Steig; from cartoonbank.com. All Rights Reserved.

Plate prior to "1935–1936": Mary Petty, *New Yorker* cartoon. © The New Yorker Collection, 1936, Mary Petty; from cartoonbank.com. All Rights Reserved.

Plate prior to "1936–1937": Richard Decker, *New Yorker* cartoon. © The New Yorker Collection, 1936, Richard Decker; from cartoonbank.com. All Rights Reserved.

Text: 10/13 Sabon
Display: Univers
Compositor: Binghamton Valley Composition
Indexer: Marcia Carlson
Printer and Binder: Thomson-Shore